What Would Murphy Brown Do?

How the Women of Prime Time
Changed Our Lives

Allison Klein

SEAL PRESS

What Would Murphy Brown Do?
How the Women of Prime Time Changed Our Lives

Excerpt from "Pick Yer Nose" copyright 1993 Ani DiFranco used by permission.

Published by
Seal Press
An Imprint of Avalon Publishing Group, Incorporated
1400 65th Street, Suite 250
Emeryville, CA 94608

ISBN-13: 978-1-58005-171-2
ISBN-10: 1-58005-171-5

9 8 7 6 5 4 3 2 1
Library of Congress Cataloging-in-Publication Data

Klein, Allison, 1976-
What would Murphy Brown do? : how the women of prime time changed our lives / Allison Klein.
p. cm.
ISBN-13: 978-1-58005-171-2
ISBN-10: 1-58005-171-5
1. Women on television. 2. Television comedies—United States. I. Title.

PN1992.8.W65K54 2006
791.432082—dc22
                        2006012046

Cover and interior design by Domini Dragoone
Printed in the United States of America by Worzalla
Distributed by Publishers Group West

For Michelle
I'm so happy we are family.

Contents

I fight with love
and I laugh with rage
you gotta live light enough to see the humor
and long enough to see some change

—Ani DiFranco

Introduction

In the spring of 2005, a *New York Times Magazine* piece about television ratings stated that "one of the great contradictions of modern American life is that almost everyone watches television, but almost no one agrees on . . . what it really means to watch television."[1]

I have been watching TV my entire life. As family lore has it, my mom turned on the TV when I was an infant sitting quietly in my baby chair, and I was hooked. Television has always been my life, a fact that feels more like a dirty little secret than an idiosyncratic personality trait. I hate to admit that I probably spent as many hours watching TV each day as I spent in school, often much more. I was the kid who always knew what happened on last night's episode, the kid who ran home after school to begin my daily regimen of television watching. Fortunately, television never dampened my love of books—as evidence has shown it can. But TV is an important part of who I am and has helped shape my sensibility.

It's no surprise that Americans watch an inordinate amount of television. Women, though, watch even more television than men. And it has always been women who television—programmers and advertisers—have sought to reach. Think daytime television and movies of the week. Early TV attempted to sell appliances that women would use as they settled in each night for another episode of family-friendly television like *Leave It to Beaver* or *The Donna Reed Show*. My mother—and all her baby boomer contemporaries—grew up watching shows where happy homemakers supported their men and were amazingly adept at keeping up their suburban homes. Of course, that generation later realized the myth of early sitcoms. Those shows failed to reveal the reality of many families in the '50s and '60s: financial struggles, single mothers, sexually active teenagers, and other real-life issues real-life families were experiencing.

In *Where the Girls Are*, historian Susan Douglas's examination of popular culture during those decades, the author explains, "I am a woman of the baby boom, which means my history is filled with embarrassment, littered with images I'd just as soon forget."[2] She and other historians have noted that without the restrictive and sometimes ridiculous images of early television, women wouldn't have found the fuel that ignited the feminist movement. Television helped make the baby boomers embrace feminism because the images of women on TV weren't representative of real women's lives and seemed downright harmful to women and girls. Douglas states that "growing up female with the mass media helped make me a feminist, and it helped make millions of other women feminists too, whether they take on the label or not."[3]

Television certainly helped make me a feminist. How could anyone watch programs like *The Mary Tyler Moore Show*, *Roseanne*, *Designing Women*, *Murphy Brown*, and *Sex and the City* without noticing that over the past fifty years or so, television has presented us with increasingly varied images of women who are not just wives and mothers, but single mothers and working girls and divorcées and women over fifty?

As 1970 is commonly cited as the year women's liberation was born, it is where my story begins. I look at the evolving image of women through the lens of the television sitcom, a uniquely female genre. The first overtly feminist sitcom, *The Mary Tyler Moore Show*, premiered that year, featuring a new kind of woman. The creators of the show, James L. Brooks and Allan Burns, said that they "thought of the difficulty of being thirty, single, and female in the very tough world of the 1970s, and we wanted to find the comedy—but also the meaning—in that." Mary Richards must have seemed like an alien creature—a long-awaited one—to the women of my mom's generation. Other than during her college years, my mother never really lived alone. She did what most women did: left her parents' house for her husband's house. By the time Mary moved to Minneapolis to "make it on her own," my mother was already married and setting up house with my father.

When I watched the series in the '80s, I was already well aware that my mother had resisted afflicting me with the images she'd seen growing up. She did this not by restricting television, but by giving me a vocabulary of feminism that helped me view TV in a different way. She'd grown up with posters of male celebrities on her walls; I grew up with female ones. In fact, one of my earliest memories is of my mother hanging a poster in my room that simply said GIRLS CAN DO ANYTHING. Granted it featured a picture of a cartoon character, Smurfette, but she was opening the door to her office which happened to read PRESIDENT on it. With this mindset, I watched television. My mother and I would cackle at Roseanne's quips and take pride in Murphy Brown's strength and achievements. I learned that I could choose to relate to TV images I felt were somewhat realistic and inspiring, and reject those that seemed belittling and sexist.

Television is a medium that depends on advertising dollars; thus many cultural, financial, and creative factors go into programming. But I always felt that in terms of TV shows, women had a lot to be proud of—and still do. Shows that addressed the issues underlying feminism advanced a whole new generation of women. The prime-time women of the '70s, '80s, and '90s worked, raised kids without husbands, and struggled with the realities of being a woman in their day and age. These are still issues millions of women relate to today.

Not only has television started depicting issues that are relevant to many, but it has increasingly featured characters who are flawed and far more human than the perfect housewives of early TV. As Betty Friedan reported in *TV Guide* in 1964, television represented American women as stupid, unattractive, insecure, martyred, mindless, bored little household drudges. I can't imagine any real women who wanted to be that way. By the time I grew up, young girls, myself included, dreamed of being Murphy Brown, a strong, successful woman with no fear of competing in "a man's world."

For me, sitcoms have always been a great place to examine women's roles, in many respects because humor offers a subtle way of questioning the status quo. In fact, sitcoms have generally been more kind to women than dramatic series, which lagged behind comedies in breaking down female stereotypes. Until fairly recently, with such series as *Dr. Quinn, Medicine Woman* and *Cagney & Lacey*, few women could be found in Westerns or cop shows.

Regardless of the way in which early sitcoms represented—or misrepresented—the American family and the American woman, the genre has, at the very least, featured women and, at the most, given them a venue for exploring (which can often mean explicitly joking about) real feminist issues. In her book *Prime-Time Feminism*, Bonnie Dow compares Mary Richards to Gloria Steinem in that both of these twentieth-century feminist icons had the ability to "make [women's] liberation marketable."[4]

In the last decades of the century, television reflected the nation's advances and struggles with feminism. As popular culture historian Molly Haskell says in her 1997 book *Holding My Own in No Man's Land*:

> *I'd suggest that it's in the field of comedy, including that much despised genre the sitcom, that television is exploding all over the place. Both within the precincts of network television and in the outer reaches of cable, there are uncommonly raunchy, innovative, sophisticated shows, many of them women-driven, that are tackling male-female conflict and sexual taboo and the undercurrent of women's rage, subjects that mainstream movies won't touch with a ten-foot pole.*[5]

During my high school years, I remember sitting on my bed reading Susan Faludi's *Backlash,* an examination of the 1980s media backlash against women. Just like the aberration of the 1950s, the '80s were a decade of neotraditionalism; but like they did in the '50s, women took what they wanted from TV and ignored what didn't reflect their reality. Regardless, I found TV heroines throughout the '80s. Elyse Keaton on *Family Ties* was an architect, a job I never knew women did. Then there was the mother of all women, Roseanne. And by the end of the decade, I had a new heroine in Ms. Brown.

The idea that women are consistently victimized by popular culture, purported by Faludi and many others, is not untrue;

it is just not the whole story. As Susan Douglas points out in *Where the Girls Are*, even early television with all its embarrassing images (for instance, flying nuns) and incongruous representations of women still suggested, on occasion, that women could be "rebellious, tough, enterprising and shrewd . . . and much of what we saw was porous, allowing us to accept *and* rebel against what we saw and how it was presented."[6] It was this first generation of women who watched TV growing up that taught the rest of us to look for inspiration, even among a mass of sexist images.

In sitcoms that have aired since 1970, I've found a lot to be proud of and a lot to struggle against. Improving the depiction of women—be they stay-at-home mothers, working single moms, or women who pursue other paths—will always be a struggle. What Douglas says about her generation rings true with mine as well: "American women are a bundle of contradictions because much of the media imagery we grew up with was itself filled with mixed messages about what women should and should not do, what women could and could not be."[7]

As television has worked to represent women in a more realistic light, writers have put female TV characters in many of the same situations that real women face. They work, take care of children old and young, deal with being married and being single. Many are our role models, and they are imperfect, like those of us who watch. TV characters can help open a window into the reality of American womanhood and help us acknowledge something we have always known. Though our lives may be fraught with obstacles, there is never an excuse for not trying to achieve our dreams.

Every now and then, when I face a notable obstacle in my own life, I ask myself, "What would Murphy Brown do?" And that is why I chose to write this book.

Chapter 1

A New Breed
The Life of the Unmarried Sitcom Woman

In 1988, a new television series premiered, introducing the world to America's first female sitcom broadcast journalist. Her name was Murphy Brown, and her creator, Diane English, invoked both the spirit of feminism as well as the many issues women face in pursuing their personal and career goals. To introduce the character, *Murphy Brown* producers used visual aids—magazine covers—that told us, with just a few words, who this woman was. The three covers of the magazines read:

She'll Ask Anything.

Fabulous at 40.

Who is man enough for this woman?[1]

In a matter of seconds, the audience knew they were seeing a new kind of woman TV character, one who would stop at nothing to get a story, one who worked hard and had the years of experience to prove it. (Thank God, the networks couldn't convince *Murphy Brown*'s producers that a successful reporter could be in her twenties.) In many ways, she exemplified how far sitcom women had come since the early days of television.

To understand the evolving role of women in society, turn on your TV and start to watch. You need only survey the last five decades, from June Cleaver to Murphy Brown to Carrie Bradshaw, to witness social history in the making. From the moment Americans started buying television sets, the situation comedy has mirrored attitudes toward the status quo: periods when we've accepted it, periods when we haven't, periods when we've fought for change.

The sitcom functions as a societal barometer because it is essentially a female genre. The first and most famous, *I Love Lucy*, both was produced by a woman and featured a precocious female character. The sitcom's twenty-two minute, two-act structure has changed little over the last fifty years, but its female characters have undergone significant transformations. Because both *I Love Lucy*, in the early years of television, and *The Mary Tyler Moore Show*, in the '70s, were so successful, TV has built a foundation of sitcoms starring and featuring women. They have reflected the evolving place of women in our society, albeit often late and tentatively. From marital status to career to child rearing, television has reflected notions old and new, the conventional and the trailblazing, and everything in between. Most notable, though, has been the evolution of the sitcom's single woman.

In the '60s, Sally Rogers, played by Rose Marie on *The Dick Van Dyke Show* (which premiered in 1961), embodied the quintessential single woman. Sure, she was funny and sassy and worked with the boys, but hers was not a fate most women would envy. She was rebuffed by the men in her world . . . and even by television critics. Consider this passage from *The Great TV Sitcom Book*:

> *There was one classic episode of* The Dick Van Dyke Show *. . . in which Sally, the ugly-duckling, man-hungry staff writer, was on a talk show asking eligible men to send her a postcard because she was looking for a husband. That was nearly twenty years ago, but you can be sure that Rose Marie's still looking.*[2]

Not only was a single woman in her thirties or older described as an "ugly duckling" (and believe me, there were worse monikers I've spared you), it was assumed she would be single forever. Although the structure of situation comedies leaves little room for characters to change much about their "situations," early TV's single women were destined to end up wrinkled, bitter cat fanciers. As historian Susan Douglas puts it, "Old contradictions don't die, they just get new outfits."[3]

While this may be true, we cannot deny the extent to which women's lives have changed since the advent of the TV sitcom. While television shows of the '50s weren't necessarily representative of real life, they reflected conventional views of women and the nuclear family. Being a single woman back then was akin to having an unexplained mental disorder or worse. In fact, in 1957, 53 percent of the American public believed that unmarried people were "sick," "immoral," or "neurotic," while only 37 percent viewed them neutrally.

By the 1960s, marriage as a national ideal, an enforceable teenage daydream, had lost some of its appeal.[4] In fact, the 1960 census reported that eighteen out of every 100 households were headed by women. Though many of these independent women were widows, almost two million were divorced, 900,000 were separated, and amazingly 1.4 million women had never wed at all.[5] As available housing increased, younger women were no longer forced to live with their families. As the '60s rolled on, more and more women entered the workforce.

With the emergence of the women's movement in the 1970s, single women became "a serious, permanent social fact."[6] Betsy Israel's *Bachelor Girl: The Secret History of Single Women in the Twentieth Century* underscores the huge changes women experienced:

> By the mid-1970s, single women would emerge as among the most economically and socially significant of all the onetime shadow population groups. Being single, like being openly gay, would finally lose any lingering taint of ugly character weakness, any hint of pathology, and come to seem an entirely viable way to live—what someone back in 1925 had first called a "lifestyle."[7]

Changes that began in the '60s started to affect women's lives both in reality and in the way they were depicted on television. As Betty Friedan, author of *The Feminine Mystique* (published in 1963), and other feminists led the Women's Strike for Equality, "a 24-hour general strike . . . of all women in America against the concrete conditions of their oppression," our first overtly feminist TV icon—Mary Richards of *The Mary Tyler Moore Show*—was taking the national stage.[8] Single womanhood was being redefined. The next thirty years of television would offer an enormous array of single women, old and young, neurotic and calm, desperate to be married and happily single. Even though television would remain a bastion of traditionalism in some ways, in other important ways it would also never be the same.

The Single Stigma

I live in New York City, a place seemingly accepting of just about any lifestyle. But it still boggles my mind how many times I have been asked (in a tone more accusatory than enquiring), "So, how come you're not married?" My mother recalls that back in the early '70s, the first question people would ask her was, "What does your husband do?" Some things change, some things don't. We may no longer assume that most women are married (or that only their husbands have a career), but it's not uncommon for a single woman to still feel like a social leper at a dinner party.

The stigma of being single hasn't disappeared, but

it's certainly lessened since the days of Sally Rogers. Most women today don't feel pressure to marry until they're in their thirties, instead of in their early twenties. But nine out of ten Americans still get married. So even though it is culturally acceptable to spend your twenties dating and working on your career, the pressure to march down the aisle intensifies as you enter your thirties.

When the world wonders why I haven't "found a man," I search for inspiration and find it where I've always found it—on television, where my sitcom buddies are out there working for themselves and staying single for, at least, a while. *Sex and the City* addresses many of the issues single women deal with, whether we live in the city, the suburbs, or a small town. As a gauge of how much our cultural version of the single woman has improved, one need only look from Sally Rogers in the fifties to Carrie Bradshaw today.

But in between them, there was Mary Richards. *The Mary Tyler Moore Show* featured the sitcom world's first unmarried heroine. The show's debut, and subsequent success, is always referred to as a historical event. As one encyclopedia of sitcoms explains, "And then, suddenly one Saturday night in 1970: *The Mary Tyler Moore Show*, starring Dick Van Dyke's ex-wife. It was funny, it was intelligent, it was moving. What a relief from the sixties."[9]

Mary Richards embodied the "career woman," a term surprisingly still with us, even as gender employment rates continue to equalize. Work wasn't the only important part of the new career woman's life. She was also single—by choice. Prior to Mary Richards, single by choice didn't exist on television. Sally Rogers and goofy over-the-hill characters were single by circumstances beyond their control and usually depicted as desperate and unfulfilled. But Mary escaped the clutches of suburban marriage because she had an aching feeling that she wanted more—more experiences with men, more independence, just *more.*

The popular culture catalyst for the acceptance of single women wasn't their entertainment value. Instead, it was a response to the times—or a delayed response. *The Mary Tyler Moore Show* broke from the sitcom status quo by making a decidedly political effort to show the 1970s "new woman" in her natural habitat.

In her job interview at WJM-TV's newsroom, Mary is asked a series of questions by her ornery future boss, Lou Grant. Even Mary can't escape the marriage question:

LOU: How old are you?

MARY: Thirty.

LOU: What religion are you?

MARY: Mr. Grant . . . I don't know how to say this: You're not allowed to ask that when someone's applying for a job. It's against the law.

LOU: Wanna call a cop? Are you married?

MARY: Presbyterian.[10]

Ah, how refreshing that Mary occupies the same world many of us live in—one where we would rather discuss our religious affiliation than explain our personal decisions about marriage, dating, and being single. Mary's response to Mr. Grant's interrogation sets the tone for the show: a woman doing her best to swim upstream in a society that still wants the womenfolk in their traditional place downstream. Seventies audiences didn't find Mary intimidating, and she was just vulnerable enough to take revolutionary steps on TV without alienating traditionalists. We have the series' creators to thank for recognizing the difficulties and excitement of a single woman taking a different path. Yet she was hardly strident about her choices. In a memorable scene from the first episode, she and her fiancé realize their relationship is over. As they part, he says, "Take good care of yourself." Mary softly says, "I think I just did."[11] It was new for television, a single woman who "took care of herself" by eliminating her boyfriend from her life.[12]

Most of the women I've met, particularly baby boomers, think of *The Mary Tyler Moore Show* as quintessentially seventies. As Bonnie Dow points out, if television scholars established a canon of "great works" as is done for literature, *The Mary Tyler Moore Show (MTM)* certainly would be included. In addition, the show is generally acknowledged as the first popular, long-running series to overtly feature the influence of feminism. *MTM* wasn't the first single-working-woman sitcom, but it asserted that work (and independence) was not just a prelude or substitute for marriage. Work was central to a satisfying life for a woman, just as it was for men.[13] "To me, Mary represented a new attitude," says one *MTM* writer, "that you could be single and still be a whole person, that you didn't need to be married to have a complete life."[14]

The Mary Tyler Moore Show set a precedent and spawned generations of "single girl" series. Even as many shows have explored the theme more progressively, "the shadow of *MTM* hangs over them."[15] It began a "quiet revolution."[16] According to *The Great TV Sitcom Book*, "Mary Richards was single. And she didn't mind. She didn't chase after men. In fact, she'd often rather spend a night in with best buddy Rhoda than go out on another boring date (she once calculated that 90 percent of her dates were bad)."[17]

If more than half of people in the 1950s thought single life was unnatural, attitudes had changed dramatically by the '70s, when studies found that only 33 percent of people had "negative attitudes and expectations" of the unmarried. Fifty-one percent viewed them neutrally and 15 percent approvingly.[18] By 1974, a study in *The New York Times* found that young, single women held themselves in higher regard than they had the year before, and felt self-assured, confident, secure.[19] By 1975, 25 percent of U.S. households were headed by single women. Over time, not only did it become it okay to be single, but the twenty-one-year-old wife archetype of yesterday came to be seen as more and more of an anachronism. She was seen as a woman who had skipped out on an important part of her young life.[20]

The single stigma was changing in real life and the television sitcom was trying to catch up. With *MTM*, the small screen was finally acknowledging a cultural shift. The networks and programmers felt that the nation was "ready" to see this change. In fact, many felt that the ideas of the '60s had progressed slowly in terms of actual change. But by 1970, things had "really crashed," wrote Betsy Israel in *Bachelor Girls.* "The changes started seeping out from there, and there was no going back."[21]

In the case of *MTM*, the networks were certainly right. Its success was not only about content but about schedule. In *Prime Times: Writers on Their Favorite TV Shows*, Nora Ephron describes her own relationship with *The Mary Tyler Moore Show*:

> *All I want to say, without being too mushy about it, is that it meant a lot to me the second time I was single and home alone on a Saturday night to discover that Mary Tyler Moore was home, too. . . . Thanks. You made it possible for millions of Americans to stay home on Saturday night and not feel they were missing anything. For that alone I loved you.*[22]

For a show to do so well on the biggest "going out" night of the week proved that there was certainly something about Mary. The show made it "respectable to stay at home on Saturday nights."[23] This had previously been the domain of the single woman, eating ice cream alone while couples dined in romantic restaurants. That is, until married couples and single women alike wanted to know what Mary Richards, a single girl, was up to each week. She was the kind of character you wanted to hang out with on Saturday nights, even if she could only stay for thirty minutes.[24]

Since *MTM*, a variety of shows have addressed the single stigma, most often when younger and older generations clash. Some of the funniest exchanges on *Ellen* occur between Ellen and her mother, a caricature of June Cleaver, who happens to have a daughter who never wears dresses nor has a boyfriend. In one episode, when her mother suggests that maybe the reason Ellen is alone is because of her constant joking (which is why we love her, by the way), Ellen responds:

LOIS (ELLEN'S MOTHER): So . . . how's your life?

ELLEN: Fine . . . fine, fine.

LOIS: Do you have a boyfriend?

ELLEN: No . . . nope . . . nope, nope.

LOIS: Are you seeing anyone?

ELLEN: You know, you know, Mom, we have lunch every Friday . . . and every Friday you ask me the exact same questions: How's your life? Do you have a boyfriend? Are you seeing anyone? How's your job? . . .

LOIS: Oops, how is your job?

ELLEN: It's fine, Mom.

LOIS: *(Disappointed)* Fine.[25]

Having to defend not being married seems to be a pretty common monkey on the backs of many women on TV and in real life. I have to defend my own choice to be single more than I ever thought I would. Just as on TV sitcoms, these defenses often happen when I'm with a group of my parents' friends. I reply with the usual stock answers of "choosing to be single." Many women I know want to get married "one day"—tomorrow, next year, or eight years from now. For countless reasons, we choose to be single for a time or forever, even if that includes tense conversations with our mothers or friends.

Ellen, Fran Fine on *The Nanny,* and Jackie, Roseanne's sister on *Roseanne*, are forced to stave off blows from their mothers about their choice to be thirty *(gasp!)* and single. Fran confronts her mother about the intense pressure she feels to get married:

> **FRAN:** My therapist says I have to get to the root of the problems that plague me, so naturally I came to see you.
>
> **SYLVIA (FRAN'S MOTHER):** I don't even know what your problem is. *(Mumbling)* Over thirty. Not married.
>
> **FRAN:** You know, my therapist is making me realize I don't need to be married to feel good about myself.
>
> **SYLVIA:** That's nice—why don't you book an appointment on New Year's Eve . . . *(hitting her)* when you're alone?[26]

Some of us are lucky enough not to feel stigmatized for being single women in our own homes, assuming, of course, none of us live with our mothers. Watching Mary Richards as "the single woman archetype," a woman determined to "make it on her own," we could bask in her limelight. Her experiences added elasticity to our notions of a woman's "place."

Following cultural trends, television featured increasing numbers of single-women in the '70s, '80s, and '90s. According to a 1991 census, both the rising age for marriage and the frequency of divorce had resulted in men and women spending, on average, more than half their lives unmarried.[27] So for every time Fran complains about being an over-thirty single woman, for every time a single woman on TV goes on a bad date and wishes she never had to go on one again, we know these women are dealing with the same laments and difficulties we face ourselves. We are all out there experiencing it together. If Alice and Ann Romano from *One Day at a Time*, Kate and Allie, Murphy Brown, the women from *The Golden Girls* and *Designing Women*, and countless others can stand up to the singles stigma, I can too. Do I still feel that my single-by-choice attitude is seen as a kind of cover for my failure to "find a man" and get married? Absolutely. Do I defy that stigma every day I continue to live a happily single-in-my-thirties life? Absolutely.

By the 1990s, TV characters like Ally McBeal and the women from *Sex and the City* had clearly internalized their acceptance of the single life of the career woman. It was no longer an overtly politicized choice; they simply saw it as normal—not a "lifestyle," but a life. This was often publicized by the media as a new type of feminism, in which women could embrace traditional values and attitudes because they had already established their independence. In essence, shows like *Living Single* (the African American precursor to *Sex and the City*), *Girlfriends*, *Caroline in the City*, and *Suddenly Susan* allowed women to covet marriage because it was a choice they made after they'd been single. *Friends* and *Will & Grace* begin with female leads deciding that they are not ready to get married. Of course, this is the world of sitcoms, so the characters invariably reach this life-changing decision while dressed in their wedding gowns, veil and all.

Though we'll probably never be able to completely rid society of the single stigma, the world is slowly moving forward, as is television programming. TV sitcom writers want to represent the status quo because viewers relate to it and find it realistic. Today, television is filled with single women: some working, some not, some divorced, some not. TV represents being single as an option, and not simply for women in their twenties. Shows like *Cybill, Once and Again,* and *Judging Amy* explore the lives of unmarried women over thirty. Television, over time, has shown us possibilities for our lives, possibilities beyond what we hear—inside and outside our own heads—about our prescribed roles as women in America. Presenting singlehood as culturally acceptable encourages women toward all kinds of independence. Every night on television, we see that being a wife and mother aren't our only options.

Mary Richards seems a bit naive in today's light, but her

life as a single professional woman by choice has helped successive generations view female singlehood in different, more expansive ways. Regardless of the waves of backlash that have affected women through the last four decades, it is now distinctly possible that there are generations of women who will not experience "single-illness" and will instead find a fulfilling life without being a wife or mother.[28] Television's single women have, at least, helped trigger some skepticism about societal marriage pressure and, at the most, even helped viewers feel confident about rejecting married life altogether.

One of my favorite examples of both how far we've come and how some things never change is an exchange between Monica Geller and Rachel Green on the pilot episode of *Friends*. After not seeing each other since high school, Rachel meets Monica in a coffeehouse in Manhattan. When Rachel asks Monica if she is married and Monica says no, Rachel pauses and says, "Well, that's okay." Monica responds, with a wonderful simplicity, as if stating the obvious, "I know." To me, her answer is both matter-of-fact and proud, making the implied question seem almost ignorant. As if Monica is thinking, "Duh, it's been okay for female lead characters to be single since 1970. Where have you been?"

Single in the City

Of the mosaic of images we conjure when we think of single women, we tend to place their species most often in a city.

Gloria Steinem, who waited until she was sixty-five to get married, explained to a reporter that she never felt much pressure to get married because she created her own kind of family/support system without being married. She looked for support from her peers, students, and friends, the way women traditionally took solace in their husbands. She also said she didn't feel immense marriage pressure because she lived in New York City. It is no surprise that there tend to be more singles in urban areas and fewer in suburban areas.

In the '50s, many television sitcoms were set in white upper-middle-class suburbs, emphasizing nuclear families and white picket fences. By the '70s, shows, particularly those featuring single women, were located in metropolises. Once again, *The Mary Tyler Moore Show,* set in Minneapolis, was out in front on this trend.

Later, *Rhoda* was set in New York, *The Golden Girls* in Miami, and *Designing Women* in Atlanta. City-dwelling singles became a staple of prime-time entertainment. Cities offer a wonderful mystique and anonymity of living, and shows about single women made use of the city as a background for their experiences.

In many ways, it was more acceptable to be a single woman in an urban environment because more singles exist in cities. These shows also represent how different kinds of people with different kinds of lives are forced to live together. We've seen how Mary was able to find camaraderie with Rhoda and Phyllis, how the women on *Friends* and *Sex and the City* found support and strength in each other. There's some comfort in knowing that no matter what you are going through as a single woman—loneliness, excitement, first dates, relationship breakdowns—a million other women in the same city are going through the same thing.

Television sets its own precedents and repeats the same formats over and over. Once again, we can thank Mary for setting a precedent, this time the urban one. Through the decades, *Alice, One Day at a Time, Murphy Brown, Friends, Caroline in the City, Suddenly Susan,* and countless other series followed suit.

No sooner had the first wave of TV's single women moved to the city than a backlash hit, trying to make women feel threatened and scared. This paved the way for the success of cop dramas like *Cagney & Lacey*, in which women helped other women who were threatened in the big city. As some were persuaded to leave for the safety of the suburbs, millions of others living alone or together braved the crime-ridden streets of the city—and loved it.

The Dating Game

A subject well explored by TV sitcoms is the issue of women and dating. Imagine all the dates you and your friends have been on and think of the comedic possibilities for a television show. Whether the man is a mismatch or "the one," TV's sitcom women have done *a lot* of dating. The "dating scene" elicits both excitement and agony for the characters and for the audience as well.

Murphy Brown, professionally accomplished, was insecure about her personal life but open to a date when the prospect presented itself. She didn't just date, either. She was attracted to a variety of men, one of whom was the character Peter Hunt, a foreign reporter. Because his career required constant travel, he couldn't make a relationship work with Murphy. In an episode titled "It's Just Like Riding a Bike," Peter returns to the news magazine *FYI* and to Murphy, unbeknownst to her friends and coworkers. When she first sees Peter again, Murphy is her usual brisk self.

> **MURPHY:** Let me guess. You were in the neighborhood and just stopped by to use the phone. Outside the building and two blocks down. Better take an umbrella, looks like rain.
>
> *(Murphy walks toward her office. Peter follows her and seems about to ask, "What is going on here?" when Murphy grabs him and pulls him into her office for a very passionate kiss.)*
>
> **PETER:** So, I'm guessing you haven't told the others about us?
>
> **MURPHY:** I like to keep my personal life personal. At least, that's what I always thought if I had a personal life.
>
> **PETER:** Did you get my letter?
>
> **MURPHY:** Yes, very steamy stuff. And a nice touch, rolling it inside a shell-casing.
>
> **PETER:** There's something about artillery fire that makes me think of you.

MURPHY: So many people say that.

PETER: I see you got the lock fixed on your door?

MURPHY: I have to be in editing in two minutes.

PETER: I can do two minutes.

MURPHY: You know, Petey, most women wouldn't consider that a selling point. You know, some of us even like to be wooed: flowers, a little trinket bestowed by the wooer on the wooee.

PETER: You think I can't do romance? I can do romance. How about tonight? I'll wear clean socks.[29]

In dating, Murphy is like many women; she knows that Peter is not the right man for her, but can't resist his adorable charm and immense sex appeal. In the end, the relationship doesn't work out, but we live through Murphy's experiences and compare them to our own.

Sex and the City focuses on dating and sex. Just thinking about the array of men the four main characters—Carrie, Miranda, Charlotte, and Samantha—have dated can make a woman feel better about her own prospects. After all, Charlotte marries a man who turns out to be impotent. Carrie dates everyone from a bisexual to a college stoner who lives with his mother to a politician whose greatest fantasy is to pee on her. With these experiences, women get to vicariously date idiots and good men as well as weirdos and neurotics. The New York dating scene certainly gets a once-over from these four women. Not only do we see their dating lives, we see how that part of their lives affects their friendships, their feelings about themselves, and ultimately their decisions about their personal lives.

Many episodes of *Friends* also deal with the subject of dating. Monica, Phoebe, and Rachel date, have relationships, and have sex. In one episode, Monica and Rachel vie for the attention of action star Jean-Claude Van Damme. In another, the girls leer at politico George Stephanopoulos, whom they can see through their apartment window. In yet another, Rachel dates a dead ringer for her friend Ross. Throughout these dating experiences, just as on *Sex and the City*, viewers get to hear what others think about the men these women choose. In the third episode of the series, Monica confides in a coworker that she is nervous about her friends meeting her new guy, Alan, since they tend to hate all the men she dates. The twist in this episode is that they adore him, which would be perfect if only Monica felt the same way.

> **MONICA:** *(To Alan)* Thanks. I'll call you tomorrow. *(Alan exits; to all)* Okay. Okay, let's let the Alan-bashing begin. Who's gonna take the first shot, hmm?
>
> *(Silence)*
>
> **MONICA:** C'mon!
>
> **ROSS:** I'll go. Let's start with the way he kept picking at . . . no, I'm sorry, I can't do this. We loved him.
>
> **ALL:** Loved him! Yeah! He's great!

MONICA: Wait a minute! We're talking about someone that *I'm* going out with?

ALL: Yeah!

JOEY: Know what was great? The way his smile was kinda crooked.

PHOEBE: Yes, yes! Like the man in the shoe!

ROSS: What shoe?

PHOEBE: From the nursery rhyme. "There was a crooked man, who had a crooked smile, who lived in a shoe, for a . . . while . . . "

ROSS: So I think Alan will become the yardstick against which all future boyfriends will be measured.

RACHEL: What future boyfriends? No . . . no . . . I think this could be, ya know, *it*.

MONICA: Really!

CHANDLER: Oh, yeah. I'd marry him just for his David Hasselhoff impression alone. You know I'm gonna be doing that at parties, right?

ROSS: You know what I like most about him, though?

ALL: What?

ROSS: The way he makes me *feel* about myself.

ALL: Yeah . . . [30]

The irony here is that the first guy her friends like is someone Monica cannot see herself with. A further irony is that although Alan really likes her, he can't stand her friends. While they are disappointed with the breakup, Monica doesn't reveal Alan's true feelings about them. All three female characters date throughout the ten-year run of the show until each finds her "it."

Suddenly Single

It wasn't only women who had put off marriage to a later date who were filling up the increasing ranks of singles. Many women joined singlehood as widows or divorcées. (Interestingly, the Mary Richards character was originally written as a divorcée, but the producers decided divorce would give the character too much of a past. Mary had the clean slate of just having left a relationship, which they felt was more appropriate for the times.) The bonds of marriage, even for women who had been married, were loosening. After the exposé of women's dissatisfaction with their roles as housewives and mothers in Friedan's *Feminine Mystique*, being separated or divorced was also losing some of its stigma. Women were actively declaring their divorced status. One of television's first divorcées, Ann Romano, wasn't embarrassed by it.

MAN: Mrs. Romano?

ANN: It is *Ms.* Romano.[31]

A variety of shows in the last thirty years have focused on women who are dealing or have dealt with divorce or separation. Cybill, an actress and mother, is constantly surrounded by her exes, each with his own issues and quirks. Cybill has already been a wife (more than once) and a mother (to two daughters). She is a semiworking actress, well into her fifties, and her motivation to date doesn't seem to have slowed. Not only is Cybill an example of the mature, been-through-it-all single woman, so is her best friend Maryann (though with more cynicism and daring than Cybill). These aren't the Golden Girls. These are vibrant women living a self-reliant life, and they are anything but spinsters. Growing up watching these shows, I never thought it "abnormal" for a woman in her fifties to live alone.

This is not to say that life for single women on TV has been a cakewalk. For instance, *Grace Under Fire* doesn't only deal with a single, divorced mother of two, it also addresses how freeing divorce can be, especially since Grace's ex-husband is an abusive alcoholic (facts taken from actor Brett Butler's real life). Whether they are single with children, single and lonely, or married and miserable, women have found more and more programs that speak directly to their experience. To go from a world in which divorce is discussed in hushed tones to a world in which divorce is par for the course has been a journey that, in my mind, has helped women face their own choices and learn that there are options outside of marriage.

Kate and Allie, both divorcées with children, make a life

together as a makeshift family in the '90s, when divorce is increasingly common.

> **ALLIE:** Kate, do you want to get married again?
>
> **KATE:** Someday.
>
> **ALLIE:** It wasn't a question. It was a proposal.[32]

Dating in midlife has created a subgenre all its own. In *Once and Again,* Sela Ward plays a recently divorced single mother who is starting a late-in-life relationship with a single father. This isn't *The Brady Bunch*. These characters are complex and the series addresses the difficulties of dating, while also being a mother in your forties.

Stepping Stone Singles

I remember a particularly funny episode of *Friends*, in which Chandler asks his platonic friend Monica if she is not married by the time she reaches a certain age to marry him. Monica's panicked response makes us laugh at the uneasiness women have with the idea that they may never marry. Monica goes on to ask Chandler so many times why he thinks she won't be married that he dives over a chair to escape the conversation. Of course, many women want to get married "one day," but some live with a stifling fear that what they want—marriage—may never happen.

Both on TV and in real life, the term "stepping-stone singles" refers to women who are single, but desperately seeking marriage: women who buy the books about how to "land a man" or play by the dating "rules." On TV, they are vestiges from an age when being single was "deviant"; but unlike the Sally Rogers–esque characters of the past, they mock the society that romanticizes the institution of marriage. In one episode of *The Nanny*, Fran is contemplating asking her boss, and love interest, out on a date.

> **GRACE:** Fran, Daddy asked you out on the first date. Why don't you ask him out on the second?
>
> **FRAN:** Mom raised me to believe that it's the man that should do the courting of the woman.
>
> **SYLVIA (FRAN'S MOTHER):** Sweetheart, I didn't know what I was saying. It was the sixties. I was taking a lot of antacids.[33]

Certainly, one of the most memorable characters desperate to get married is Rhoda Morgenstern, Mary Richards' neighbor. Like Mary, Rhoda is a single woman in the big city, but she has a very different attitude about being single. While Mary is happy with her independence, Rhoda and her mother lament the fact that Rhoda's not married. Most of the comedy is based on that very personality trait. When hearing about any man at all, Rhoda's response is, "Is he married? Sorry, force of habit." On her own show, Rhoda eventually gets her wish and marries her boyfriend, Joe. As viewers, we are happy to see our favorite character get what she wants, even if it isn't what we want.

I wasn't particularly happy, when *Sex and the City* ended, that the women who had been single and free for six years, all settled down in one form or another. But at the same time, all their years of dating woes, marriage fears, and personal decisions represent the many ways women can be single and the many ways our choices about men, relationships, and sex affect our lives. Even if their experiences culminate in marriage, I doubt many women, especially Carrie Bradshaw and friends, are unhappy about all the years they learned about themselves and what they wanted out of life before becoming part of a couple. No matter how much these women need men, they prove that they can, if they have to, live without them.

Single as a State of Mind

I know that there would be no single life on TV without Mary Richards and a lot less validation of that life without *Sex and the City*.

On the very first episode of *Sex and the City (SATC)*, Carrie Bradshaw, a writer, examines the state of being single today in New York City. "Welcome to the age of un-innocence. No one has breakfast at Tiffany's, and no one has affairs to remember. Instead, we have breakfast at seven AM and affairs we try to forget as quickly as possible. Self-protection and closing the deal are paramount. Cupid has flown the co-op. How the hell did we get into this mess?"[34] We all can agree with Carrie that sometimes single life feels like a mess we have gotten ourselves into, but it is also amazing to hear a woman talk about seeking love and happiness through singlehood in the same way men do. Asserting that women should be self-protective, but can also indulge in "affairs," is something that many women today can relate to.

Single women in sitcoms have given us a great deal to work with. At the end of *SATC's* first episode, Carrie meets Mr. Big and introduces herself as a writer working on a column about women who have sex like men. What an introduction. Even when Carrie realizes that she wants to be in love and doesn't want to feel guilty about her sexual conquests, she spends the next five years doing just what she was examining in her column: living a single life with no regret, embarrassment, or stigma.

Today, single adults without children compose the majority of the population, and this doesn't seem to be changing. Unlike previous generations, we aren't booming with babies. In fact, being single in America today isn't half as embarrassing as it was before 1970. Television is entertainment, and entertainment makes things appear better, more interesting, and even more glamorous than they really are. In a way, this has helped single women feel less ashamed of their situation as they see wonderful dynamic, women like Carrie Bradshaw, and the women of *Living Single* and *Friends*. My own New York City apartment may barely compare to the rent-controlled luxury of Monica and Rachel's pied-à-terre, but like those fumbling, funny, driven characters, I too have a space of my own to live my single life. I have pushed alongside them through the ups and downs of being single (without any plan in sight to get married).

In *The Improvised Woman: Single Women Reinventing Single Life*, one of my favorite books about the experience of being a single woman, Marcelle Clements explains the confusion and difficulties single women face:

> *Many single women sporadically careen back and forth between being viewed (and perceiving themselves) as distinctly rejected—"pathetic" is the word that comes up—or as possessing the eminently enviable aura—"glamorous" is the euphemism. My guess is that many women feel both, depending on whom they're with. After all, as a rule hardly anyone feels particularly talismanic to themselves, unless they're in the manic phase of their cycle. Conflicting messages proliferate from the same source: "In my department . . . most people are married," said one woman, "and they like to have me as this sort of wandering, sexy, romantic figure, but they would also like to have me married because they think it would make me happy and because it would make me less threatening.*[35]

The truth about women's history is that regardless of the choices offered to them in their time and place, women always feel the push and pull of tradition versus progression. It is one thing to watch self-reliant single women on TV, but quite another to be one yourself. These TV shows have externalized all those internal struggles many of us feel. Ally McBeal may be a successful single lawyer, but she is an emotional roller coaster. Some find her annoying—no one likes to listen to anyone complain without taking action—while others find her inspiring. (Ally works in the same office as her ex-boyfriend and his new wife, setting herself up for misery.) Ally McBeal actually made the cover of *Time* with an accompanying feature story that asked if she was the face of "new feminism." In my opinion, she is just one of the faces, and for me, she is bolstered by a lifetime of single female TV icons living the lives they chose for themselves.

So many women in my TV family have helped expand the available options for women's personal lives. *Sex and the City* feels like the culmination of years of struggling to show everyone that being married is no better than being single. As opposed to being seen as old, desperate, and pathetic, the *SATC* characters are hot middle-aged women who live in a world where being single is not only a choice, it's often the preferred one. As Marcelle Clements remarks, single women can seem almost "glamorous." If the *SATC* women are anything, they are definitely that. Even if single life isn't a party-hopping, fabulous-clothes-wearing romp around New York City, Carrie, Miranda, Samantha, and Charlotte give us a glamorized version of ourselves, the same way *Leave It to Beaver* once offered 1950s America a sanitized version of the wife and mother. As the oft-quoted Virginia Slims advertisement boasted in the late '60s, "You've come a long way, baby!"

Chapter 2

Unequal Unions
Marriage on Television

> **PAUL:** There's my beautiful bride.
> **JAMIE:** Bite me.
>
> **—Mad About You**

Anyone who watched prime-time TV in the '50s and '60s saw the institution of marriage through the lens of a conservative ideal, an airbrushed, picket-fenced life where everyone was quite happy in his or her highly defined roles. Take, for example, *Leave It to Beaver's* June and Ward Cleaver. While he braved the male business world, she stayed home and raised the children, vacuumed in her high heels, and had a delicious dinner ready when Ward walked through the front door after a day at the office.

Just as the Cleavers and Ozzie and Harriet Nelson depicted societal attitudes about marriage in the early days of television, couples depicted in later sitcoms showed the reality

45

that all marriages were not states of wedded bliss. In the early '60s, Betty Friedan's *Feminine Mystique* shed light on the fact that many housewives felt inferior to the idyllic representations of themselves on TV, which also made them depressed. Ironically, television's bubbleheaded housewives of the '50s and genies and witches of the '60s served as catalysts for the women's liberation movement and eventually for network programmers to change the image of women in marriage.

From the 1970s onward, women's traditional role within marriage has been dramatically challenged by Maude and Walter Findlay *(Maude)*, Roseanne and Dan Conner *(Roseanne)*, Louise and George Jefferson *(The Jeffersons)*, Steven and Elyse Keaton *(Family Ties)*, Paul and Jamie Buchman *(Mad About You)*, and the title couple in *Dharma & Greg*. Even today's more conservative family sitcoms, including *Everybody Loves Raymond* and *According to Jim*, which center around the male lead characters, feature TV wives and mothers with more power, more competency, and more strength than their '50s and '60s TV predecessors. These women may exist within a more traditional sitcom family format (they do not work outside the home), but they rarely defer to their husbands' wishes. They argue for equal division of labor within the home and voice differing opinions within their marriages. The cultural and social changes that have occurred since the mid-twentieth century cannot be abandoned even within series that consciously adhere to a traditional nuclear family ethos. Debra Barone, wife and mother on *Everybody*

Loves Raymond, expects much more help from her husband than June Cleaver ever did from Ward.

> **RAY:** Morning, honey. Anything for breakfast?
>
> **DEBRA:** How about pancakes?
>
> **RAY:** Oh, great.
>
> **DEBRA:** *(Handing him a list)* I need eggs, butter, milk, syrup, and pancakes. While you're out, could you go to the bank, a hardware store, and the dry cleaner's?
>
> **RAY:** I'll just have cereal.
>
> **DEBRA:** Ray!
>
> **RAY:** Well, what do you do all day while I'm at work?
>
> **DEBRA:** *(Picking up both twin boys)* I entertain men, Ray.[1]

The prime-time nuclear family has evolved since the whitewashed era of the 1950s. Few women can look at their early TV counterparts and identify with them. My mother's and grandmother's marriages looked very different from that of the Cleavers and Rob and Laura Petrie of *The Dick Van Dyke Show*. These early prime-time moms and housewives reflected sanitized versions of dependent women. But they represented a select group, alien to the real-life experiences of most American women. Moreover, these characters were not effective in keeping women in their place. In fact, many women recognized the falseness of those images of marriage and womanhood, and used them to help buttress a movement—women's liberation—that would fight the confinement of marriage and the lack of opportunities beyond their domestic role within the nuclear family.

With the introduction of family comedies like *Maude, Good Times,* and *Roseanne,* television expanded its representations of marriage in the '70s, '80s, and '90s. Those shows tackled such issues as infidelity, divorce, financial problems, and power struggles. Though Lucy Ricardo may have disobeyed Ricky time and again, everyone knew who was really in charge. But when we were privy to conversations between Maude and her husband, Walter, we saw that the balance of power was up for grabs, reflecting the reality of the typical American home. By 1980, only 15 percent of American marriages consisted of a father who worked and a mother who stayed home with the children, down from 70 percent in the 1950s.[2] It was not simply that TV had changed; marriage in America had changed and even television couldn't ignore that fact. I can't imagine any 1950s TV wife turning to her husband and barking "Bite me!" as Jamie Buchman in *Mad About You* does. It may not be eloquent, but it is wonderful to know that TV wives get frustrated and angry (just like women in the real world). I'm sure even June Cleaver felt like turning to Ward every once in a while to say, "Bite me."

The Evolution of the TV Wife

While baby boomers (those seventy-six million Americans born between 1946 and 1964) and their parents watched the sanitized images of TV marriages, successive generations have seen them on reruns. Early-evening prime-time slots have generally been a place to examine, explore, and expose marriage in America. The "domestic" or "family" comedy, as it is known, has been a television staple throughout the medium's short existence. The sitcom is unlike film, a finite two-hour involvement with characters, where the final credits roll just as the male and female leads overcome obstacles in order to finally get together. Marriage is barely represented in the movies (where there is greater emphasis on romance), but marriage has always been depicted on television. Historian Susan Douglas has not-so-fond memories of the types of women she saw in early family comedies: "At night on TV . . . there were the infamous family sitcoms, like *Father Knows Best*, *Leave It to Beaver*, *The Adventures of Ozzie and Harriet*, and *The Donna Reed Show*, with their smiling, benevolent, self-effacing, pearl-clad moms who loved to vacuum in high heels."[3]

Even though my own mother always worked outside the home, a situation barely represented on the TV she watched growing up, she treated housework as just that—work. She wanted to keep a clean home, but never defined herself as a wife by her dusting or vacuuming. Nevertheless, as I got older, I saw how early television's images of marriage, as unrealistic as they were, did affect my mother. Even today, she doesn't like to leave the house without makeup, something I do without even noticing. I feel that mascara and lipstick are a bit dressed up for, say, the grocery store. But my mother was raised on an entirely different TV diet. She believes that beds should always be made and dishes always washed, which, to me, seem like vestiges from an earlier era. At the same time, I can almost hear my own mother's mother reinforcing these domestic rules to her, making them the very definition of a good wife.

Even for younger generations, it is difficult not to internalize these images, so much so that "kids not even born when *Bewitched* premiered in 1964 nonetheless grew up with Darrin and Sam"[4] through the magic of cable TV, nostalgia programming, and endless reruns. Our ideals about marriage still feature black-and-white images of merry suburban housewives living in marital bliss. Of course, television slowly incorporated modernism into its programming. We still remember Ralph Kramden's famous rejoinder, "To the moon, Alice," but we also remember Maude taunting her husband with the caustic phrase, "God'll getcha for that!"

And Then There's Maude

The perfect white-suburban, upper-middle-class stay-at-home moms, the typical television women before 1970, have slowly morphed into characters that not only escape the stereotype, but subvert it. One of the first overtly feminist wives on television was Maude. She ran her house with her scratchy voice and sassy quips. I don't think anyone, including her husband, Walter, wanted to mess with Maude. Strength of character, solid convictions, and the amazing ability to speak her mind are just some of the traits that made her a revolutionary departure from the June Cleavers of television. As the first spin-off of the groundbreaking sitcom *All in the Family, Maude* is based on the character who had been introduced to America as Edith Bunker's cousin and the diametric opposite of political reactionary Archie Bunker. She is liberal. He is working-class. She is upper-middle class. The irony is that *both* Archie and Maude speak their minds without censure or fear.[5] In fact, the *Maude* theme song pays homage to the strong, mouthy, infamous women who came before her, including Lady Godiva, Joan of Arc, and Betsy Ross. Like the inimitable female trailblazers who came before her, Maude was also "enterprising, socializing" and "everything but compromising." As the song proclaims, "Right on, Maude!"

The overtly political show deals with some very nontraditional marital problems—alcoholism, unwanted pregnancy, depression, infidelity, life, death, and everything in between. *Maude* premiered in September 1972, on the heels of *The Mary Tyler Moore Show* and amidst the political turmoil brought about by the feminist movement. If you could be Mary Richards when you were single, you could be Maude when you got married. Maude was my Murphy Brown before Murphy was ever created. Though Maude is a wife, mother, and grandmother, she is far from traditional. Ballsy, outspoken, and as stubborn and determined as any male character, Maude was an entirely new creation. I could relate to the family in this series, feeling ostracized myself for coming from a divorced household: Walter is Maude's fourth husband, and Maude is Walter's second wife. Even if I was a little girl, I knew this marriage offered Maude more equality and independence than previous TV marriages had offered women. Maude clearly had the final say in her household and her marriage.

> **MAUDE:** Walter, if you don't want my daughter and my only grandchild living here with us, just tell me.
>
> **WALTER:** And . . . ?
>
> **MAUDE:** . . . and, I'll rip your heart out.

Lucy Ricardo and Laura Petrie were the wives of the past; Maude was the wife of the future. This highly successful show added a new dimension to the representation of married women on television. As a character (and as a series), Maude shook things up: "With one hand, she unbuttoned the stuffed shirts of convention, and with the other, she gave the finger to authority."[6] Just as I've tried to channel the courage and boldness of Murphy Brown, I have also asked myself, "What would Maude do?" She gave women the inspiration and strength to speak their minds, even if only to their husbands.

Retro-Sexism and *thirtysomething*

I admit the shameful fact that I am a child of the shameless '80s, growing up in that strange decade of extreme conservatism, capitalism, and consumerism. It was a time when both my family and the nation at large were bombarded with messages about the importance of the nuclear family, while more and more marriages were ending in divorce. Just as my family was becoming increasingly "nontraditional," our country was experiencing what writer Susan Faludi labeled "a media backlash" against women. In the '70s, *Maude* took charge of her husband and her marriage; but the '80s brought us a slew of retro-wives, modern versions of June Cleaver and Harriet Nelson.

The '80s backlash was tame in comparison to what women of the '50s experienced.[7] Nevertheless, the emphasis on "family values" during the 1980s attempted to stigmatize those who didn't live in a nuclear family, which ironically most Americans did not (and still don't). TV programmers clearly wanted to follow the prevailing ethos of the time. Thus, the quintessential TV wife of the 1980s was Hope Steadman on the drama *thirtysomething*. The show was created by ABC to appeal specifically to "yuppies" (the widely used term for the young urban professional demographic).

The show seemed a bland step back to a time when women were housewives, first and foremost: An overachieving Princeton graduate, Hope gives up her career to raise her daughter and care for her husband, Michael. The show's other lead couple, Elliot and Nancy, are more modern and acknowledge the fact that they have problems, which leads to a separation and eventually a divorce. Nancy is unhappy with her role as a housewife, having given up her career as an artist. If the housewives are depressed and troubled, the single women on the show fare even worse. Reflecting the conservatism of the time, the show attempted to glamorize traditional gender roles. If you had enjoyed *Maude* or *Roseanne,* Hope and Nancy weren't nearly as interesting as the two female characters who pushed the limits of what viewers expected from "the little woman."

In analyzing television programming over the years, many historians and social critics acknowledge that sitcoms have been more open to women's progress and expanding roles than other television formats, including news, dramas, and late-night programming. But author Susan Faludi describes how even on sitcoms, women were losing ground in the eighties.[8] In her examination of the 1987–88 season, to which Faludi refers as "the backlash's high watermark on TV," she found that 60 percent of new shows had no regular female characters and 20 percent had no women at all.[9] "Women's disappearance from prime-time television in the late '80s repeats a programming pattern from the last backlash when, in the late '50s and early '60s, single dads ruled the TV roosts and female characters were suddenly erased from the set," she writes.[10] With shows such as *My Two Dads* and *Full House*, the prime-time sitcoms of that period overwhelmingly featured male single parents. In fact, Faludi found that two-thirds of the sitcom children featured in the 1987–88 season lived with only a father or male guardian, a figure that stood at only 11 percent in the real world.[11]

Of course, there were notable exceptions to these findings, as well as millions of female TV viewers who were savvy enough to ignore the stereotypes and focus on more realistic female representations. Like me, Susan Douglas found her share of inspiring female TV characters in the '80s.

> Feminism is constantly being reinvented, and reinvented through determination and compromise, so that women try, as best they can, to have love and support as well as power and autonomy. As they do, they have certainly taken note, with Susan Faludi's help, of a backlash filled with wishful-thinking pronouncements about the "death" of feminism and the heralding of a new "postfeminist" age. But they have also taken heart in Roseanne, L.A. Law, Murphy Brown . . . in the various defiant, funny, smart, and strong women they see on TV.[12]

While the consumer-driven, Reagan-filled '80s were not kind to women on television, there were some notable exceptions. Hope Steadman may have reveled in her neoconservative domesticity, embodying "the good mother . . . bathed in heavenly light as she floated about the kitchen, rapturous over breast-feeding," but countless real women saw through these sanitized images. In fact, the show never ranked higher than twenty-fifth in the Nielsen ratings. A new group of women were about to take the stage, the ones who resisted and even ridiculed these ideals.[13]

What Doesn't Kill Us . . .

Roseanne was no Hope Steadman. Premiering in 1988, *Roseanne* not only showcased a working-class family, but was based on the premise that Roseanne—overweight, caustic, and sharp—was in charge . . . of everything. She took control of both her children and her husband with a crass blend of humor and an overt acknowledgment of what women have to go through in our society as wives and mothers. As a stand-up comedian, Roseanne Barr had based her comedy on the world she knew—as a housewife and mother, or "domestic goddess," as she termed it. Her routines—and eventually her eponymous sitcom—reflected how she felt about that job and how *she* chose to go about being a wife and mother.

Like *Maude, Roseanne* deals with very real issues rarely addressed in television marriages. Roseanne and Dan Conner don't have it easy. They struggle with money, with making time for their kids and for each other. They have to work on keeping their fifteen-year marriage on track. They fight on equal ground (many would say with Roseanne having more power than her husband) and they deal realistically with marriage issues many domestic sitcoms shy away from.

From the start, it was clear that this was a completely new TV family. Besides the fact that both Roseanne and Dan are a little overweight, a little slovenly, and very honest, they present marriage in a way few had ever seen on television before. Their opening dialogue in the show's pilot, titled "Life and Stuff," sets up a marriage in which grievances and unfair cultural standards are acknowledged. It is morning in the hectic Conner household when Dan enters the kitchen.

> **DAN:** Is there coffee?
>
> **ROSEANNE:** Dan, isn't there coffee every morning?
>
> **DAN:** Yes.
>
> **ROSEANNE:** In the fifteen years that we've been married, has there ever been one morning where there wasn't any coffee?
>
> **DAN:** No.
>
> **ROSEANNE:** Then why do you have to ask me every morning if there's coffee?
>
> **DAN:** Is there toast?[14]

This addresses women's traditional domestic role (makers of coffee) and husbands' tendency to take that role for granted. Roseanne Barr explained that TV had seen too many "moms" and too few "matriarchs," so her goal was to make "radical television by rendering the mundane with grace and uncommon insight."[15] In the pilot episode, as Roseanne and Dan Conner assess their duties and responsibilities for the day, her vision for the series is abundantly clear.

> **ROSEANNE:** Dan, the sink's all backed up again.
>
> **DAN:** I'll plunge it right after breakfast.
>
> **ROSEANNE:** Well, I don't want you to plunge it. I want you to fix it now.

DAN: You got it, babe.

ROSEANNE: Now, this is the third time this week. You gotta fix it today.

DAN: Absolutely.

(Eldest teen daughter, Becky, enters the kitchen.)

BECKY: Mom, my book bag just fell apart!

ROSEANNE: I just bought it yesterday.

BECKY: Mom, please, you gotta take it back!

ROSEANNE: Alright, I'll do it after work.

As Roseanne recognizes the increasing obligations and errands that will fill her day, she turns to her husband for help—something the perfectly organized and competent wives of earlier television would be loath to do.

ROSEANNE: Could you meet with Darlene's teacher today?

DAN: I can't do it today, babe. I'm putting in a bid on a job, and if I get it, me and Freddy start construction this afternoon.

ROSEANNE: Well, how about this book bag? Can you exchange that? Can you fit that into your tight schedule?

DAN: Either that or fix the sink.

ROSEANNE: Okay, fix the sink. I'll do everything else, like I always do. I'll have to get off work an hour early, lose an hour's pay, totally rearrange my whole schedule. *(Sarcastically)* But I don't mind.

DAN: Are you ever sorry we got married?

ROSEANNE: Every second of my life.[16]

The overt joking about the constant work of a wife and mother helps defuse Roseanne's obvious anger about cultural double standards. Every statement she makes sheds light on what is really going on in American homes.

Roseanne reflected the fact that many dads were remote when it came to daily family life. Historian Susan Douglas writes, "Unlike Ozzie or Dr. Stone or Ward, who were always hanging around the house in their cardigans, eager to help Mom reason with the kids, my father and most fathers I knew were not around the house much, and when they were, they stayed far away from the metal cylinders Mom did get to deploy—Pledge cans and vacuum cleaner hoses. No wonder so many of our mothers were pissed."[17]

Roseanne was the first TV mom I saw who was pissed, just like the majority of the women I knew, including my own mother. When Roseanne argued against women's confined roles, I knew I'd met my role model if I ever decided to get married. She was as close to real as I had ever seen on television. She was brutally honest about the struggle of married women and did her best to humorously point it out at every turn.

Roseanne Barr also inspired me to try my hand at stand-up comedy. (The world of stand-up did not prove to be my cup of tea—too many late nights in smoky clubs and too much missed TV.) When she burst onto the comedy scene in the 1980s,

Roseanne was an entirely new species: a wife and mother who went into the male-centered world of comedy to specifically make fun of being a wife and mother. She wasn't traditionally attractive or thin, but she possessed a bold confidence expressed most vividly in her famous statement, "The thing women have get to learn is that nobody gives you power. You just take it." The success of Roseanne Barr's stand-up comedy persona, in which she famously dubbed herself a "domestic goddess," directly inspired the character she would play in her sitcom. Just as it came through in her standup comedy, Roseanne was not a typical mother, and she made sure that if she was to star in a sitcom—the penultimate achievement for standup comics—she was to be a matriarch. She even had to fight to name the show *Roseanne* rather than "Life and Stuff." Of course, television shows are not simply mirrors that reflect reality, but are "careful, deliberate constructions."[18] TV historian and critic Todd Gitlin likens them to "funhouse mirrors" that distort reality by magnifying some aspects of real life, while ignoring or demonizing others.[19]

When *Roseanne* debuted, the roles of married women on television, and in real life, were in flux—so much so that experts' advice about how to be a "good wife" was continually changing. From Betty Friedan to Phyllis Schlafly and Helen Gurley Brown, our society was inundated with mixed messages about women at home and at work. And it wasn't only suburban middle-class wives. Television finally was beginning to represent working-class marriages and their unique struggles.

In *Roseanne's* pilot episode, Roseanne returns home from a hectic day of work, followed by a meeting with one of her children's teachers, followed by returning her daughter's defective book bag. She confronts her husband about their unequal workload.

> **ROSEANNE:** How come that sink ain't fixed yet?
>
> **DAN:** Oh, I'm gonna get right on it.

As their conversation progresses, Roseanne learns that Dan didn't get the bid on the job and spent the day fixing cars with his friends.

> **ROSEANNE:** So, you had, like, the whole day off?
>
> **DAN:** No, I didn't have the whole day off. I was busy, uh . . . making contacts.
>
> **ROSEANNE:** With what? Dwight's truck and a six-pack?
>
> **DAN:** Oh, c'mon, Roseanne. I was hoping to kick a little work my way. I got my last two jobs from Dwight.
>
> **ROSEANNE:** Well, maybe he can get you your next wife?
>
> **DAN:** Maybe.
>
> **ROSEANNE:** Oh, well, what would I ever do without you? You just sit there and drink your beer, hubby, I'll fix the sink myself.

DAN: The hell you will! I'll fix the sink, Roseanne.

ROSEANNE: Oh, talk is cheap, Mr. Fix-It.

DAN: Fixin' the sink is the husband's job. I am the husband!

ROSEANNE: Yeah, and I'm the wife, so it's my job to do everything else, right?

DAN: Oh, don't give me that.

ROSEANNE: Oh, well, it must be true. I put in eight hours a day at the factory and then I come home and put in another eight hours. I'm runnin' around like a maniac taking back book bags, talkin' to teachers, and everything else, and you don't do nothin'.

DAN: Whoa! Hey, I do plenty around here!

ROSEANNE: Like what?

DAN: Clean the gutters.

ROSEANNE: And?

DAN: What's the point here, Roseanne?

ROSEANNE: The point is that you think this is some magic kingdom where you just sit up here on your throne. And you think everything gets done by some magical wizard. Oh, *poof*. The laundry's folded. *Poof*. Dinner's on the table.

DAN: You want me to make dinner? I'll make dinner.

ROSEANNE: And I'll spend the rest of the night washing dishes.

DAN: I wash dishes.

ROSEANNE: When?

DAN: Thursday.

ROSEANNE: In 1972.[20]

Honest and fearless, Roseanne exposes the reality of marriage, not the fantasy. She tells Dan that she is angry and with good reason. "I got a news flash for you," she says. "You better come down off that throne and start helping me out around here 'cause I am getting fed up!"[21] Many wives can relate.

Behind the scenes, Roseanne Barr was also making headlines. Though the show's first season was both successful and critically acclaimed, it was also "famously difficult," with stories of Barr often walking off the set and once staging a sit-in over a dispute with the head writer.[22] The offscreen difficulties of this powerful determined woman were not all that different from those onscreen. I can't imagine the battles she was forced to fight to preserve her vision in the male-dominated network TV world. Regardless of the tabloid sensations, I saw a woman who did whatever she had to in order to be heard and to push the envelope of what was acceptable on television.

Television was slowly following the changes that were occurring in real marriages. With *Maude* and *Roseanne,* the pressure to be the perfect wife and have dinner on the table when the man of the house arrived home was lessening. But television's depiction of the perfect wife was steeped in myth from the beginning. As Stephanie Coontz argues in her book *The Way We Never Were: American Families and the Nostalgia*

Trap, early television depicted life the way we wished it to be, and it was no more a "golden age" than any other time in American history.[23] Shows like *Roseanne* and *Maude* helped television shatter that myth and catch up with real life.

It wasn't just women's roles that were becoming more realistic. Throughout the '70s, and to a lesser degree in the '80s, some sitcoms were starting to look beyond the comforts of the white upper-middle-class world. Working-class families were now making inroads into the genre with shows like *All in the Family, Good Times,* and *Roseanne.* Just as *The Mary Tyler Moore Show* spawned new versions of the single working girl sitcom, working-class family comedies found their own place in our collective popular culture.

The New TV Marriages

Depicting the working-class marriage wasn't the only break-through sitcoms made during the '80s. Late in the decade, audiences saw all types of marriages being examined as even more conventional marriages were changing. For example, *Mad About You* gave us an urban marriage that adhered very little to its traditional TV past. The wife and husband have much in common—they are both educated (she at an Ivy League school), they're passionate about their careers, and they have similar attitudes toward in-laws, household responsibilities, and their marriage in general. While Roseanne struggles with the constraints of the American wife,

Mad About You's Jamie Buchman is a woman who takes equality in marriage for granted. She and her husband, Paul, address their marital woes with the same kind of humor and neuroticism. Until they decide to have a baby, the gender issue in their marriage is, essentially, moot.

The first episode *of Mad About You* opens with the Buchmans in bed. Jamie is snoring so loudly she is keeping her husband awake. When Paul wakes her, Jamie tells him to run the shower for her and make the coffee, in radical contrast to Dan Conner. In this new version of the American married couple, Paul and Jamie are presented as equals—sometimes Paul makes the coffee, sometimes Jamie makes the coffee. This seems a lot closer to the egalitarian marriage I would like to have someday.

The first conversation we hear between the Buchmans is about sex—and, lo and behold, it is Jamie who brings up the topic, upset about the infrequency with which she is getting sex.

> **JAMIE:** It doesn't bother you that we haven't had sex in five days?
>
> **PAUL:** Hello?
>
> **JAMIE:** I just don't understand why it doesn't bother you. It's been almost a week.
>
> **PAUL:** It's not a week.
>
> **JAMIE:** Sunday will be a week. What's going on with us?

PAUL: What's going on with us is that we're married five months and the sexual part is over. I thought you understood that, I'm sorry.[24]

Jamie continues to push the issue, and Paul, explaining how busy they have been, insists that there's nothing wrong with their marriage. It is refreshing to hear a woman talk about her own sexual needs without any shame. Considering it wasn't all that long ago that Lucy and Ricky slept in twin beds, *Mad About You* offers a more realistic depiction of marriage between equals rather than a dependent relationship that avoids even a hint of sexuality.

JAMIE: What can I say? I'm a woman. I have needs. I'm young and vital.

PAUL: And beautiful.

JAMIE: *(Looking in mirror)* Is my head getting bigger?

PAUL: And neurotic.[25]

They leave for work together, both carrying briefcases, both running late, and both on very equal terms. They accept each other, make fun of each other, and know that marriage is not perfect. Other than being white, upper-middle-class New Yorkers, they were a departure from the traditional television marriage, because they interacted as equals.

Depicting marriages between equals is a growing trend on television. In *Dharma & Greg,* a blue-blooded, rich lawyer and a

Jewish hippie yoga teacher marry after knowing each other for only three days. Regardless of their dramatic differences, there seems to be no hierarchy in their relationship. Sometimes Greg agrees with Dharma's "hippy-dippy" ideas, and sometimes Dharma helps her husband impress his upper-crust family and friends. The two spouses compromise between the traditional and nontraditional. In the third episode of the show, after Greg has relinquished his high-style life to live in Dharma's alternative loft, she uses her plumbing skills to make Greg feel more at home in her space. Along with her mother, Abby, and her friend Jane, Dharma begins renovating the bathroom; when Kitty, Greg's mother, enters the loft, she's shocked to find three women working on a job traditionally reserved for men.

> **KITTY:** Dharma, I'm sure I'm going to regret asking this, but why are you installing a shower?
>
> **DHARMA:** Don't got one.
>
> **ABBY:** Yeah, but she does have the bathtub from our old place in Half Moon Bay. I gave birth to her in that tub.
>
> **KITTY:** And that's where Gregory bathes?
>
> **JANE:** Yep. Seen it with my own eyes.
>
> **KITTY:** Why do you people live like this?
>
> **DHARMA:** 'Cause we can't camp on the beach anymore. Besides, Kitty, I love it here. I mean, I did all of this work myself. Did you know this used to be a battery factory?

KITTY: Ah. And to your credit, you've nearly disguised that fact.

DHARMA: Thanks. I just wish once I get this shower installed, that Greg'll feel more at home.

KITTY: So you're doing this for Gregory?

DHARMA: Yeah. I want him to feel totally comfortable.[26]

Dharma and Greg illustrate TV's new marriage—they are individuals as well as equals, and much of their humor is derived from poking fun at traditional marriage. Of course, there are traditional elements to the show, mainly introduced by Greg's conservative parents, but they are balanced with nontraditional elements, often introduced by Dharma's parents—who, by the way, never married.

The difference and individuality displayed by these new characters give TV women more complexity and color. After motherhood, the most traditional role for a woman is that of wife, and now we have a variety of ways to look at that role.

Some Things Change, Some Things Don't

Since 1970, television has showed us marriages that have changed and marriages that have stayed the same. Real-world marriages have made strides in equalizing the distribution of household and familial duties. Unfortunately, no matter how many strong, even intimidating, wives are depicted on television, traditional notions of women's roles and "women's work" won't disappear overnight. We see Dan Conner cling-ing to a world in which "wifely" duties are clearly delineated throughout the *Roseanne* series. But Dan and other husbands know that these duties will be shared more and more. Femi-nist wives still face the inequality of labor in their marriages but are vocal about the inherent unfairness of gender-biased expectations. Dual-income couples are now the norm. That does not mean that housework (historically, devalued as actual work) is divided more equally now than it was fifty years ago.

In her landmark book *The Second Shift*, Arlie Hochschild examines the ways in which societal changes in power, the economy, and cultural values occur inside of marriage as well as outside of it. Problems that seem personal or specific to a marriage are often "individual experiences of powerful eco-nomic and cultural shock waves that are not caused by one person or two."[27]

What happens outside our homes finds a way inside them, and sometimes that way is through our television sets. Since 98 percent of Americans own a TV, television programming is a part of our lives and its depiction of marriage is not irrel-evant to our ideas about married life. In America, women are increasingly taking a different path from the one followed by their mothers and grandmothers; but men diverge from their fathers' path less often.[28] As Roseanne tries to explain to her husband, when she gets home from work, she faces another full eight hours of work for the family, a "second shift." Based on her research involving dual-income couples, Arlie Hoch-schild finds exactly what angers Roseanne.

> *If women begin to do less at home because they have less*
> *time, if men do little more, if the work of raising children*
> *and tending a home requires roughly the same effort,*
> *then the questions of who does what at home and of what*
> *"needs doing" become key. Indeed, they may become a*
> *source of deep tension in the marriage . . . [29]*

Television hasn't shied away from addressing this prob-lem. *Maude, Good Times, Rhoda, Family Ties, Roseanne,* and *Mad About You* explicitly address inequality and separation of labor in marriage. Even more conservative series like *The Cosby Show, Growing Pains,* and *Home Improvement* occasion-ally address the difficulties of dual-income marriages and how couples negotiate the workload and their roles.

Unlike the shows my mother and grandmother saw, I've seen all kinds of marriages on TV, from best friends deciding to marry (like Monica and Chandler on *Friends*) to the marriage of a boss and employee from separate worlds on *The Nanny* to the nonsexual marriage between a gay man and a straight woman on *Will & Grace*. I feel grateful that marriages explored on TV have been this varied and focused, in some cases, on issues of equality. *Roseanne* and its counterparts acknowledge the realities of marriage. I know, without ever having been married, that marriage is not a perfect white-picket-fence sepia-tone den of tranquil-ity like everything else in life, it has its own set of problems, disappointments, and expectations. More realistic sitcom marriages have helped younger generations of both sexes think carefully about the decision to marry as opposed to simply succumbing to the cultural pressure.

The balance of power in marriage today may still lack full equality, but the only way to move forward and change that is to acknowledge that reality. I thank the television shows I have watched for helping to lay bare what really goes on behind closed doors.

Chapter 3

Because I Said So!

Parenting in Prime Time

> I figure that if the children are alive when I get home, I've done my job.
>
> **—Roseanne**

In today's world, when women's equality is often seen as a given, who would want Donna Reed for a mother? (Or, for that matter, uptight, cardigan-wearing Ward Cleaver as a father?) For me and many TV viewers, women like Alice, Maude, Roseanne, Elyse Keaton, Grace, Cybill, Lois (of *Malcolm in the Middle*), and even Marge Simpson represent a new version of motherhood that confronts issues midcentury sitcoms never tackled. When I watch reruns of *Father Knows Best* and *The Donna Reed Show,* I see a world where the problems of being a parent and running a household are so minor—a boy loses his sweater (a real storyline from *Leave It to Beaver*), a teen makes two dates for the same night—as to be irrelevant to real-life parents. Of course, these "problems" are deftly addressed, usually by Dad, with some "well-pointed words of advice," and the child automatically "learns the moral lesson" only to be faced with another minor infraction the following week.[1]

Real-life white, suburban middle-class children of the '50s and '60s weren't little angels who made only minor screw-ups. Early family sitcoms were not ready to depict the dirty reality of drugs, teen pregnancy, defiance, and delinquency. Television shows featuring perfect children didn't reflect the experience of many American families.

The "perfection trap" of early sitcoms still has a tight hold over the American family. That's partly because we look nostalgically to a past that never existed, and partly because culture, politics, and mass media continue to extol the nuclear family's virtues even though most of us don't live in one. Child-rearing—whether a person is married or divorced, black or white, working- or middle-class, gay or straight—has changed dramatically in the last fifty years; for most people, the nuclear family exists only on TV.

It didn't represent sitcoms many households in the fifties, when women made up nearly 30 percent of the workforce.[2] As Susan Douglas explains, "All too many of us witnessed the tensions and the resentments in our mothers, and these shaped, quite powerfully, how we negotiated our way through the media dreams before us."[3] Throughout the '50s and '60s, real life and television were going in opposite directions. There were some signs of progress, like sitcoms featuring witches and genies—expressing female power through magic. But inevitably, Samantha of *Bewitched* and Jeannie of *I Dream of Jeannie* submit to their husbands' or "masters'" wishes.

Cultural assumptions, like nostalgic sitcoms, are slow to adjust to reality. By 1955, more women (including married women with children) had jobs outside the home than in any previous time in our nation's history.[4] Yet they were stigmatized by a culture that believed a woman's place was in the home. In *Feminist Chronicles,* Reka Hoff, who worked as a lawyer in 1956, recalls the hostility she and other career women faced and their constant need to defend themselves: "If unmarried, their career is designated a 'substitute' for marriage; if married, their career is designated a 'substitute' for motherhood; if a mother, their career brands them as selfish or neglectful."[5]

Attitudes didn't change much in the 1960s. Nevertheless, women were beginning to make strides in equalizing power within their families. The ethos of the patriarchal family was eroding as families looked less and less like the Cleavers. With more women "bringing home the bacon" just like Dad—and still performing most household duties—the line between who was "head of the household" and who was a dependent was increasingly blurred. In 1967, half of all U.S. women in their thirties worked; by 1982, three-quarters of all U.S. women in their thirties were in the same situation.

Within the household, the balance of power continued to shift during the '70s and '80s. Mothers became the dominant parental enforcer, as was clearly shown on *One Day at a Time, Maude, Good Times, Alice, Roseanne, Kate & Allie, Grace Under Fire, Valerie,* and *The Nanny.* Some of the mothers in these shows "wore the pants" because they were widowed or divorced, but others were just the kind of mom nobody wanted to mess with.

I related to the idea of women taking charge of the kids. It was what my brother and I knew. As Susan Douglas points out, even on the most traditional shows in the seventies and later, "our mothers could still see . . . women resisting and making fun of the credo that 'real' women found fulfillment in diaper pails and macaroni recipes, or that they thought obeying their husbands made much sense."[6] Roseanne never told her children, "Wait until your father gets home"—at least, not without a heavy tone of sarcasm or irony. And neither did my mother. Sitcom mothers were getting tougher, funnier, and far less perfect; they often seemed unsure of how to be the best parent, but they were determined to try.

Wait Until Your Father Gets Home

Whenever I watch *Roseanne,* the quips about her all-encompassing power over her household and husband make me smile, if not laugh out loud. In one of my favorite episodes, the writers decided to "break down the fourth wall" (theater-speak for removing the invisible curtain separating actors from audience by introducing elements that remind the audience they're viewing fiction). Roseanne sits in her kitchen with the icons of traditional TV moms—June Cleaver, Ruth Martin *(Lassie)*, Louise "Weezy" Jefferson, and Mrs. Arnold *(The Wonder Years)*. Roseanne discusses how she runs her household. Each TV mom laments how her character was rarely featured on her respective show. When June Lockhart complains that Lassie had more lines than she did, Roseanne asserts, "In my house, I'm the boss and Father knows squat!"[7]

It isn't just talk, either. Roseanne is queen of her domain. But even with all her power, she—like all parents—is still figuring out how to best raise her children. Dan Conner is the first husband I ever saw on TV complaining that, compared to his wife, he has no say in his own house. Many times he is right; it's as though Roseanne is always saying, "Hey, you knew what you were getting into when you married me." Truth is, Roseanne does a good job of running the show; when she and Dan join forces to reprimand the kids or make rules, they make a good team because the subtext of the show is that Dan accepts Roseanne's dominance generally without question. He loves who she is and they love each other enough to plow through the frustrations of living in a matriarchal environment.

For television viewers in the '80s, *Roseanne* turned the tables on the traditional notions about family. The matriarchal structure was so accepted on the show that when Dan's brother-in-law, Fred, taunts him, "Well, at least I'm not afraid of my wife!" Dan says defensively, "I'm not afraid of my wife." Fred responds, "Oh, have you remarried?"[8]

Like *Good Times, Roseanne* deals with the realities of working-class parents. When Mom and Dad are busy worrying about how to pay the bills, the kids' minor messes and squabbles are seen as just what they are—minor. Another highly popular '80s family sitcom, *The Cosby Show,* featuring an upper-middle-class family, the Huxtables, with five children and a brownstone in Brooklyn, brought back a retro brand of parenting. On occasion the Cosby kids do something "bad" or break the rules, but it all seems minor—a scratch on the station wagon, a bad grade now and then. The Cosby parents' biggest problem is their daughter, Denise, who drops out of college and isn't sure what she wants do with her life.

A great deal of *The Cosby Show*'s humor is had at Denise's expense. She seems flaky and confused, not unlike many real kids. (Her life wraps up neatly, when she marries a military man who already has a daughter: a built-in family in which Denise can fulfill a dream we never saw coming—that of being a mother.) Denise is the only character many people can relate to: Her siblings are overachievers who attend Princeton and NYU, not surprisingly, since Dr. Huxtable (Bill Cosby) is an obstetrician and Mrs. Huxtable an attorney. It was a conscious decision by Bill Cosby to create a very family-friendly sitcom, with nothing overt about race even though they were one of the only black middle-class families on TV. I never knew a family who lived that life. It's also important to note that *The Cosby Show* premiered at a time when America was being smothered by a "return to traditionalism." The show serves as an emblem of nuclear family nostalgia, while *Roseanne* and *Murphy Brown* subvert that "norm." (Remember also that both shows were created and controlled, primarily, by women.)

Not long after this tumultuous time period, TV's most famous fictional broadcast journalist, Murphy Brown, decides to become a single mother. This strong, secure character becomes unsure of herself in the face of motherhood as she imagines explaining the big questions about life to her future child. For example, what will she tell him about death? Though many real-life critics chided the show for the purportedly unrealistic representation of Murphy's life changing so little after the birth of her son, I prefer Susan Douglas's analysis: "Murphy Brown also gave all the traditional stereotypes about motherhood the raspberries and continued, even after the birth of her child, to be as insensitive, narcissistic, and bossy as before."[9]

This was the era of the "realistic parent," when the conventional Huxtables met their realistic counterparts in the Conners. In a hilarious episode of *Roseanne*, former hippies Dan and Roseanne, come face-to-face with their own past and their current responsibilities as parents when they find marijuana in the house. They automatically assume one of the kids brought it home. It turns out that it belongs to Dan and Roseanne. In the episode, Dan, Roseanne, and Roseanne's sister, Jackie, run to the bathroom to "relive the sixties." They realize that smoking pot as grownups with kids isn't the same as passing around a joint at a sit-in in 1968. When Dan asks why they ever smoked pot, Roseanne explains that it was a different time. "There was a war going on. It was just more fun back then."[10] The paranoia induced by the weed reminds them of the mistakes they made when they were young and also puts into perspective how much having children changes your life. I think about that episode often because someday I may have to explain to my children why I made some dumb choices in my youth.

Roseanne was ahead of her time in recognizing how hard it is to be a "cool" parent and how having children changes everything. The episode drives home the fact that those youthful decisions, stupid as they might seem in hindsight, are part and parcel of the teenage experience.

I was a typical teenager. I did well in school, wasn't on drugs, and, for the most part, behaved myself; but I was also, as my mom called me, "a snot." I talked back, slammed my door, and gave my mother the silent treatment, just like most teens. In the midst of my angst-ridden teen years, I recognized TV versions of myself, like Roseanne's daughters, Becky and Darlene. Becky was basically the good daughter. She did well in school, was involved with her peers, and spent the bulk of her time with her friends "at the mall." Darlene, on the other hand, was a loner, wore black clothes, and on occasion, skipped school altogether. Almost every teenage girl I knew related to Darlene. We identified with her feelings of discontent and applauded her amazing sarcasm (she had a team of writers creating her lines, elevating her responses beyond the ubiquitous "Duh" or "Whatever").

Roseanne and Dan had various problems with their kids over the course of the series, some typical, some not; but every time the show, or other progressive family sitcoms like it, examined those issues, it made us all—parents and children— feel a little less alone.

In the episode "No Talking," Roseanne grounds Becky for her back talk and bad attitude and Becky responds by waging a war of silence against her mother. Not only does she refuse to talk to Roseanne, but she defies her again by sneaking out of the house. When Roseanne discovers that the grounded teen has defied her authority, she explains, "See, that's why she's grounded—'cause she's acting awful and her attitude stinks." Any parent who has ever had to deal with a teenager knows all about "attitude." When Roseanne demands to know where she's been, Becky explodes: "Do you need to know where I am every moment of my life?" Dan answers, "Yes, she does." Roseanne grounds her for another week and Becky flips out with an "I hate you" and a slam of the door. Becky continues to defiantly ignore her mother, but speaks to her dad like a little angel. Roseanne does what she always does, uses humor and a little intimidation to make her point: "Becky, you know what this silent treatment does to me, don't ya? It just makes me want to talk more. In fact, it just makes me want to talk constantly until you have no choice but to listen." You've got to love Roseanne.

Roseanne worries, though, that Becky may be going through something she refuses to talk about. Dan tries to be the voice of reason, saying, "Oh my God, she's acting like a teenager." But nothing will calm Roseanne. She wants to take Becky's door off the hinges.

> **DAN:** Will you listen to yourself? I'm more worried about you than I am about her.
>
> **ROSEANNE:** Well, I'm worried about me too. She's driving me crazy. I tried joking with her. I tried yellin' at her. I even tried being reasonable, but she still won't say one word to me.
>
> **DAN:** It's a real struggle for power.
>
> **ROSEANNE:** Yeah, and I'm losing.[11]

In no time, everyone is mad at each other because of Becky's obnoxiousness. Later, when Roseanne and Jackie are cleaning Becky's room, they find her diary. Roseanne has to decide if she will violate her daughter's privacy (like her mother did to her) or accept that Becky is a perfectly normal fourteen-year-old. As Roseanne holds the diary, Jackie says, "There are just some things you don't need to know." This is one of those situations many parents of teens face. Roseanne decides to have a heart-to-heart with Becky and tell her she'd come across her diary and almost read it, but didn't want to violate her daughter's privacy the way her own mother had hers: "You know, I guess I just hoped that you and I would have a better relationship than I had with my mom. Maybe I don't understand everything you're going through, but you don't understand everything I'm going through, either." As Roseanne replaces Becky's bedroom door, she says that Becky can keep it closed if she likes, but "I hope sometime you'll let me in."[12] This episode says a lot about what teenagers need—a little space, a little understanding, and the knowledge that you, the parent, will be there when they need you.

In the *Murphy Brown* episode titled "It Came from College," Murphy agrees to host Veronica, a friend's college-age daughter, for a weekend. Murphy has no desire to do it and posts a time schedule at work for her colleagues to sign up and volunteer for time slots when they'll be responsible for entertaining the guest. Of course, no one steps forward. When Veronica arrives (played by a young Anne Heche), Murphy is impressed by her overwhelming social conscience. She shows sincere respect and admiration for Murphy, a boost to her ego. They share complaints about mothers and typical ultimatums like "As long as you live under my roof . . . " Murphy and Veronica agree that mothers are overprotective and sometimes silly.

Veronica proceeds to pull out a cigarette and mentions that her mother hates that she smokes. Murphy's reaction is "mature" and "uncool": "Well, maybe she's just protecting you from, uh, you know, lung cancer."

Things don't get much better from there. Murphy does not want to listen the rap group, Public Enemy, Veronica wants to play. Murphy agrees that being a teenager is tough, "never being listened to, never being respected, and worst of all, never being trusted." And Veronica responds with, "Can

I borrow your car?" Murphy is as obsessed with her Porsche as she is with herself but acquiesces, and soon the *FYI* staff is berating her for not asserting more control over the teen. In the episode's final scene, Murphy waits at home for Veronica to return with the car. She is reading *Talking to Your Teen* and *When Your Kids Drive You Crazy.* Murphy believes she can research her way out of the situation. But after waiting until "four in the morning," she relies more on instinct than on research. During her confrontation with Veronica, she spews, "And don't use that tone with me!" Veronica announces she is going to bed, but Murphy yells, "Get your little keister back here, young lady, you've got some explaining to do!"[13]

No matter how cool a parent wants to be or how "mom-like" it seems, setting boundaries and instilling discipline are a necessary part of parenting, as the Conners and Murphy Brown learn with the rest of us.

Single Motherhood

Since their earliest days, television sitcoms have been obsessed with the perfect family. But the single mother began making inroads into that world in 1968 with the debut of *Julia,* a show about a nurse raising a son on her own, featuring Diahann Carroll, the first black woman to star in her own comedy series. In *Alice,* a sitcom based on the feminist film *Alice Doesn't Live Here Anymore,* the lead character was also raising a son on her own. One of TV's most famous single mothers is, of course,

Murphy Brown, criticized by then–vice president Dan Quayle for having a baby out of wedlock. What he and other politicians left out of their "family values" speeches was the fact that there had always been single mothers struggling to support, feed, and care for their kids. By circumstance or choice, death or divorce, single mothers on TV, as in real life, were forced to be both mother and father to their children, as witnessed in the single-parent households on *Maude, Roseanne,* and *Grace Under Fire.* Other shows, such as *The Nanny,* portrayed women acting as substitute mothers for others' children.

It wasn't always easy for these women to be both mother and father to their children. In an episode of *Alice,* titled "Sex Education," Alice is forced to discuss the birds and the bees with her twelve-year-old son, Tommy. Like most parents, Alice does not have an easy time of it.

> **ALICE:** Oh, Tommy, I don't know . . . there's no way . . . there's no way to define love. When it happens, you'll know. It's a very special feeling for a very special person, and caring and responsibility are all a part of that kind of relationship. Well it's more than just, oh . . . oh . . .
>
> **TOMMY:** Okay.
>
> **ALICE:** Okay?
>
> **TOMMY:** Boy, this caring and responsibility and love . . . it's all so complicated. I can see now why I was an only child.[14]

Helping your children grow up to be healthy, happy

adults is enormously difficult for two parents, let alone one. One of my favorite single TV moms is Ann Romano from *One Day at a Time*, a highly successful 1970s sitcom about a single mother who is divorced, raising two daughters in Indianapolis, and has returned to using her maiden name. She is proud of being able to handle two daughters—and eventually a job at a public relations firm—on her own. Like Roseanne and Dan Conner, Ann Romano doesn't have an easy time with her daughters. Norman Lear, creator of the show (and many others, including the groundbreaking *All in the Family*), said that he wanted to produce a show that would make divorced women "comically respectable."[15]

In the midst of dating and working, Ms. Romano has quite a challenge raising her daughters, Julie and Barbara. Among her many trials as a single mom: Julie wants to drop out of school; Barbara will do anything to be popular, including refusing a date from an unpopular but nice boy; Julie protests oil prices and dates a forty-two-year-old man; and both girls must face the fact that their mother is dating various men. Ann is described as a mom who "dispensed with the milk and cookies of former sitcom mommies, and instead dispensed good advice to and respect for her separate-but-equal daughters."[16]

Boys Will Be Boys

Being a parent has always been a dance of discipline, compassion, and understanding, but it often slips into the murky world of the double standard—one set of rules and expectations for sons, another for daughters. In the early days of TV, girls were polite and chaste—all-around "good girls." They didn't have sex (actually, we just didn't hear about it), break into their parents' liquor cabinet, or sneak marijuana into their rooms. As society became more complex, the experiences of children and teenagers grew increasingly complex as well. Mothers found themselves having to talk to their daughters about issues that for so long had only been the domain of the boys.

Over time, TV parents began raising a new breed of child: the rude and moody adolescent (Darlene on *Roseanne,* Zoe on *Cybill*) who wanted the same things out of life that boys did. This required a new kind of parenting for both real and fictional families.

Roseanne helped usher in parenting methods that challenged the status quo, in the same way her kids did. She rejected the double standard (or at the very least recognized its existence). She, like real-world parents, found herself addressing many of the same parenting issues with both her daughters and son. Gone were the "boys will be boys" days.

When Kathy, her snobby neighbor, confronts Roseanne about her son being a "bad influence" on Kathy's son, Todd, Roseanne rises to the occasion. The fact that Kathy looks down on the Conner brood helps to provoke Roseanne even more. After Todd gets a scraped knee, Kathy again confronts Roseanne, just as Becky tells her mother she got her first parking ticket. All is chaos in the homes of America.

KATHY: Todd just told me he cut his arm playing at a construction site. Did you know they were there?

ROSEANNE: Oh yeah, they just told me.

KATHY: Roseanne, I left him here assuming you would keep an eye on him.

ROSEANNE: They took off on their bikes.

KATHY: And you allow your son to just leave whenever he wants?

ROSEANNE: Yeah, I encourage it.

Roseanne does not take kindly to Kathy's suggestion that Roseanne lets her children run rampant. Kathy's response offers Roseanne evidence of what she already suspected—that Kathy is convinced she's a better mother than Roseane.

KATHY: I always know where my son is.

ROSEANNE: Well, I've got three kids and a job and I can't be everywhere, so, okay, I've gotta trust my kids, and they're still alive. So, obviously, I've done something right.[17]

Roseanne tells the woman that she is an "amateur" mother because she still checks to see if her son is breathing during the night. In the end, Roseanne puts the situation of "eight-year-old boys" in perspective. They get scrapes, they disobey, but, hey, they are still alive and well.

In other episodes, Becky dates a very "bad boy" and

refuses to stop even after being forbidden from doing so; Becky asks her mother for help in getting birth control; Darlene's boyfriend moves into the house; Darlene becomes the first in the family to go to college; Becky elopes and moves into a trailer park. These are issues real parents have to cope with. Roseanne and Dan are no different, dealing with their children's flaws, mistakes, and faulty logic.

Another show that deals heavily with parenting issues is *Yes, Dear,* in which two sets of in-laws, each with children, live on the same property. The two moms are sisters; the more uptight and upwardly mobile couple, Kim and Greg, live in the main house, and Kim's sister, Christine, lives with her husband, Jimmy, in the guesthouse. As such, they garner a lot of comedy by comparing contrasting parental styles. In one episode, Greg and Kim are faced with the fact that their two-year-old son, Sammy, has been bullying other kids. Like many new parents faced with a question they can't answer, they head to the books. They find that parenting tends to involve both book work and some trial and error.

> **KIM:** It doesn't matter why he's doing this. We just have to get him to stop.
>
> **GREG:** You're right. You're right. Do what you have to do.
>
> **KIM:** What do you mean?
>
> **GREG:** I don't know, talk to your friends, read your books, watch your parenting videos. Do what you do.

KIM: I think this is a problem we should solve together. . . . I'm tired of trying to solve all these problems by myself. If what I come up with doesn't work, I don't want to feel like I'm the one who screwed things up. I want us both to come up with a plan, and fail or succeed together.

GREG: You're right.

As the couple rifles through the books on bullying they checked out of the library, they are confronted with a very typical situation: They really have no idea what to do.

KIM: What did you think of that one?

GREG: I don't know what to think. This book says he should spend more time with other children. The last book said that he should stay away from other children. They all seem reasonable. How do you know which one to pick?

KIM: Well, you decide which ones you don't want to use, and then one by one you try the ones you do.

GREG: Well, what if you try all the ones you want to try and then you find out that one of the ones you didn't try might have been the one that worked. I mean, that's insane!

KIM: Welcome to parenting. My name is Kim. I'll be your wife.[18]

Parents try to do the right thing by their children in a world where no one knows all the answers. When people talk about parenting, it always reminds me of something Maya

Angelou, also a mother, once said: "You do what you know how to do. And when you know better, you do better."

Sex, Drugs, and Rock and Roll

As television progressed through the decades, many shows began addressing the more gritty issues of family life—sex and birth control, lying, disobeying. Prime-time audiences began to see sons who were less than manly and daughters who were having sex; teens who lived in a world where drugs were available; disenchanted adolescents who cut class and dropped out of school. The taboos of yesteryear were no longer being swept under the sitcom's suburban rug.

On an incredible episode of *Roseanne,* Dan and Roseanne deal with their daughter's sexuality when she asks to go on the pill. As the episode opens, Becky whisks Roseanne's sister, Jackie, to her room. Shortly afterward, Jackie ushers Becky downstairs and informs Roseanne that Becky has something important to talk about.

> **BECKY:** Well, Mark and I are getting along really good now. And I know you guys aren't crazy about him, but you gotta admit that he's trying real hard.
>
> **ROSEANNE:** Okay.
>
> **BECKY:** Um, well . . . I was thinking, you know, just in case we decide to, um, that it's time for me to, um, get some birth control.

Roseanne is speechless—not an easy feat.

JACKIE: Isn't it great, Roseanne? That Becky has such a wonderful, progressive, open-minded mom that she can talk to about that?

ROSEANNE: Uh-huh.

BECKY: I was gonna go to a clinic, but Jackie thought that I should go see your gynecologist.

ROSEANNE: Uh-huh.

BECKY: Really? So this is okay with you.

ROSEANNE: Uh-huh.

BECKY: I can't believe how great you're being about this. I'm so glad Aunt Jackie made me tell you.

JACKIE: I thought that we should take her.

ROSEANNE: *(Screeching)* Oh yeah, we'll take her.

BECKY: Great. Thanks, thanks so much, Mom.

Becky leaves happily, and Jackie tries to convince Roseanne, who is visibly shaken and stunned, that Becky's coming to her was a good thing.

ROSEANNE: Are you crazy? She wants me to go get her birth control and that's a good thing?

JACKIE: Will you just sit down?

ROSEANNE: No, Jackie. I need to lay down in a great big pine box.

JACKIE: She came to you, she confided in you, she trusts you. That's a good thing.

ROSEANNE: I cannot handle this.

JACKIE: Yes, you can.

ROSEANNE: No, I know I can't do this. I know. I know I can't do this.[19]

Suddenly, we hear a baby crying in the distance as Roseanne's friend Crystal comes to visit with her infant son. We see Roseanne listen to the baby crying for a few seconds, then her demeanor changes as she utters, "I can do this." She realizes that as uncomfortable as she is with Becky coming to her in need of birth control, the prospect of Becky *not* coming to her could end up being a lot worse. She decides to do what is best for her daughter, regardless of how much she wishes she and Dan didn't have to deal with this problem. This episode explores the ways in which, no matter how much you dislike the decisions your kids make—smoking pot, drinking, or having sex—you can't ignore these issues. Roseanne's biggest problem is that she keeps wishing this was something she "didn't have to know," but once she knows, she faces it. In fact, when she can't think of something supportive to say to Becky as she heads into the gynecologist's office, Roseanne says, "Go get 'em." It is the last thing she wants to say, but she knows that parenting requires a whole lot of things that many people never imagined.

TV Parenting 101

When I was growing up, I longed to be part of a fictional television family. Roseanne and Grace (of *Grace Under Fire*) were not the kinds of moms you wanted to piss off, but when faced with problems with their children they knew which battles to choose. Every now and then, I wished that when I had made a mistake I knew my mother would go ballistic over, I had a TV mom who would be able to put it in perspective with a good joke or quip, or sage advice (bolstered by a team of writers).

The two sets of parents on *Yes, Dear* are very different: Kim buys organic vegetables, Christine thinks fast-food French fries count as a vegetable serving. Christine and Jimmy rely on their instincts when it comes to their kids; Greg and Kim rely on researching every aspect of their children's life. They realize their differences, and make an effort to allow room for everyone's methods.

By being forced to live together, the couples learn to accept each other's differences with respect and without judgment. Of course, these issues are played out over and over again. At the end of the pilot episode, Kim comes to a conclusion about parenting: "We need to take things as they come, stop worrying about every little problem."[20] The uptight parents learn not to worry so much, but still run back to the books when they get nervous. The point is that different kinds of parents—and people—have much to learn from each other when they keep an open mind and understand that all parents are always learning.

Watching parents struggle with their kids and parenting issues on television can help us feel less alone with our own problems. It may even be possible to learn something. TV parents have given us many tools. The humor enforced by the situation comedy genre helps give us perspective on the things our kids do and don't do, when they misbehave, and when they make difficult decisions. It also allows us to see that there are many ways to be a parent and each way deserves respect. Television also shows us that although our children may not make the decisions we would wish, sometimes they *need* to make their own mistakes.

Through the TV "window," many shows allow us to see a family that is not our own and realize the importance of accepting our kids for who they are, no matter who that may be. In a late episode of *Roseanne,* the Conners are preparing for the birth of Roseanne's last child. They decide to make a video for the yet-to-be-born baby. In the video, Becky and Darlene read a letter they found written from Roseanne to Dan the night before their wedding, two decades earlier.

> *Dan,*
> *We're getting married tomorrow. As cool as it is that you are going to be my husband, it is even cooler that you are going to be the father of my children. 'Cause I really want our family to be different than the families we grew up in. Our kids are gonna get a better shot than that. We're*

gonna make sure that they know they're worth something and that no matter what they do, no matter how mad they make us, or how bad they screw up, they can always come home.[21]

Chapter 4

Doing "It" for Fun

The New TV Sexuality

> Teenagers are God's punishment for having sex.
>
> **—Roseanne**

Regardless of the mores of the times, sex is a subject that remains highly personal in any era. Ideas about sex are often intertwined with our notions about religion, family, and peer groups, our attitudes about intimacy, privacy, gender, and youth. Some of our ideas and influences may be transparent; others may be subconscious and unexpected. I hardly consider myself a prude, but even I was surprised the first time I heard a "blow job" joke on television. On the show *Friends*, the women characters have read a self-help book in the nature of *Women Who Run with the Wolves*, a book riddled with hokey metaphors about how women are "the wind" and men are the "lightning-bearers." Rachel is dating Ross, who comes into the coffee shop to whisk her away to a movie.

> **ROSS:** Rachel, we gotta go.
>
> **RACHEL:** No. Why do we always have to do everything on your timetable?
>
> **ROSS:** It is not my timetable, it is the movie's timetable.
>
> **RACHEL:** How do you expect me to grow if you won't let me blow?[1]

Ross looks flustered and starts mumbling things like "Well, um, I don't, um, have a problem with that." It is, of course, his reaction that really inspires the joke, because it reflects just what a nineties audience might be thinking. This series took place at a time when our culture had reached a level of openness about sex that was unprecedented. From Britney Spears to *Sex and the City*, America certainly seemed to be okay with women's (and strangely, even girls') sexuality. For the women on *Friends*, for instance, sex was just part of the urban young-adult world they lived in—a world that accepted the women on the show dating, having sex, having one-night stands. These facts about their sex lives never changed how the audience viewed them.

For *Friends'* Phoebe, Monica, and Rachel, sexuality is simply part of their characters. We are talking about network

TV—not cable or HBO (where later the sexual life of four single women would become the basis of *Sex and the City)*. Phoebe is probably the most sexually uninhibited. After all, as a young girl, she had lived an alternative life on the streets of New York City. Monica, a more traditional character, is nevertheless sexually active. Rachel seems to be somewhere between Monica and Phoebe. When *Friends* debuted, I was in college. The show struck a chord with me and many others of my generation. Here was a group of twentysomethings who did not judge one another about sexuality, regardless of how different their feelings on the subject were. This was one of those milestones in television history when you could actually measure how far our culture had come in accepting women and their sexuality.

From Separate Beds to Sexual Tension

In a world where the Ricardos slept in twin beds, early TV made strange bedfellows out of sitcoms and sex. My mother grew up at a time when TV couples never shared a bed, something I cannot fathom. (My mother confided that she once thought her parents never had sex. I knew my parents had sex though it was certainly uncomfortable to think about.) Sitcoms' married couples were also a part of the sexual revolution of the sixties; families are, after all, "part of the wider society, as well as being the structures in which intimacy was experienced."[2]

Gradually, the wives and mothers of prime time were portrayed not just as stereotypes but as individuals and sexual beings. I'm not just talking about young wives and mothers. Starting in the '60s, and continuing today, people of all ages have become more open about their sex lives; the culture has been rethinking its ideas about gender, sex, and women in general.

The early '70s saw a flood of books—generally directed at couples—that were essentially manuals on how to have a better sex life. Couples in America were admitting that sex was an important part of their lives, even if this meant we had to imagine Maude and Arthur "doing it." They certainly weren't the only ones. James and Florida *(Good Times)*, David and Maddie *(Moonlighting)*, Cliff and Clair *(The Cosby Show)* were all doing it. It wasn't always explicitly discussed, but it was clear that these couples, as well as later sitcom couples such as Jamie and Paul *(Mad About You)* and Dharma and Greg, were sexually attracted to each other.

Wives, mothers, even grandmothers were discussing sex openly:

MAUDE: With you two schoolboys around, a girl isn't safe in her own bed! I could have been violated!

WALTER AND ARTHUR: *(Together)* By who?

MAUDE: God'll get you for that. Both of you.[3]

Just as *The Mary Tyler Moore Show* serves as the origin of single-woman feminism on television, Maude serves as the icon for feminism within marriage. A wife, mother, and grandmother, Maude isn't particularly feminine or sexually submissive, but as we watch her run her household with her iron voice, we know she has sex and we also know she likes it. When *Maude* debuted, sex was just beginning to show its face on television as a normal part of married people's lives. This show, and a few others, set a precedent. In a short time, we went from a mindset that sex was nonexistent in marriage—even when women had children—to sex being a natural and acknowledged part of married life. The seventies were a pivotal time when even grandmothers, such as Maude, were doing it for fun.

Maude and Walter started a televised sexual revolution within marriage, whose standard was carried by many other couples over the years. In the '80s, only a decade after TV brought us such shows as *Green Acres, The Flying Nun,* and *The Brady Bunch,* a new age of television was dawning, featuring families that in many ways resembled our own. When *Family Ties* premiered in 1981, we had, for the first time, a set of former-hippie baby boomers raising kids in the suburbs. The show features a strong, professionally successful wife and mother and a less successful, emasculated father and husband. This series is often seen as a bastion of '80s traditionalism, its premise being that two reformed hippies are raising a hyper-conservative Republican son, played famously by Michael J. Fox. However, the show's traditionalism was mixed with a general acceptance that parents were people too, had careers, interests—and sex.

Family Ties' parents weren't traditional in the way that

Hope and Michael of *thirtysomething* were traditional. The former was a much more overtly political sitcom than the latter drama of life in the suburbs. *Family Ties'* adults dealt with real issues that included sex: when they didn't have time for it, when they did, and their desire for each other. Post–*Family Ties*, it became a hallmark of family sitcoms to have the parents get caught canoodling or even making out by their children, something that was always met with an "Eww" or "Gross." On other traditional shows since then—including *Home Improvement* and *The Cosby Show*—everyone was doing it. On *Roseanne,* the Conners had a healthy sex life, as did the married women who appeared on *Designing Women*. It's hard to imagine a time when sex did not exist for married women on TV, since it's such an integral part of today's sitcom family. If all I watched on television when I was growing up were couples who seemed not to have sex lives, I can't imagine how I would feel about sex and marriage today.

Seeing shows in which couples enjoyed the fruits of their marriage helped us see sex in a new way. We may not have liked it, but we all knew that parents—TV ones and real ones—were having sex and this was all a part of marriage. These new TV marriages were more exciting than the sexless marriages of television past, but they were also more complicated and thus more real, preparing us all for a future in which men and women negotiated matters related to sex as opposed to hiding from them.

The Power of the Pill

In 1960, the FDA's approval of the birth control pill set in motion a cultural shift that, in many ways, we are still experiencing today. How big a change this would mean for women and our culture, in general, cannot be overstated. According to author Deborah Felder, since 1960, the pill, as it is colloquially known, "has been part of the daily routine for more humans than any other prescribed medication in the world. It has been called 'the first medicine ever destined for a purely social, rather than a therapeutic, purpose,' and the impact of oral birth control has reached into nearly every aspect of women's lives in the second half of the twentieth century."[4]

Women could finally control their biological "destinies," as Freud had written a century earlier. Women's sex lives were to change forever because they no longer had to be the bearers of all problems and consequences of sex. They had control over their reproductive lives and thus were, on some level, released from the restriction that possible pregnancy put on their sex lives. This made men and women more equal sexually, each making personal decisions about their bodies and their lives. In her book *A Century of Women*, Felder recounts how invention of the pill affected just about everything.

> *According to* Newsweek *in 1967, the Western world's morals and manners had "changed more dramatically in the past year than in the preceding fifty," and the Pill was at the center of that acceleration as both the cause and*

*the effect of a radical transformation of science, society,
and culture, expressed in a variety of forms in modern
women's lives.*[5]

The 1960s' ideals about sexual openness and expression
certainly influenced the succeeding decades. While the sexual
revolution was acknowledged by nonfiction writers and news
programs, these ideas only made their way into television programming in the '70s.

Once TV producers and writers decided to address political issues in the public sphere, they were facing political
issues that were also personal issues. Kate Millett's book
Sexual Politics (published in 1970) made famous the phrase
"The personal is political." While the pressing issues of the
sixties included the politics of war, government, and genera-
tional change, the issues of the seventies focused on sexual
discrimination, abortion, and countering the inequality of
women in many realms, including their sex lives. This forced
TV producers—many of them male, including the creators of
The Mary Tyler Moore Show and *Maude*—to explore women's
struggle for equality and freedom.

During the '70s, one of the most common sitcom plots
featuring single women concerned the prospect of dating and
what that entailed. Of course, it entailed a discussion about
sex. When *MTM* debuted in 1970, Mary wasn't simply a single
woman trying to make it in the working world, she was also
an attractive woman who dated men and reveled in the experience of making decisions about her sex life without the input

of her conservative parents. According to one sitcom encyclopedia, "Mary didn't just date—she *dated.* (One time she didn't even come home!)"[6] The new freedom born in the '60s and more fully realized in the '70s was a breath of fresh air. Not only could women decide to make their own money and have their own jobs, they could also decide who they wanted to have sex with and how to take the necessary precautions so they wouldn't get pregnant.

In one famous episode, Mary's mother reminds her not to forget to take her pill. Mary simply responds, "I won't." She doesn't need to justify her actions or defend her desires; she simply takes responsibility for her own sex life, something new on television. I can't imagine learning anything about sex, even in subtle ways, from watching fifties reruns. I learned more about sex from 1950s movies than I ever did from TV shows from that decade. Then, women like Mary Richards slowly began to claim their sexuality, culminating in the sexually confident women of *Sex and the City* several decades later. When Carrie, Miranda, Charlotte, and Samantha discussed their escapades—oral sex, S&M, one-night stands—over cocktails and brunch, June Cleaver and Harriet Nelson must have rolled over in their TV graves.

It is hard to imagine what our world would have been like without the pill, and without women being able to initiate "a fundamental change in sexuality from the primacy of procreation to that of pleasure."[7] One of the best descriptions I've read of its importance comes from a 1990 *Ladies' Home Journal* article about the pill's thirtieth birthday:

It's easy to forget how truly liberating the Pill seemed to be in 1960. Nothing else in this century—perhaps not even winning the right to vote—made such an immediate difference in women's lives. . . . It spurred sexual frankness and experimentation. It allowed women to think seriously about their careers because they could postpone childbirth. And it sparked the feminist and pro-choice movements. Once women felt they were in charge of their own bodies, they began to question the authority of their husbands, their fathers, their bosses, their doctors, and their churches. As founding feminist Betty Friedan has said: In the mysterious way of history, there was this convergence of technology that occurred just as women were ready to explode into personhood.[8]

This new level of personhood that women have achieved has its positives and negatives. It could be argued that sexual freedom brought on a host of other problems, including intimacy and commitment issues, ideas about motherhood versus careerism. But that does not discount the incredible freedom the pill bestowed on women, giving us control over our bodies for the first time.

Sex and the City is one of the most obvious markers of this change. In this series, women surpass being judged by what goes on inside the bedroom. We have finally arrived to a place where having a sex life is more acceptable than it has ever been.

Claiming Desire

Historically, women's sexual desires have been denied. Even the women my mom grew up with didn't talk about sex except in hushed tones. Girls who "did it" were bad and girls who didn't were good—a "truth" reinforced by all aspects of our culture, particularly during the sexually repressed 1950s. Nevertheless, there were always real-world women who indulged their sexual desires, even in the face of societal condemnation. As society began to lessen its hold on women's sexuality in the '70s, women onscreen and off began to explore sexuality and desire.

On television, women in the 1970s began expressing some level of desire, even if it was initially understated. Mary Richards definitely desired men and we knew it, but due to her naive demeanor, it was a somewhat uncomfortable thought. Later, with *Alice* and Ann Romano of *One Day at a Time,* we saw women who clearly had sexual desires. Ann Romano was involved in a variety of sexual relationships with men, and this while raising two teenage daughters. Murphy Brown dated a wonderful array of men throughout the show's run. The marriage comedy *Mad About You* began with Jamie, the wife, upset about the lack of sex in their relationship. No matter how open-minded and sexually sophisticated audiences considered themselves, *Sex and the City* pushed the envelope even more.

In an episode from the first season entitled "Secret Sex," Carrie Bradshaw, the New York City relationship and life-style writer, mulls over what so many women consider before going on dates: *Do I or don't I?* As she is trying on dresses with her three cohorts, they discuss sex and dating with honesty and humor.

SAMANTHA: Oh honey, it's fabulous! Bravo!

MIRANDA: It's tits-on-toes, baby, but you make it work.

CHARLOTTE: Let's just say it, it's the naked dress. I mean you're obviously going to have sex with him tonight.

CARRIE: Come on, it's our first date.

MIRANDA: She's not going to have sex, she's just gonna look like sex.

CARRIE: That's right. I'm just a trailer.

SAMANTHA: Please. *(Pouring a glass of wine)* If it happens, it happens. Bottoms up!

CHARLOTTE: Wait a second. . . . If you're serious about this guy, you can't sleep with him on the first date.

SAMANTHA: Oh, God.

MIRANDA: *(Walking away)* Here she goes again with *The Rules*.

SAMANTHA: The women who wrote that book, they wrote it because they couldn't get laid. *(Samantha and Miranda settle in on the couch with their drinks while Charlotte and Carrie follow behind.)* So they constructed this whole bullshit theory to make women who *can* get laid feel bad.

CHARLOTTE: *(To Carrie)* But if you're serious about a guy, then you have to keep him in a holding pattern for at least five dates.

CARRIE: Oh, you've gone up.

CHARLOTTE: Yes. Because the number of dates that you wait to have sex with a man is directly proportional to your age.

MIRANDA: Forget the math—just don't screw on the first date and you're fine.

CARRIE: Third date.

CHARLOTTE: Too soon.

SAMANTHA: Reality check: A guy can just as easily dump you if you fuck him on the first date as he can if you wait until the tenth.

MIRANDA: When have you ever been on a tenth date.

CHARLOTTE: And by then at least you're emotionally involved.

SAMANTHA: Exactly. I mean, isn't it better to find out if sex is good right off the bat before anybody's feelings get hurt?

CHARLOTTE: But it's okay to have hurt feelings.

MIRANDA: And you always handle those so well.

CARRIE: Well, there is something to be said for being straight.

SAMANTHA: Since when did you become such a Victorian?

CHARLOTTE: The Victorians were onto something. They valued romance.

MIRANDA: True romance cannot exist without good sex.

SAMANTHA: Yet, you can have good sex with someone you don't like or respect or even remember.

(The door buzzer sounds.)

CARRIE: Alright. Well, ladies, I'm going out for dinner. Good night.

ALL: Bye!

CHARLOTTE: Have fun.

CARRIE: Bye!

(Carrie closes the door and is walking down the hall.)

CARRIE, VOICEOVER: The truth is, I was dying to sleep with him. But isn't delayed gratification the definition of maturity?[9]

HBO gave us the sexually mature and desiring women of the year 2000. They dealt with sex the way men always had: They did it *and* they talked about it.

When academics refer to "postfeminism," they describe a world in which many equalities for women are taken for granted and accepted at face value. These equalities include sexuality, women's desire, and sexual freedom. The term *postfeminism* is bandied about in reference to the show *Ally McBeal*, whose lead character certainly owns her sexuality. She shows us early in the series that she met the love of her life in preschool when she bent over to "smell his butt."

Ally believes that even at a young age, she was expressing her desire for a man. Ally's biggest problem is how much her desires distract her from everything else in life. With the trauma she constantly experiences, it's hard to understand how she can be a lawyer or accomplish any work. As annoying as that is, it rings true for some of us. I like seeing a real woman who has desires, often for men who aren't right for her, and how these desires affect her life. I think hers is the plight of many women in her socioeconomic and age bracket.

I love the way Ally McBeal expresses her desire. In one episode, she fantasizes about having sex in a car wash with a hot man she barely knows. It's great. When she lusts after a man who works at the coffee shop she frequents, we see her inner desire via a funny special effect in which her tongue rolls out of her mouth and reaches across the room to lick coffee foam off the man's nose. Our innermost desires are played out through Ally's thoughts.

It isn't only young women who have experienced the acceptance of women's sexual desire on TV. The women of *The Golden Girls* also had sex. Even in the '80s, older women were getting it on. In that series, four women, the youngest at least in her sixties, live together in a house in Florida. They are single because of widowhood or divorce and live their lives, in some ways, just as the *SATC* women would later.

Sluts, Whores, and Real Women

No one would ever accuse Mary Richards, Rhoda, Kate, or Allie of being promiscuous. On 1970s television, the old ideas about labeling a woman a "slut" if she had sex before marriage began to change. As more and more women explored their sexuality in real life, the word "slut" began losing currency. (Even today, in colloquial conversation, some women refer to each other as "slut" or "whore" as a joke.) In her book about 1950s and 1960s pop culture, Susan Douglas explores how ideas about the definition of "slut" started to blur. "The legacy of the 1950s was that no 'nice' girl ever, ever, went all the way before marriage, and no nice woman ever really liked sex. But by the early 1960s, there were indications to the contrary, in best-selling books, in suggestive ads, in pop music and in James Bond movies."[10]

It wasn't until the '70s that prime-time television reflected changing attitudes about women (and even teenage girls) and sex. The tide was turning in favor of the "sluts" and not the "good girls." Who wanted to be a flying nun when you could be Mary Richards, who had a sex life (because she took the pill)? No matter the extent of the media backlash in the 1980s, there were some ways in which we would never go back. As Susan Douglas writes, the rigid code "meant to keep middle-class girls' pants on until after they got married—the double standard—was starting to crumble."[11]

On an episode of *Murphy Brown*, Murphy is desperately trying to get the plum assignment of interviewing an elusive author, played comically by liberal activist Martin Sheen. When Frank, Murphy's coworker—who also wants the assignment—argues that he should get it because of his deep connection with the author, Murphy blurts out, "I slept with him!" Frank concedes, "You win."[12] Murphy then explains that she was in college and the older, idealistic writer was visiting and she got caught up in the moment. No one would ever refer to Murphy Brown as a slut. Her sexuality is part of her character, and it sometimes leads her into relationships with men who are vastly different from her based solely on lust.

In the hilarious finale of the episode, Murphy interviews the author. She discovers he is far from what she remembers, a situation I'm sure many women identify with when they see ex-boyfriends or husbands. Not only is her former lover is a conservative Republican, he does not even remember their tryst. She is livid. Martin Sheen turns to her during a commercial break after he realizes he may have slept with Ms. Brown: "It was you. I always thought the blond was Diane Sawyer."[13] It has to kill Murphy's ego in the same way it would a man's—something everyone wants, male or female, is to be remembered. (Well, maybe not; there are some things we would like ourselves or others to forget.) Moreover, Murphy, just like many women, makes bad choices; but in the world of sitcoms, as in real life, women are no longer considered "sluts" for doing so.

Times have changed. Things that were taboo when my mother was growing up are now taken for granted. But even in this postfeminist world, there are lingering remnants of more restrictive attitudes. I doubt my own mother has ever walked into a pharmacy to buy condoms. But while many women of my generation have done that, we also know it to be a "dodge everyone's eyes" shopping experience. In a way, we are evolved, but we can still feel the stare of the checkout woman as she rings up our box of ribbed and lubricated protection. Not everything changes overnight. For middle-aged and older women who grew up with a restrictive set of sexual mores, their relationship to sexuality has been complex.

In the 2002 *New York Times* bestseller *The Bitch in the House*, a title featuring another word women have reclaimed, writer Cynthia Kling discusses sex and how she and the women of her generation have dealt with the idea of sex, sluts, and desire.

> *Recently at a party I found myself listening to a group of middle-aged women talk about when they'd discovered their erotic selves. For one, it was a college relation-ship with a sweet, willing, and curious boy; another had embarked on a series of experiments in her twenties— testing bisexuality, aggressiveness, and hetero sluttiness to see where she fit on the bell curve.*[14]

There are all sorts of ways to be a "slut" today, but the word doesn't have the negative force it once did. We live in a world where we get to live our sex lives how we live our lives—on our terms, just like Mary Richards, Murphy Brown, Kate, Allie, and the women of *SATC*.

Sitcoms' women have been exploring their sexual desire

for decades now. In fact, on the pilot episode of *Friends*, Monica sleeps with a man on the first date without judgment or indictment. Characters like Cybill and Maryann on *Cybill*, Fran on *The Nanny*, *Ellen*, Caroline and Annie on *Caroline in the City*, the women of *Living Single*, and Phoebe, Rachel, and Monica on *Friends* are open (and funny) about sex—they talk about it, do it, and *(gasp)* enjoy it.

On *Sex and the City*, the four sexually adventurous and independent women own their sexuality like they own their shoes. They question themselves and their logic, just as they question their footwear purchases. In the end, no matter on what date (it was indeed the first) Carrie had decided to sleep with her conquest, Mr. Big, she accepts herself and she questions herself, as many real women would probably do as well.

> **CARRIE, VOICEOVER:** Late that day, the cream of New York gathered to toast the maiden voyage of my bus.
>
> **SAMANTHA:** Where's Mr. Big?
>
> **CARRIE:** Couldn't make it.
>
> **CHARLOTTE:** What do you mean he couldn't make it?
>
> **CARRIE:** I don't know. It's a work day.
>
> **CHARLOTTE:** Oh, but this is your bus party. Oh . . . I told you, you shouldn't have—well, never mind.
>
> **CARRIE:** What, he's not here because I slept with him on the first date?

CHARLOTTE: Basically, yes. When you sleep with a man on the first date, the relationship will never be anything more than just sex.

CARRIE: Uh-huh. Cheers. *(Toasts with champagne)*

CARRIE, VOICEOVER: I didn't want to admit that she was right.

(A bus drives up.)

SAMANTHA: Ah, here it comes!

CARRIE, VOICEOVER: I just wanted to see my bus and get the hell out of there.

(The side of the bus does not have an advertisement on it.)

CHARLOTTE: Oh—shoot.

SAMANTHA: Ah, quiet . . . *(Another bus arrives.)* Here you come!

(They all gasp. The advertisement has a mustache drawn on it.)

CHARLOTTE: Oh . . .

SAMANTHA: Oh, don't worry, sweetie, don't worry. Nobody in New York notices a bus until it's about to hit them.

CHARLOTTE: That's right.

Meanwhile, Miranda has decided to have a one-night stand with a guy she met at the gym. In the final scene, Carrie goes to see Mr. Big to find some answers to the questions she's been asking herself.

CARRIE, VOICEOVER: Very late that night, fueled by a massive quantity of champagne, I decided to say goodbye to Mr. Big.

(She knocks on his door, and he answers sleepily.)

CARRIE: I just came here to tell you that if you're embarrassed or ashamed to be involved with me in any way then we can no longer see each other.

CARRIE, VOICEOVER: The truth is, I blame myself. I wore the naked dress on our first date. I slept with him too fast. And now I'm on a Fifth Avenue bus with a penis [graffitied] on my face.

MR. BIG: What are you talking about?

CARRIE: You don't introduce me to your friends. You bring me back to that restaurant where men take women they don't want to be seen with. You won't come out and meet my friends. You have me in a niche for certain events, certain restaurants, certain people, like I'm only a particular fragment of the kind of person that you think you should be dating.

MR. BIG: But I've only gotten to know a particular fragment. Although I'm beginning to know more.

CARRIE: Well, this is not me. This is me *(she flings her arm and spills her drink)* reacting to your perception of me.

MR. BIG: Oh, okay. Well, I think Feng Hau is the best Chinese food in the city, so that's why we went there. And uh, oh, the guy we met in the street, I couldn't remember his name—which probably means I have Alzheimer's, so that's what that was about. And this afternoon I had courtside tickets to the Knicks' and that's all, folks.

CARRIE, VOICEOVER: I should have been jumping for joy, but I only felt a hard knot of fear.

CARRIE: So, you and me, then maybe this is for real?

MR. BIG: Could be.[15]

It may not be perfect, but at least we, as women, can each decide for ourselves where we are sexually. We've reached the point where we can revel in our "sluttiness" as opposed to being oppressed by it.

We still must deal with the aftermath of all this change. Do women judge themselves for their sexual escapades, just as men have always done? Sure they do. Are sexually aggressive women still judged by the culture at large? Absolutely. But every day that women continue to dilute the age—old meaning of the monikers "slut" and "whore," we get closer to a place where we can judge ourselves—and others—less, and begin to explore exactly what we want from our own sex lives.

Chapter 5

Father Knows Squat

Gender and Sexual Politics in Prime Time

> The thing women have got to learn is that nobody gives you power. You just take it.
> **—Roseanne**

Long gone are the days when TV moms threatened, "Just wait until your father gets home!" Times have certainly changed, and so has the traditional nuclear family. "In 1967," Stephanie Coontz writes, "half of all women in their thirties were married mothers who remained at home full-time; by 1982, only a quarter of all women in their thirties could be found specializing in that way."[1] With definitions of "family" and "gender role" evolving, television slowly presented us with varying alternatives to traditional ideas about what it meant to be a man or woman, husband or wife. For instance, TV's single mothers took on the role of disciplinarians, a duty previously reserved for dads. Women on *Alice, One Day at a Time, Kate & Allie, Valerie, Grace Under Fire,* and *Designing Women* served as both maternal and paternal figures.

Traditional roles between spouses also evolved, as evidenced by the 1992 pilot of *Mad About You,* which opens with wife Jamie ordering husband Paul to get up and make the coffee, a far cry from a world in which the responsibility for food preparation (and any other household duties) was solely placed on women.

It wasn't only inside the home that roles were changing. The female leads on *Laverne & Shirley, Roseanne,* and *Grace Under Fire* held jobs in manufacturing plants, traditionally deemed male positions. When real women began to engage in activities previously reserved for men—working outside the home, disciplining the children, handling financial matters—television, at its own pace, began changing to fit this new reality. Feminism was the driving force behind many cultural and societal changes in the last half of the twentieth century—the advent of the birth control pill, the legalization of abortion, the movement toward equality in the workplace, our ability to make our own choices about our sex lives, and the statutes enacted to protect women from rape, assault, and domestic violence.

Television, as a mass media, tends to veer somewhere toward the middle when it comes to politics and culture in order to appeal to the largest audience and thereby sell expensive advertising time. It also has perpetuated many negative representations of women (who can forget *Charlie's Angels* and *Baywatch*?). But we can't lose sight of the ways in which television has represented and even furthered the status of women in America. As a mirror of popular culture since the 1950s, television has served as a barometer of attitudes toward American women.

A Past That Never Was

More people than I care to think about are walking down the street right now—male or female, white or black—dreaming of their future with images that often include a quaint house in the suburbs, a cozy family life, a Christmas tree, a white picket fence, maybe two kids, maybe two dogs, maybe the American dream. The problem is not that people want certain things out of life; it is that too often people look to a future that harkens to a past that never existed. In her extraordinary book *The Way We Never Were*, Stephanie Coontz explores how we get caught in what she terms "the nostalgia trap." Many of the images that fill our fantasies are just that—fantasies—and the interaction between genders and appropriate roles within families is something that has always been in flux. No medium has perpetuated the "perfect" family myth more than television. But not all TV viewers have bought into it.

I remember a time in college when I was knee-deep in a women's history course that stirred in me a deep anger. I am still an "angry" feminist. Even today, when women make up more than half the population, they still make up less than 8 percent of Congress. That should make anyone—man or woman—who believes in a representative government angry.

When I was in college, I had no way to express my anger about the various representations of women on television. I eventually stopped watching altogether for fear that seeing one more bikini-clad dancing girl in a beer commercial would put me over the edge or make me throw something heavy through the screen. And I am a middle-class, straight, white woman; I can't imagine the anger black, Asian, Hispanic, and gay women must feel at their representation in the mass media. However, women television viewers have their own opinions about what they watch, and respond to it in different ways. Historian Susan Douglas writes about watching early television, "If my memory serves me correctly, I didn't learn to yell back at the TV set on my own; I learned it, in part, from Mom."[2] So did I.

Mass media representations of women are like anything else. We each interpret them in our own way. Maybe there are women who feel empowered by beer commercials or think Jeannie didn't have it so bad. I'm sure, on some days, we all think Jeannie didn't have it so bad. Whatever our opinions about the images we see, we adjust to media images in different ways and the good news is that for some of us—myself included—the choice over what TV we support and what we boycott empowers us as viewers and consumers. Maybe we don't control what is broadcast into our living rooms, but researchers have found that TV viewers "*do* resist the homogenizing pull of TV, by ignoring it when it's on, yelling 'Bullshit!' at the commercials, channel clicking or deconstructing the news."[3] While boycotting may work for some people some of the time, the bigger question is what do we do with all the daily images on TV? What meaning do they have?

No TV image was as ubiquitous as that of the traditional 1950s family, which had no relevance at all to black families, or gay people, or families headed by women, or any family where both parents worked so they could pay the rent and put food on the table. Fifties television left out a lot. It was a decade that gave rise to corporate America and "suburbanism." It exalted the nuclear family and clearly delineated gender roles. In the '50s and '60s, according to Stephanie Coontz, women could rely on "a common life course—a predictable pattern in which women fell in love, got married, had sex, and bore children. Marriage, after all, was central to everyone's establishment of adult status and identity, and since we were women, marriage and childbearing would occupy the bulk of our active adult lives."[4]

With these conformist expectations imposed on women, some form of revolution was inevitable. The "perfect" wife and mother paradigm was an impossible standard to live up to, as Coontz points out:

> *A successful 1950s family, moreover, was often achieved at an enormous cost to the wife, who was expected to*

subordinate her own needs and aspirations to those of both
her husband and her children. In consequence, no sooner
was the ideal of the postwar family accepted than observers
began to comment perplexedly on how discontented women
seemed in the very roles they supposedly desired most.[5]

Nowadays, the many options women can chose from can make life confusing. There is a certain allure to a life that is neatly laid out in front of us. But if we are to follow that course, no one ever asks what *we* want out of life or allows us to explore other options; this is the kind of life that becomes stifling and unfulfilling.

The year my mother was born, 1949, *Life* magazine reported that "suddenly and for no plain reason" American women were "eerily restless."[6] Under a "mask of placidity," many wives and mothers were seething with anger, resentment, and unhappiness. Soon, print media was exposing the plight of wives and mothers, but television programming didn't follow.

When writer Betty Friedan, also a wife and mother, began investigating what she termed "the problem with no name" in 1957, she found multitudes of women who were seriously unhappy with their lot in life. Many women found solace in alcohol, drugs, or anything else that could dull their feelings of discontent. Friedan published *The Feminine Mystique* in 1963 and it became a bestseller. It challenged the previous decade's ideas about women, particularly those idealized TV images—the very ones everyone was trying to live up to, but never could achieve. The women of that era might have been told that a clean house made for a fulfilling life, but many knew better.

Like my mother, who always had exceptionally high expectations for housecleaning, Susan Douglas's mother also succumbed to her duty, though it was increasingly clear that mimicking "perfect" TV wives and mothers was simply not possible.

> My mother despised doing housework, and she was extremely unpleasant to be around when, on her weekends "off," she vacuumed, stripped the beds, cleaned the oven, ironed, and so forth. Yet she was determined to have the house neat and clean at all times, because a clean house was the primary way you were assessed as a wife and mother. June Cleaver made having a spotless house look so effortless; for Mom, it was so hard.[7]

It wasn't just housekeeping that real people could not keep up with. For real Americans to approach the level of material comforts shown on *Leave It to Beaver* and *Father Knows Best*, most families needed both Mom and Dad in the workforce. To have their houses approach TV's standards of tidiness and cleanliness, most moms would have had to come home from work and mop till they dropped.[8]

Regardless of the era, the idea that women can be "perfect"—perfect wives, perfect mothers, perfect executives, perfect superwomen—is always a fallacy. If life were that easy, well, maybe we wouldn't even need the entertainment of television. In the '50s, women were expected to be flawless wives and mothers, just as in the '80s and '90s the media projected the image of women who "could do it all." As women know, those unrealistic images set us up for all kinds of impossible expectations both collectively and individually. Even though the word *feminism,* in some circles, is strangely taboo—we've all heard women say, "I'm not a feminist, but . . . "—it was the fight for equality with men (also known as feminism) that allows us to live today in a world where myriad options are open to us, options that extend beyond what our bodies can do and empower us to be valued as much for our thoughts, ideas, and creativity as we are as for our breasts.

The Effects of Feminism

Feminism as a force for social change has dramatically altered life for modern women. Today, few women realize that their fight to vote began in 1820 and lasted 100 years, until women were granted full suffrage in 1920. Societal changes often happen slowly and popular culture does its best to keep pace. While television shows lagged behind what was going on in our real lives, there was nothing women could do but launch a revolution.

It's also important to understand our relationship with television. It may be a mass medium, but because most of us watch it in our homes, in our pajamas, with our kids, it feels more personal than many other forms of entertainment.

As reality (versus fantasy) became more standard on TV, sitcoms needed to showcase characters that were relatable to real women, characters who experienced the same set of dichotomies most women face: sex, work, marriage, motherhood. The clear-cut path for women (and men as well)—getting married, raising a family, having a husband as the go-to guy of the household—was no longer featured as ideal, in part because real people were aware that life, especially women's lives, was never that simple.

This is as true today as it was when the single, thirty-year-old Mary Richards abandoned a traditional path and meandered her way through a new world, one that was slowly endorsing women's independence—personal, financial, and sexual. To give characters more believability, the creators of the show and Mary Tyler Moore, herself, drew upon the new options open to women in the real world, just as the writers of *Sex and the City* drew upon their own dating and sexual experiences. In fact, one great sitcom writer, Cindy Chupack (who has written for more traditional shows like *Everybody Loves Raymond* as well as *SATC*), wrote a memoir, titled *The Between Boyfriends Book,* about the many experiences she's had with men, not unlike the experiences of the four lead characters in *Sex and the City*. For writers, creating experiences for women characters has become an effort in realism. I have heard many television writers talk about how they listen to real women's conversations and, on occasion, record conversations with their own friends. This should be no surprise—women have a lot going on in their heads and in their lives. I, for one, am happy to see issues laid bare on television as opposed to living in a society in which mass media refuses to acknowledge the daily successes, struggles, and insecurities that every American woman has felt at one point or another. This new world of television gives us women who are admirable and strong, yes, but also riddled with insecurity, fear, and uncertainty just like most American women.

Compared to the one-dimensional prefeminist representations of women, we now have complex TV characters who are a far cry from June Cleaver. Murphy Brown is a recovering alcoholic; Roseanne is always fighting a weight problem; Carrie Bradshaw's financial ignorance has her spending the bulk of her salary on shoes. Even as I want to be like Murphy Brown, I am drawn to her flaws and foibles as much as to her strength and ambition. To me, this is the essence of feminism: we deserve the same rights, options, and responsibilities afforded to men, but we are no better, no kinder, or more together than our male counterparts.

However, we've had a history of patriarchy to fight against, both on and off TV. I'm sure there are many women who never wanted to be like Mary Richards or Murphy Brown, but I think few would deny that the more varied characters we see on TV—be they stay-at-home moms or CEOs— the more we can begin to feel at ease with our own options, decisions, and lives.

It is generally accepted that *The Mary Tyler Moore Show*

ushered in feminism on television; but as critics, historians, and feminists have often worked to designate what feminism has meant at each point in our history (from careerist feminism to difference feminism to class-based feminism), the kind of feminism Mary Richards brought to America is generally called "lifestyle" feminism, where women could choose a "lifestyle" of work or independence or putting off marriage, options deemed unacceptable and deviant before the women's liberation movement. Because this new type of woman may have been threatening to the cultural dynamic in 1970, the show's writers and producers tried not to be overtly political, but they could not avoid the underlying revolution that was taking place. Writer-producer James Brooks explained that he wanted Mary to live in a world in which "women's rights were being talked about and it was having an impact."[9] This impact was not just seen on Saturday-night television; it was becoming part of many American women's lives. Women were waiting longer to wed while others were ending their marriages.[10] In addition, the passage of the Equal Credit Opportunity Act made it easier for women to buy their own property and establish their own credit.[11]

In her evocative interviews with women, Betsy Israel underscored the extent to which real women in the '70s were changing. In an interview with an art appraiser who, at the time, was turning thirty, she found how "women's lib" was changing the way women made decisions about their lives, even minor decisions.

*I was tired of living out of a big version of a suitcase—
not having the nice things in the style I wanted them in
because, goddamit, I was supposed to have these things
selected from my registry, or to pick them out together
with my husband, with whom I was to establish a real,
permanent home. . . . I didn't even have a nice car. Everything was on hold and I was just too far along in all the
other areas of my life to live without a decent shower
curtain or wineglasses.*[12]

So many women were single or single with children; they
no longer had to wait for a man to create their own lifestyles.
That is not to say that many women would not have been happy
finding a life partner, husband, or boyfriend, but they knew
they could live on their own until that happened. I always
thought Rhoda Morgenstern was a great example of a woman
who, yes, wanted a man desperately, but was clearly strong and
brash enough to live without one for as long as necessary.

In some ways, feminism hijacked the '70s. The political
activities centered around women's rights were in the media
spotlight. In the '90s, when I was in college and attended
women's center activities and events, I could still find some
committed activists and a few other believers, but I'm sure it
was nothing compared to the early '70s. Our efforts to bring
then–attorney general Janet Reno to speak to our student body
were a great deal different from the 1970 "Women's Strike for
Equality" protest in New York City, the first large women's
liberation protest that garnered a lot of media attention. The
turnout was so large, it even surprised the organizers; the

event was covered in *Newsweek, Time, Life,* and on the front page of *The New York Times.* Feminism was big news in the '70s. Even the bastion of tradition *Ladies' Home Journal* did an eight-page insert on "The New Feminism" in 1970.[13] Feminist celebrities like Betty Friedan and Gloria Steinem got lots of publicity. This mirrored the more subdued revolution taking place on television, symbolized by Mary Richards and later by Maude Findlay.

Mary Richards was both revolutionary and traditional. She was described by Ella Taylor in *Prime-Time Families* as a combination of "girl-next-door sweetness and 'old-fashioned' attachment to honesty and integrity, on the one hand, and spunky New Woman, on the other."[14] The show was walking the tenuous path of social change, "endorsing modernity at the same time as it hallowed tradition."[15] I think Mary Richards had to invoke the "feminine" qualities of nurturance and emotionality because TV programmers wanted to ease into the new world of feminism. Had Maude come before Mary, it might have precipitated a backlash. Audiences responded well to *The Mary Tyler Moore Show.* It wasn't simply a new feminist statement; it was an extremely successful one, which launched three spin-offs. And it's still popular, decades later, in syndication and on DVD.

Academic Andrea Press investigated what real women thought of *The Mary Tyler Moore Show* and found that middle-class women identified very strongly with Mary. They saw her as both realistic as well as a positive representation of female independence.[16] I wonder if women related to her because, at times, she was visibly unsure of her own choices. I think this same lack of certainty makes many women identify with the characters of *Sex and the City* as well; they question and opine and discuss their every move just as most real people do. While Mary's insecurity was usually demonstrated with a "typically" female response such as crying, whining, or stuttering, it did not detract from the fact that she could stand up to men like her boss, Mr. Grant, or anyone else who got in her way.

In a rare pop-cultural moment, *Mary Tyler Moore* got television on track with what was occurring in society. As mentioned previously, television progresses more slowly than other media. The structure and format of sitcoms remains the same. *MTM* successfully carved out a new "single career-woman" genre, and shows have been attempting to re-create its success ever since. It is not that writers, creators, and producers lack innovation. It has more to do with com-mercial reality. As a business, television wants to appeal to the largest audience possible. Shows based on single women have been hugely successful since *MTM* was introduced—*Murphy Brown* in the '80s, *Friends* in the '90s, and *Sex and the City* most recently.

In creating a nonthreatening feminist, *MTM* paved the way for the type of feminist audiences would love to hate: Bea-trice Arthur as Maude. *Maude* premiered two years after *The Mary Tyler Moore Show,* and the American TV audience was ready. The show's theme song compared Maude with Joan of

Arc. Maude Findlay—divorced, taller than most men, brash, deep-voiced, and unyielding—was no Mary Richards, but could never have been created without her. Maude was not the kind and caring nurturer that Mary was; Maude was the kind of woman who would get arrested for speeding and argue the case in court. On the telephone, she was commonly confused with a man; she was the kind of woman who kicked her husband out of the house when he said, "It's either politics or me."[17] She was stubborn like a man and never shied away from a fight. As a young girl, I watched *Maude* reruns in the eighties. Even then, she was an admirable representation of a woman who refused to be told what to do, even when it was to her detriment; she played the role of a tiger instead of a kitten. In response to her unexpected success, Bea Arthur, an incomparable comedic actress, once said, "There is no one like me." There was no one like her character, *Maude,* either, and even today she serves as a model of female strength we see all too seldom on television.

Were the Eighties Really So Bad?

Growing up in the '80s, I saw a materialism, greed, and cult of accumulation that seemed unprecedented. It was the decade of Gordon Gekko, the über mover and shaker in Oliver Stone's film *Wall Street*, who pronounced proudly, "Greed is good." But movers and shakers have historically been men, as underscored in Susan Douglas's *Where the Girls Are:*

*Throughout our lives we have been getting profoundly con-
tradictory messages about what it means to be an American
woman. Our national mythology teaches us that Americans
are supposed to be independent, rugged individuals who
are achievement-oriented, competitive, active, shrewd, and
assertive go-getters. . . . Women, however, are supposed
to be dependent, passive, nurturing types, uninterested in
competition, achievement, or success, who should conform
to the wishes of the men in their lives.*[18]

As Douglas explains, "It doesn't take a rocket scientist to
see that these two lists of behavioral traits are mutually exclusive, and that women are stuck right in the middle."[19] This
was certainly true in the entertainment and popular culture of
the 1980s. As evidenced in Susan Faludi's *Backlash,* the 1980s
were a decade when America adopted a form of neotraditionalism that was not particularly friendly to feminism.

President Ronald Reagan claimed that women's equality
was so complete that there was no need to "appoint them to
higher office." That pretty much characterizes the faulty logic
of the decade. The press, pundits, and politicians of the time
saw women as "so equal" they should give up any further fight
for equality and, even better, give up careers and independence that would never *really* fulfill them in the same way
that being a wife and mother would. Think about the films
from that decade in which working women eventually found
more happiness at home or with a man *(Mr. Mom, Crossing
Delancey, Baby Boom, Parenthood, Three Men and a Baby).* To
some degree, television followed suit. *Baby Boom* was a short-

lived sitcom, based on the film by the same title. Its premise is that a New York advertising executive "lioness" gives her career up to raise an adopted baby in rural Vermont. She falls in love and starts her own gourmet-baby-food business, a more "acceptable" exercise in female entrepreneurship by '80s standards. *Baby Boom* was indicative of the decade's discomfort with feminism.

One of the decade's most popular shows, *thirtysomething*, was emblematic of the era's reevaluation of women's roles, '80s-style. Many women I know felt that *thirtysomething* did much to glamorize the mundane life of housework and diaper-changing. As Faludi notes, the '80s were a time when women faded into the background, much as they had done in the TV shows of the '50s and '60s:

> *Women's disappearance from prime-time television in the late '80s repeats a programming pattern from the last backlash when, in the late '50s and early '60s, single dads ruled the TV roosts and female characters were suddenly erased from the set. . . . An analysis of prime-time TV in 1987 found 66 percent of the 882 speaking characters were male—about the same proportion as in the '50s.*[20]

There were some exceptions. I see the backlash of the '80s inadvertently serving as a great catalyst for women's anger and discontent with how they were portrayed in mass media in general and on television in particular. It is no coincidence that the late 1980s brought us the sitcoms *Roseanne*, *Murphy Brown*, *Designing Women*, and *The Golden Girls*, all overtly feminist shows. The decade even gave women some prime-time drama in the form of the cop show *Cagney & Lacey* and the divorcée-on-the-loose dramedy *The Days and Nights of Molly Dodd*. Both series were kept on the air by the vehement reaction of women viewers when the shows were threatened with cancellation. Even on traditional shows of the decade such as *The Cosby Show* and *Family Ties,* the mothers were also very successful career women, a lawyer and architect respectively, and were proud of that success.

In surveying the history of women's representation on television, the bad is often as instructive as the good. We clearly see the inequality of women in many sitcoms, from *Roseanne* to *Murphy Brown* to *Grace Under Fire*. Women have done their best to assert whatever independence and power on TV they could. As mentioned earlier, the show *Roseanne* was originally to be titled "Life and Stuff," but the matriarch herself put her foot down. This was *her* show, based on *her* stand-up comedy, and if men had always been able to use their names for show titles (Dick Van Dyke, Bill Cosby), there was no way Roseanne was going to acquiesce to something else. This is one of the victories in our short history of feminist television that makes many viewers, including me, very proud.

Equality That Is Still Not Equal

Okay, so we've entered the new millennium, and where are we in relation to the equality of the sexes? Unlike the 1950s, a time when discretionary income doubled and many families were able to survive on only one income, we now live in an era when most people, both married and single, struggle to make ends meet. We live in an economy where most women *have to work*. There is a host of evidence showing that, as a society, we are still trying to keep up with the Joneses, or the Cleavers, but increasingly, the only way to do so is to mire ourselves in everything from multiple mortgages to credit card debt. As many Americans struggle to pay rent or make mortgage payments and put food on the table, the media and daytime television still feature shows in which stay-at-home moms battle it out with working moms over who is better—an indulgent topic with little relevance for most of us.

The irony of '50s television was that while TV moms almost never worked, most real moms did. Even all those '50s TV moms were *working* actresses. Most women today don't have the luxury of being stay-at-home moms. One of the biggest injustices (first recognized by feminism) is the lack of worth and value attached to the myriad things women (working outside the home or not) must do to take care of their homes, their husbands, and their children. Unfortunately, this has been a perennial problem. As Susan Douglas asserts, "By 1963, women like my mother were in an untenable position. They worked all the time, yet their work inside and outside the home was taken for granted and poorly valued."[21]

The trend for women with children to work outside the home has continued to grow. In 1975, 47 percent of all American mothers with children under age eighteen worked; by 2000, the rate had risen to 73 percent.[22] With so many mothers working, it stands to reason that the division of labor within the home would move toward equality as well. Unfortunately for most working moms, this is far from true, as sociologist Arlie Hochschild indicates in her book *The Second Shift.* But the subject is part of our social and cultural dialogue, and even more traditional sitcoms like *Everybody Loves Raymond* address the issue.

We have found strong allies in female TV characters who acknowledge the inequalities they face. I can only hope that writers and producers, particularly women writers and producers, continue to create TV shows that feature women who address these struggles and acknowledge how far we've come and how far we still need to go to achieve equality.

Chapter 6

Dream Jobs and Drudgery

TV Women and Work

> I like my job. It's who I am.
>
> **—Murphy Brown**

Like Mary Richards of *The Mary Tyler Moore Show,* I rejected others' expectations of me and headed for the big city. But I was leaving academia in 2000. Mary was rejecting marriage. In 1970! Mary Richards went where few TV women had gone before: to work. As a *TV Guide* article of the era explained, "Television . . . does not provide human models for a bright thirteen-year-old girl who would like to grow up to be something other than an ecstatic floor waxer."[1]

Mary Richards was a trailblazer. She challenged conventional notions of what girls should do when they grow up. By the time I went to New York decades later, I wasn't making a statement about choosing a career over being a wife and mother, as Mary had done. I was simply exercising my freedom to choose what *I* wanted. Nevertheless, women of my generation still must confront what I like to call the three Ms: marriage, motherhood, and makeup application. These pressures swirl in our heads along with media images of women dancing happily around their dishwashers. But the fact that I had grown up with Mary Richards meant I had another image in mind: a cheerfully optimistic theme song playing as one of the most important female TV characters of all time throws her hat up in the air as if graduating into her own independence. This was a new kind of TV woman— one who may have been alone, who may have just started to embark on a new adventure, but would very likely "make it after all."

My favorite definition of a feminist is "a woman who assumes self-dependence as a basic condition of her life."[2] Even today, Mary Richards fits the bill. As corny as it may sound, after arriving in New York, I walked around the city conjuring up images of Mary's wide-eyed appraisal of Minneapolis. (It wasn't all rosy for me, though. Mary had no trouble affording her spacious apartment; I could barely fit into mine.) Like Mary, I considered self-dependence a basic condition of life. With a journalism degree in hand and not one ounce of television experience under my belt, I decided to become a TV news producer. If Mary could do it, why couldn't I?

Like many women, I was influenced by the women I grew up watching on television. My ideas about gender roles didn't come from feminism, per se. They evolved from, in historian Susan Douglas's words, "the perspective of someone who, like most women, watched from the sidelines, yet who found being a spectator an increasingly political and politicizing act."[3] None of the little girls I knew wanted to be the kind of housewife they saw on black-and-white television, presuming they wanted to be housewives at all. *The Mary Tyler Moore Show,* along with *Julia* and *That Girl,* presented us with alternatives to the life of the happy homemaker, which seemed, to me at least, uneventful and unfulfilling. (Who could have imagined that decades later, *Desperate Housewives* would portray the life of wife and mother as downright ominous?)

The *Mary Tyler Moore Show* was just the beginning. Soon a new feminist voice was speaking to audiences through more and more women characters. *Alice, One Day at a Time,* and *Laverne & Shirley* depicted the lives of different types of "working women." Some had children *(Julia, Kate & Allie),* some enjoyed professional success *(Murphy Brown, Caroline in the City, Veronica's Closet),* some were still trying to make it big *(The Betty White Show,* which portrayed the life of a struggling actress and was a precursor to *Cybill),* and some struggled with dignity and humor at low-paying jobs *(Alice,* Florida on *Good Times, Grace Under Fire).* Shows such as *Ally McBeal, Buffy the Vampire Slayer,* and *Living Single* featured characters for whom feminism was just a part of life.[4]

The Beginnings of TV Feminism

At the beginning of the '70s—the decade in which feminist ideals created a fundamental shift in society—Mary Richards was already different from the TV women who preceded her. She lived alone, something few television women did. She worked outside the home by choice. She wasn't afraid to give up the traditional role of wife and mother. At the time, no other female character who had rejected society's expectations and blazed her own trail was cast in a positive light.

Mary Richards represented a woman we could all be (albeit an upper-middle-class white woman), in part because she could be simultaneously weak and strong, contradictions that made her real. The creators of the show, James L. Brooks and Allan Burns, explain, "We thought of the difficulty of being thirty, single and female in the very tough world of the '70s, and we wanted to find the comedy—but also the meaning—in that."[5]

Previously known to audiences as Laura from *The Dick Van Dyke Show*, Mary Tyler Moore embodied the character that many view as one of television's first attempts at representing the realistic experiences of women. Mary Richards was lithe and beautiful, but she was by no means perfect. She had some stereotypical female traits: She could be naive, weak, and, at times, whiny. She was also strong, independent, and hardworking. She had rejected suburban marriage and family and bravely struck out for the big city. She lived alone and worked for personal fulfillment, not to support children or as a part-time hobby. It was a life and attitude that many female TV viewers had never before seen.

Mary wasn't the only working woman to appear on the show. Rhoda, her neighbor, and Sue Ann Nivens, one of Mary's coworkers, were also single working women. Though clearly an important support network, they also presented a contrast to Mary. Rhoda was desperate for a husband. Mary, on the other hand, had rejected a marriage proposal and did not seem eager to seek another. In the pilot episode, when describing what her life could have been had she gotten married, she exclaims, "I could've married him! Can you imagine what that life would have been like?"[6]

The idea that women can (and, some believe, should) work outside the home, though unquestioned in most circles today, has had a rocky history in America. After working during World War II, more than a few women resented being forced back into traditional domestic roles. In 1944, one in three women defense workers had previously been full-time homemakers and about 2.7 million mothers were in paid employment. The war had presented women with opportunities to earn wages and learn new skills.[7] But by the end of the war and the end of the decade, a conservative political and social climate prevailed. Though many women continued to work outside the home, television was to become traditionalism's best ally in attempting to keep them at home. In fact, in a 1949 *Fortune* magazine poll, 46 percent of respondents felt college should prepare women for marriage and family.[8]

Few young women today are aware of just how sexist our society was only decades ago. Katha Pollitt, author, *Nation* columnist, and professor, sees it firsthand.

> *My students are only vaguely aware of the legal and cultural restrictions Betty Friedan wrote about. It came as news to them that not so long ago married women had trouble getting their own credit cards, help-wanted ads were segregated by sex, and women were routinely expected to resign their jobs if they became pregnant.*[9]

For women who grew up in a time when they were afforded few of the protections and rights they have today, Mary Richards seemed revolutionary. After all, in 1964 *My Living Doll* premiered, a show starring leggy Julie Newmar as a female robot programmed to do anything she is told, particularly "only to speak when spoken to" and "to obey all orders" given by her male "boss."

During the 1950s, television was both culprit and accomplice in attempting to show women their proper place. "Remember, ladies," the televisions seemed to say, "how wonderful it is to cook and clean while wearing a strand of pearls and a smile." Years later, *Grace Under Fire*'s Brett Butler mused, "As far as I know, the only woman who's been allowed to be consistently independent, adventurous and unmolested is Lassie, and they used all boy dogs to play that part."[10]

Real women often felt the same way. In 1960, Herma Snider, a typical American housewife and mother, wrote in *Redbook,* "I pride myself upon being of average intelligence

The Mary Tyler Moore Show

On her own for the first time in her life and
working at WJM, Mary Richards was TV's
first independent single woman of the '70s.

Maude

The character Maude Findley was created
by the show's producer, Norman Lear,
to be the antithesis of *All in the Family*'s
Archie Bunker—she was a feminist, outspoken, liberal, and, of course, a woman.

One Day at a Time

Anne Romano of *One Day at a Time* dealt with the complexity of being both mother and father to her teenage daughters.

Cagney & Lacey

Chris Cagney and Mary Beth Lacey changed the course of TV history as the first female police partners.

© CBS/Photofest

Designing Women

This show about a Southern-women-owned
interior design firm resonated so strongly
with female audiences that CBS was forced
to issue an apology after repeatedly
moving the show's timeslot.

Wearer of many hats, including Mom and 9-to-5er, Roseanne also started her own business, a diner, with her sister, Jackie, and friend Nancy.

Roseanne

The Conners, a typical working-class family living in the heartland of Lanford, Illinois, was one of the most popular TV families of the 1980s.

Murphy Brown

Candice Bergen, perfectly cast as the
no-nonsense TV journalist, had to fight for
the part—network executives wanted to
cast Heather Locklear instead.

Friends

Rachel, Monica, and Phoebe of *Friends* invited us into their many candid—and often hilarious—heart-to-hearts about life, love, and finding their place in the world.

Sex and the City

One of HBO's most successful series, *Sex and the City* attracted droves of female viewers with its frank conversations about the sexual and romantic lives of Carrie, Miranda, Samantha, and Charlotte. The series finale, in 2004, drew in 10.6 million viewers.

and understanding. During my high school and college days I had dreams of a career in journalism. But after my marriage these dreams were abandoned." She described the drudgery of being trapped in the home, a rut where she existed on "cigarettes and cleanser fumes. . . . Meanwhile, the mind that I thought I had camphored away refused to stay put; it yearned for a chance to flex its muscles on something besides the grocery bills and the perpetual 'why?' of three small boys."[11]

This was a common malaise for women who longed for a life outside the home. It also made clear the realities of a world in which men weren't similarly forced to abandon their dreams. "I yearned for a full, satisfying life and I felt that the world was passing me by," Herma Snider wrote. "Each night as I tucked my sons into bed, I thanked God that they would grow up to be men, that they would be able to teach, write, heal, advise, travel or do anything else they choose."[12]

On television, the few women who held jobs outside the home were minor characters, like Sally Rogers on *The Dick Van Dyke Show*. The real stars of the '50s were the men or the kids—Lucille Ball being the exception; but *I Love Lucy* was still a domestic comedy, albeit starring a mischievous wife and mother. The titles of many popular shows—*My Three Sons, Father Knows Best, Leave It to Beaver*—barely acknowledged women's existence. Shows that did acknowledge them, did so by defining them through their relationships with men: *My Little Margie* (who, by the way, was twenty-one), *Our Miss Brooks, How to Marry a Millionaire, The Farmer's Daughter*.

The predominance of female subservience on television had a way of making real women feel that harboring career ambition should be kept a deep, dark secret. Anna Quindlen, best-selling author and former *New York Times* columnist, compares that era to an earlier one: "At twenty-five, I should have worn a big red A on my chest; it would have stood for ambition, an ambition so brazen and burning that it would have reduced Hester Prynne's transgression to pale pink."[13]

In the '60s, working women didn't fare much better on television. It was a decade of farce, starring flying nuns, genies in bottles, identical cousins, and *My Mother the Car* (I did not make this up). If '50s shows were not representative of women's reality, the '60s took us to a new level of absurdity.

Gender representation on television was seriously off the mark. Women, young and old, who compared themselves or their mothers to June Cleaver, Harriet Nelson, or Donna Reed were inevitably disappointed. In *The Feminine Mystique,* Betty Friedan discovered this firsthand when she interviewed a suburban housewife and found that "as she made the beds, shopped for groceries, matched slipcover material, ate peanut butter sandwiches with her children, chauffeured Cub Scouts and Brownies, lay beside her husband at night—she was afraid to ask, even of herself, the silent question—'Is this all?'"[14]

In her examination of women's roles in the public sphere, Marie Wilson asked herself that very question "I grew up in the 1940s and 1950s, when women were truly limited to a supporting role. I was Homecoming Queen and a class officer (but not the president). I was a cheerleader. I won beauty contests in my hometown of Atlanta. I married poor but with promise, then nearly went mad in the isolation of a small apartment with a baby. . . . If you strip away the particulars, I have led an American woman's life."[15] That life provided her with the catalyst to create the White House Project (which addresses the role of women in politics) and to become president of the Ms. Foundation for Women, for which she developed Take Our Daughters to Work Day. Not bad for a beauty queen.

Marc Cherry, the creator behind 2003's hit suburban satire *Desperate Housewives*, says that he created the show because he was inspired by the sacrifices his mother made to have a family. (In this case, maybe psychiatrist Carl Jung was right when he suggested that the largest psychological influence on children is "the unlived life of the parent.") Cherry saw his mother as lacking role models that fell somewhere between "Betty Crocker and Betty Friedan."[16] In the pilot episode of *Desperate Housewives,* Mary Alice Young, the narrator of the series, eerily explains, "I spent the day as I spend every other day—quietly polishing the routine of my life until it gleamed with perfection."[17] She then retrieves a revolver from her closet and kills herself in the back yard of her "perfect" suburban home. That's quite a statement about the darker side of the "feminine mystique."

For historians, the '50s, as television, rarely resembled

the lives of Americans. In reality, women in the '50s made up nearly 30 percent of the workforce, a fact barely acknowledged by TV shows at the time.[18] Most sitcoms of that era depicted an idealized portrait of the middle-class housewife.[19] In other words, television offered, at best, a sanitized representation of womanhood and, at worst, a false one.

In 1970, when television introduced Mary Richards, viewers finally saw a single woman who was more representative of the general population. Still, Mary Richards lived a life many had never seen depicted on television before. The average age of women marrying for the first time had been steadily increasing (and continues to rise to this day).

Watching reruns of *MTM* as I was growing up in the '80s, I was inspired by Mary Richards and find many of her experiences still pertinent today. When I worked at a cable network, as an associate producer (like Mary), I also was faced with a gruff, intimidating, and unapproachable boss. Though my superior was a woman, I was just as afraid of her as Mary was of Mr. Grant. One evening, I was forced to work late rewriting a news piece my boss disliked—okay, hated. Like Lou Grant, my boss had no qualms about expressing her opinion, no matter how harshly worded.

Ironically, that night I arrived home to see a rerun of the pilot of *The Mary Tyler Moore Show*. (Thank goodness for Nick at Nite.) In her job interview (and first interaction) with Mr. Grant, both Mary and the audience begin to realize what she has gotten herself into.

MARY: It seems you've been asking me a lot of personal questions, which don't have a thing to do with my qualifications for this job.

MR. GRANT: You know what? You've got spunk.

MARY: *(Blushing)* Well . . . yeah.

MR. GRANT: I hate spunk! Tell you what. I'll try you out for a couple of weeks, see if it works out. If I don't like you, I'll fire you. If you don't like me, I'll fire you.

MARY: That certainly seems fair. What's the job?

MR. GRANT: The job is that of associate producer.

MARY: *(Stunned)* Associate prod—

MR. GRANT: Something wrong?

MARY: No, I like it. Associate producer.

MR. GRANT: The job pays ten dollars less a week than the secretarial job.

MARY: *(Mentally calculating)* That'll be fine.

MR. GRANT: If you can get by on fifteen less a week, I'll make you a producer.

MARY: No, I think associate producer is all I can afford.[20]

A boss like Mr. Grant is far from ideal, but certainly not far from reality. The antagonism established between these two characters offered me a humorous way to relate to the pitfalls of my own work life. And it isn't just Mary who stands up to her boss. Later, Murphy Brown *rules* her boss, Miles Silverberg. Roseanne's manufacturing plant superiors seem downright afraid of her. Fran (of *The Nanny*) has her boss wrapped around her little finger. And Alice gives as good as she gets from her gruff boss, Mel. For Mary Richards and these other characters, standing up to the boss requires backbone, but also diplomacy. Each time I was forced to confront my own boss, I tried to keep this in mind. The only difference between Mary and me, as I saw it, was that nervousness would force her to giggle, stutter, and stammer verbally, while it gave me nausea, night sweats, anxiety attacks, and whole mornings spent in the bathroom. (I still do not understand why characters on television rarely get diarrhea, incapacitating panic attacks, heart palpitations, insomnia, and tearful trips to the bathroom, just like the rest of us. Maybe seeing our icons act so "real" would still be a little too much for the American viewing public.)

Women I know have had similar experiences. One friend has counted the number of times a day her male boss refers to her as "sweetie," "sweetheart," or "honey," a condescension he never employs with men. Even though our work environments may always be filled with sexism and discrimination, characters like Mary Richards give us role models of women who press on regardless (even if now and then, it brings them, and us, to tears).

MR. GRANT: I do not remember asking you for any help. Here's the last order I can give ya, Mary. Lay off!

MARY: I don't wanna lay off![21]

Because the lives of sitcom characters, for better or for worse, don't change much over the course of a series, we get comfortable with what we expect from our heroes. Mary is not about to give up her dreams, and by extension, she taught me not to give up on mine. She also struck a chord with the viewing public at the time; the series consistently ranked in the top twenty rated shows for its entire seven-year run. It also won twenty-five Emmys and spun off two other successful sitcoms with independent female leads.[22] (In 1974, a writer for *The Mary Tyler Moore Show*, Treva Silverman, became the first woman to win an Emmy for a sitcom.)

The Mary Tyler Moore Show was considered smart, literate, and of higher quality than the farcical television of the 1960s. For many women, it represented much more than just a new TV series. Unlike female characters in other popular sitcoms of the era (e.g., *All in the Family*), Mary is never presented as an object of ridicule or humiliation.[23] She symbolizes the independent woman of the 1970s. In her early thirties, Mary doesn't shun marriage and family, but is not desperately grabbing for that idealized feminine brass ring (or engagement ring, as the case may be). Female viewers, then and now, adore her.

Mary is a truly multidimensional character. She works, yes, but dates as well. She likes men and even the idea of marriage, but won't give up her professional dreams for those personal goals. Mary Richards demonstrates to me what "The personal is political" means. She rejects, or at least delays, women's stereotypical roles—marriage and motherhood—and is, in my mind, a feminist exclamation point. Mary, and the audience who watches her, is not sure where she'll end up: Married? Promoted? President of the network? The world is rife with possibilities for a female TV character, and in TV's realm of constant replication and formula, that is quite a feat.

For all her independence, Mary Richards is warm, loving, and vulnerable.[24] This is the crux of her comedy—often demonstrated when she has to muster enough courage to stand up to Mr. Grant. This also makes her more real. Women characters on television, and in pop culture in general, are complicated because the search for a more realistic depiction of female characters is also a search for the female identity, the battleground for strong versus weak, tough versus demure.[25]

In one episode, Mary proves her courage by singlehandedly going to bat for Mr. Grant—her colleagues being too fearful—when his job is threatened. She convinces the intimidating, male television station owner to give her boss another chance, and Mr. Grant is irritated by Mary's audacity.

MR. GRANT: *(Pointing to Mary)* The little lady's got a big mouth.

STATION OWNER: Now, watch that, boy, that's a woman.

MARY: Yeah, but it's a woman with a big mouth.[26]

With his job secured, Mr. Grant confronts Mary: "I suppose you feel like Mary Poppins or something?" Increasingly confident, she responds, "Well, no. Actually, I'm a little disappointed. I thought I was next in line for your job."[27]

Portraying a single working woman on TV was a dicey proposition in 1970 and ensuring Mary's likability was always a consideration. No matter what Mary's voice or dialogue betrays about her weaknesses, there is no doubt her behavior is brave. Mary Richards, an everywoman's woman, showed us that it doesn't matter whether we live in Minneapolis or Memphis, work as a television producer or teacher—each one of us "can make it after all."

Working for a Living

Network sitcoms in any era offer clues about the status quo of women in America, but they're certainly not fully realistic portrayals. Popular culture, in all its forms, is meant to entertain, thus placing limitations on overly mundane or uninteresting content. After all, it is doubtful viewers would be thrilled to watch countless hours of Murphy Brown sitting in a room editing tape or the stars of *Designing Women* calculating payroll taxes. Sitcoms, by nature, aren't meant to represent real experience as much as they are meant to draw on real experience for humor. Even so, since the '70s, TV has recognized and addressed as much as it can the real experiences of women, including the struggles working women face—feeling caught between their jobs and their families, or, dealing with on-the-job sexual harassment.

I knew more about women who worked because they had to than about women who lived in the pristine world of home and hearth. My great-grandmother immigrated to the United States from Russia and, like many other Jewish immigrants who came through Ellis Island, she had no money and could not speak English. Many women of this generation, dubbed by author and broadcaster Tom Brokaw "the greatest generation," worked because they had to. Even by the '70s, many working-class men clung to the ideal of having a wife who could stay at home, but the economy of the household increasingly required two incomes.[28]

In the 1950s, regardless of the happy homemakers displayed on television, the percentage of women in the workplace grew at a rate four times greater than that of men.[29] My own great-grandmother had not come to America dreaming of cleaning other people's homes or pressing ribbons in a garment factory, but she worked to afford her own daughters a better life. For my family, and many first- and second-generation immigrants, the American dream was on display on television, though not always attainable in real life. Women of color, who have always been a large part of the workforce, are still barely represented on television.

Early sitcoms offered viewers a goal. If you could rise above your working-class station, you could own a house in the suburbs, or even a coveted washing machine. The subtext of suburban family comedies like *Leave It to Beaver* and *Father Knows Best* told American audiences that this dream was attainable. This dream, though, rarely addressed the reality of working-class existence: Working-class women have always worked. Even in the '50s, nearly 40 percent of black and Hispanic women worked.[30] Although this wasn't represented by the sitcoms of that era, my grandmother and great-grandmother served as reminders of that reality when I was watching reruns decades later. The world we knew was portrayed on *Roseanne* or *Good Times* more than on *The Adventures of Ozzie and Harriet.*

Since the '70s, Bonnie Dow writes, television has done important "cultural work in representing feminism for the American public."[31] TV sitcoms were a new place to work out the problems many women face—problems that run deeper than what to prepare for dinner or who will pick up the kids after school. Women on shows like *One Day at a Time, Alice, Roseanne,* and *Grace Under Fire* work because they have to work. They work full-time to support either themselves or their children, and they deal with the difficulties that come with it. After *MTM*, it wasn't long before TV women were expected to earn a paycheck, if not launch an entire career.[32]

Working-class sitcoms don't judge women as harshly for working outside the home as their middle-class counterparts had in the past. After all, if it wasn't a choice—these women worked to survive—they couldn't really be blamed for taking a job to support themselves or their families. Not all women were afforded the options of characters like Rachel Green on *Friends*.

> **MONICA:** C'mon, Rachel, you can't live off your parents your whole life.
>
> **RACHEL:** I know that. That's why I was getting married.[33]

Women's work in prime-time sitcoms moved steadily from a hobby or adjunct to family life into the same realm as that of men, much like in real life, where women in greater numbers were entering higher education, the professions, and the workplace.[34] With the enormous success of *The Mary Tyler Moore Show,* and the series it spawned, either directly or indirectly *(Roseanne, The Nanny, Grace Under Fire)*, television could now move on to working-class America.

Few TV fans think of working-class comedies without drumming up images of Archie Bunker or *The Honeymooners*. But it was *Roseanne,* debuting in 1988, that broke the mold for working-class women. Though not a workplace comedy, *Roseanne* often deals with the intricate relationship between women and work, especially when working women are also wives and mothers.

Roseanne's sitcom character is a brash, loudmouthed, working-class mother and wife who jokes about and mocks the unfairness of her situation and is especially blunt about her views of men and sexism. Her humor aggressively attacks whoever and whatever denigrates poor women—husbands, family and friends, the media, or government welfare policies.[35] She is the perfect example of the "unruly woman," troublesome to men, challenging to everyone, and strong beyond most women ever seen on TV before. That is exactly what Roseanne, the producer of the show, wanted: "I never want her to be perfect. I want her to be flawed. And all the characters on the show are flawed, as are all women, and all human beings."[36]

Roseanne made it clear that no working-class family sitcom could ignore the realities of the work world. For this family, employment is not based on gender or power, but on financial necessity (just like it was in mine). This sitcom deals with life's nitty-gritty—bills and insurance, paychecks and payments—the same thing I saw my mother deal with in managing family and work. If there are money problems, everyone is forced to deal with them.

Roseanne is also a powerhouse to a degree rarely seen before on television:

> ROSEANNE: *(To her son, D.J.)* Me and your dad, we're exactly equal in this house. You know why? 'Cause that's the way I want it![37]

Even when accused of being bossy, Roseanne caustically defends herself.

> **ROSEANNE:** I don't boss Dan around. I'm helping him get in touch with his submissive side.[38]

Outside the home, Roseanne may not have chosen the job she goes to each day, but she persists with humor and often sheer might. When Roseanne must face her intimidating manufacturing plant boss—who happens to call all the women in the plant "girls"—she doesn't shy away from a fight.

> **ROSEANNE:** You are a lot of things, but you ain't no manager.
>
> **MR. FABER:** Sweetheart, you just bought yourself a bunch of trouble.
>
> **ROSEANNE:** No, sweetheart, you did.[39]

In the end, the manager of the plant should never have pitted himself against Roseanne, who successfully organizes a walkout, with every single female factory worker quitting right along with her. As she exits, Roseanne gets the last word: "I guess we're not gonna make our quota today, honey bunch."[40]

Establishing a working-class premise helped *Roseanne* expand the boundaries of women on television, partly due to the fact that less gender-specific stereotypes are expected of working-class women and women of color. Working gives characters like Roseanne and Florida pride and fulfillment they wouldn't get solely from their work as wives and mother.

Paying Our Dues

Work isn't always a source of pride for women on television. By the 1990s, many women on television had careers, though not always the ones they wanted. And in real life, after working for three years in television production in New York, I was burned out. I decided to become a waitress. Yes, after taking out a twenty-thousand-dollar loan for graduate school and working my way through the ranks at a popular national cable station, I was serving people food. I wasn't particularly proud of my new station in life, but I also knew it wasn't permanent (or so I hoped). After all, only several years before, Rachel Green on *Friends* had done the very same thing. She, like Mary Richards before her, made a choice to escape marriage, move to New York City, and try to "make it after all." When Rachel tries to explain to her father why she eschewed his plans for her life, she attempts a metaphor:

> RACHEL: All of my life, everyone has always told me, "You're a shoe! You're a shoe, you're a shoe, you're a shoe!" And today I just stopped and I said, "What if I don't wanna be a shoe? What if I wanna be a, a purse, y'know? Or a hat!" No, I'm not saying I want you to buy me a hat. It's a metaphor, Daddy![41]

Life does not go as smoothly for Rachel as it once had for Mary Richards. Instead of finding her dream job in the fashion industry, Rachel is forced to be a waitress at a coffeehouse. I could empathize. I too had come to New York to achieve my dreams and, like Rachel, found the life I dreamed of elusive.

As I carried trays of drinks (not so much carried as consistently dropped), I felt Rachel's embarrassment. In one episode, she is confronted by a group of catty women she knew growing up.

RACHEL: What are you guys doing here?

FIRST WOMAN: Well, we were in the city shopping and your mom said you work here and . . . it's true.

SECOND WOMAN: Look at you in the apron—you look like you're in a play. Let's talk reality for a second. When are you coming home?

RACHEL: What? Guys, I'm not.

SECOND WOMAN: C'mon, this is us.

RACHEL: I'm not. This is what I'm doing now. I've got this job. I even do my own laundry. This is what I'm doing now.

FIRST WOMAN: Waitressing?

RACHEL: I'm not just waitressing. I . . . um . . . I . . . uh . . . I write the specials on the specials board. And, I, uh, take the dead flowers out of the vase. Oh, and sometimes Arturo lets me put the little chocolate "blobbies" on the cookies.

THIRD WOMAN: Well, your mom didn't tell us about the "blobbies."[42]

I've done the same thing—exaggerated my position and hoped no one would treat me with that same blend of disappointment and condescension. Disappointment is often part of women's work lives. After the embarrassing encounter with her old friends, Rachel whines, "Everyone I know is either getting married, getting pregnant, or getting promoted, and I'm getting coffee. And it's not even for me!"[43]

For most, the path to achievement includes a lot of pit stops. Waiting tables can be liberating—the variable schedule, not feeling indebted to some corporation, no claustrophobia-inducing cubicle—but, at the same time, it can be demeaning and unrewarding. It is also the kind of job that helps make Rachel a more well-rounded person. Realizing that the workingclass has it harder than she had imagined, Rachel gains a newfound respect for those she once shunned.

RACHEL: So, like, you guys all have jobs?

MONICA: Welcome to the real world! It sucks. You're gonna love it![44]

When Rachel finally gets fed up with waiting tables, her friends convince her to "get the fear" and quit the job. According to Chandler, nothing forces you to look for a job more than not having money coming in. She does quit and finds a job in the fashion industry—not the dream job she was after, but certainly one that puts her on the right path. I too needed to "get the fear." If Monica worked in a cheesy '50s diner on her way to becoming a chef, and Rachel would take *any* job in fashion, I certainly could do the same. These women reminded me that life doesn't hand you anything. (Well, sometimes it hands you your grandmother's affordable New York City apartment, like Monica on *Friends,* but this is rare.) Sometimes, life even takes hard-earned things away.

> **RACHEL:** Look! Look! Look! My first paycheck! Look at the window. There's my name. Hi, me. God, isn't this exciting? I earned this. I wiped tables for it. I steamed milk for it, and it was totally . . . *(she looks at the check)* not worth it. Who's FICA, and why's he getting all my money?[45]

Rachel and Monica show us that, even though it is frightening—and possibly unrewarding—if we don't go after what we want, we may never get it.

One of the benefits of the sitcom format is that the longer a series is on the air, the more the writers are forced to expand the boundaries of their characters in the unending effort to find new story ideas each week. The advantage of this well-established sitcom practice is that domestic comedies blend into workplace comedies and vice versa. Roseanne's work outside the home was always a part of the show, sometimes causing her guilt about not being home with her kids and sometimes creating the anxiety and tensions that come with the workplace territory. These complications are the lifeblood of sitcoms.

> **JOB INTERVIEWER:** *(To Roseanne)* I like you already. You drove the wrong way down an alley that's forbidden to cars and you parked in the fire lane. The point is: You got here on time. You know how to get things done.[46]

Work outside the home doesn't always offer women TV characters a route to positive self-esteem. Clearly, Roseanne was forced to give up her dreams of becoming a writer for the reality of daily life.

> **DAN:** Thermostat's fixed. You just turn this little doodad here, the heat goes on in the basement, and it's ready for you to resume your writing career.
>
> **ROSEANNE:** Well, you know, I don't think I'm gonna have much time to pursue that career, now—what with the new job I got today.
>
> **DAN:** Did you get that waitress job?
>
> **ROSEANNE:** Yes, I did. Well, it was between me and the other woman they hired.
>
> **DAN:** Well, it beats sweeping up at that beauty parlor.
>
> **ROSEANNE:** Well, the way I look at it, I'm still workin' with hair, only now, it's in the food.[47]

Few would argue that Alice dreamt her whole life of becoming a waitress in a greasy-spoon or that Grace (of *Grace Under Fire*) planned on working on a manufacturing assembly line. Many women in '80s and '90s sitcoms worked out of necessity—Kate (of *Kate & Allie*) wasn't always happy with her job as a travel agent planning vacations for others, and Cybill joked about her dissatisfaction with many of her acting parts.

Often, many of the problems sitcom women face at work actually begin at home. When Roseanne gets a job sweeping floors at a hair salon, she is surprised to find that she enjoys the job, in part because of a supportive network of women. Her family, though, makes fun of her promotion to "shampoo girl." They frequently question her job choices.

BECKY: You got a job?

ROSEANNE: Yeah, I'm workin' in the restaurant over at Rodbell's Department Store.

BECKY: The one in the mall?

ROSEANNE: Yeah.

BECKY: Where I hang out with my friends?

ROSEANNE: Yeah.

BECKY: My mother is going to be there?

ROSEANNE: Yeah, it's a kick in the head, ain't it?

BECKY: You've ruined my life!

ROSEANNE: Well, you don't think I took the job for the money, do ya?[48]

Roseanne isn't the only character forced to defend her work. Caroline (of *Caroline in the City*) finds herself in the same position.

CAROLINE: *(Speaking on the phone)* The ad should read, "Colorist wanted to assist nationally syndicated cartoonist." No, it's not *Beetle Bailey*. Mine's about a woman. No, that's *Cathy*. Mine's *Caroline in the City*. It's a witty, kind of carefree— Oh, yeah? Well, then, we're even. I think your ads are stupid.[49]

The dual-career married couple on *Mad About You* battle, on occasion, over their respective careers. When Jamie is stressed about nabbing a new client, Paul offers little support.

JAMIE: *(Speaking on the phone)* I don't want to hear it, Rick. Just drag your disorganized butt out of bed and fax it to me right now! *(She hangs up the phone.)*

PAUL: Wow. Wow. I have never been more scared in my life.

JAMIE: What?

PAUL: You just spoke very harshly to your underling.

JAMIE: I happen to be under a lot of pressure.

PAUL: Hey, I know that.

JAMIE: No, you don't. If it doesn't involve you directly, you're not interested.

PAUL: I'm not interested? I mean, how can you say that?

JAMIE: Tell me the name of this account that I've been trying to nail for the last three months.

PAUL: What is this? A pop quiz?

JAMIE: Tell me.

PAUL: Must I constantly prove my love to you?

JAMIE: You have no idea what I do.

PAUL: I don't know you're in public relations?

JAMIE: Which means I do what?

PAUL: It means you relate . . . uh . . . publicly.

JAMIE: You're an embarrassment to husbands everywhere.[50]

Not only do many women on TV have to defend their choice of work, they also have to deal with the expectations of a society that still predominantly defines women not only as wives and mothers but also by their appearance. As she prepares for a job interview, Roseanne looks in the mirror and muses, "They're not gonna hire me. They're gonna hire some chicky with a tight skirt and a loose everything else."[51] Eventually, Roseanne comes to the conclusion that many women are forced to face: No matter what paths are open to them, "the weaker sex" is still faced with the limitations of a society run by men and the shortsightedness of those who believe in women's biological destiny.

In a particularly poignant episode titled "Confessions," Roseanne's mother, Beverly, a classic traditionalist, confesses what her expectations had been for Roseanne.

> **BEVERLY:** We were never worried about Roseanne. We knew what she was gonna be.
>
> **ROSEANNE:** Oh? What?
>
> **BEVERLY:** Safe and comfortable. And a good mommy, just like you are now.
>
> **ROSEANNE:** So, uh, what are you saying, Mother? You're saying that all I could be is some ordinary housewife?
>
> **BEVERLY:** Oh, Roseanne, you have a nice house, beautiful children, a husband. There's nothing wrong at all with being ordinary.[52]

Roseanne is stunned by the statement. Weeping, she tells Dan just how much she is hurt by the fact that her mother never thought she could be "a great astronaut or the president" instead of "some great organ donor." At dinner that night, the family attempts to cheer her up by pointing out everything she does as a wife and mother. Roseanne, on the other hand, doesn't see it the same way.

DAN: Not only is Roseanne a really good cook, but she keeps this house running like a well-oiled machine.

JACKIE: I don't know how she manages, well, with her job and all the other stuff she does.

ROSEANNE: Like what stuff?

JACKIE: Like . . . like . . . the, um . . . PTA. I don't know how they manage without her.

ROSEANNE: I quit that two years ago, Jackie.

DAN: Well, obviously your work there was finished, honey.

JACKIE: She sold over fifty tickets to the Elks' glaucoma dance.

ROSEANNE: Which means I must know how to dial a phone, huh? You know, D.J. has Scouts every Saturday, which also means I had to master the fine art of driving. Boy, I'm just a regular Renaissance woman, aren't I?[53]

In moments like these we see the complexities of women and their work. Roseanne isn't always pleasant and appropriate, but she fights against inequality and dissatisfaction, often with just her words (like a good little hell-raiser). She has enough humor, chutzpah, and drive to inspire all of us—including men—to question what society believes women should be.

Mike Wallace in a Dress

Unless your dream was to be exclusively a wife and mother, television didn't offer much inspiration before 1970. If you liked pearls, you had it made. My mother's generation was taught to behave like Donna Reed and Harriet Nelson, even as the women's rights movement was gaining steam. When *The Mary Tyler Moore Show* created a workplace sitcom with a female lead, big changes ensued in television programming.

Other sitcoms about working women followed. One of the most successful of that genre was *Murphy Brown* (which premiered on CBS in 1988), a workplace comedy set at a fictional network newsmagazine show and starring a character few of us are likely to forget. Murphy Brown, a broadcast journalist, was the toughest, most stubborn and powerful woman audiences had seen to date. As a national broadcaster, Murphy's character was watched by millions of people on the fictional newsmagazine *FYI*. As a feminist icon, Murphy Brown inspired millions of real life women. One of her attractions was that she was flawed, just like the rest of us.

The pilot episode features her return from rehab at the Betty Ford Clinic. Her problems with alcohol well-documented, Brown's career image and personal life have taken a big hit. The premise of the show is to follow Murphy's comeback.

Diane English, the creator of *Murphy Brown*, says that if she created the show today, she would write a different character, one less hard, one who possesses some of the softer 1990s feminine traits or what some scholars (and *New York Times* writers) would call "postfeminist" traits. However, working women who were out proving themselves in the 1980s had to be tough. Therefore, Murphy had to be able to play in a man's world by men's rules. She found her own way of doing so, as countless real women were doing at the time.

As a teenager, I found Murphy Brown to be an incredible phenomenon—the same way Mary Richards was for viewers in the '70s. Murphy, though also an independent "career woman," seems light-years away from Mary Richards. Murphy never stutters; she yells. She speaks her mind. She isn't intimidated by anyone, famous or infamous. Her work is exceptionally important to her, so much so that she compares not working to having her oxygen cut off. The actress who portrayed Murphy Brown, Candice Bergen, described the character as "Mike Wallace in a dress."[54] She is a marked contrast to the sedate, demure TV women of the '50s.

Clearly, no one ever said to Murphy Brown, "Good girls play nice," or "Women don't need careers, dear." By watching her, I gained the strength to stand up for myself and speak my mind. I wondered how she would respond to men who said things like, "Girls are just not good at math," or if told she should defer to men. Murphy would do almost anything to get what she wanted and helped show viewers what it took to "make it" in the workplace. It may have been a fictional workplace, but the lessons were real. When asked how she got a difficult interview, Murphy explained, "I just kept at him, always there, sticking like a wad of gum to his shoe. He just finally decided it was easier to give in."[55] Murphy fought her battles the same way a man would—Diane English made sure of that—and I tried to follow in her footsteps.

In a working world composed primarily of men, I followed Murphy's example and forced myself to speak up, give my opinion (even if it differed from others'), and, sometimes, be a "bitch." That was what was expected of Murphy.

> **ANCHOR JIM DIAL:** At ten o'clock, Murphy Brown is gonna get off that elevator, late as usual. She will insult at least three people, grab a cup of black coffee, and bum a cigarette. Then she will lock herself in her office until she comes up with the perfect piece for next week's show, as usual.[56]

After all, it was the same thing men did (though they weren't labeled with the "b-word"). Murphy Brown—and I—decided that we were not going to be judged for taking charge, or if we were, we would refuse to care.

Murphy Brown isn't always inspirational. In episode after episode, Murphy's personality gets her into trouble, from being excluded from presidential invites to having to fight tooth and nail to get interviews with people who fear meeting her face-to-face. Murphy Brown's flaws don't only make her more realistic, they also make her more sympathetic. Audiences want to see Murphy succeed precisely because she is flawed. She is as conflicted as those of us who watch her. She is sarcastic, sometimes childish, a viciously loyal friend, a single woman weary of dating, and, eventually, a single mother. She may have enjoyed a myriad of advantages, from a financially stable family to a college education to a strikingly beautiful face—television is still a visual medium, after all—but it doesn't mean her life is always easy.

> **MURPHY:** Do you have any idea what it's like to do what I do? To go for thirty-six hours without sleep because you were in an editing room trying to make an impossible deadline? To travel all the way to Abu Dhabi without knowing whether the emir is going to feel like talking that day? And then, half of America writes in to find out where Corky Sherwood buys her lipgloss.[57]

One reason *Murphy Brown* stands out in our memories is due to the media firestorm over election-year comments made by then–vice president Dan Quayle, criticizing Murphy's decision to become a single mother.

In a 1992 speech to the Commonwealth Club of California about the current state of the country, he famously claimed, "It doesn't help matters when prime-time TV has Murphy Brown—a character who supposedly epitomizes today's intelligent, highly paid professional woman—mocking the importance of fathers by bearing a child alone and calling it just another lifestyle choice."[58] It was not only Murphy Brown's choice to procreate that appeared irresponsible to people like Mr. Quayle, but that she was a high-profile working woman and as such was a likely role model, the type of person many women admired regardless of the fact that she was fictional. That the White House was commenting on the actions of a television character made clear how truly influential people felt Murphy Brown was, and there was the fear among some traditionalists that she would influence other women to make nontraditional "lifestyle" choices. It also underscored the fact that popular culture *matters*—real women may indeed look to their television counterparts as a source of inspiration.

> **CORKY:** Murphy, what's the secret to your success?
>
> **MURPHY:** It's not that complicated, really. Never be afraid to take a chance. When you see that brass ring, go for it, and never let anything get in your way.
>
> **CORKY:** What about voice lessons?[59]

Other women on television inspire us to go after jobs and careers in more subtle ways. Elyse Keaton, from *Family Ties,* is an architect and earns more money than her husband. Jamie Buchman of *Mad About You* is married to a semi-struggling documentary filmmaker. Jamie herself graduated from Yale, is a public relations professional, and, during the series, starts her own PR firm. Ellen owns her own bookstore. Caroline *(Caroline in the City)* writes a nationally syndicated comic strip. Cybill is an aging Hollywood actress, and no matter how much she hates the bitparts and cheesy dialogue she's forced to spew in B movie roles, she succeeds in achieving her dream of acting. She may not be on the A-list, but she is proud of being a working actress, continually reminding herself and everyone around her that "there are no small parts."

In the pilot of *Alice,* aspiring singer Alice is offered the opportunity to audition for an entertainment agent and she goes for it, explaining, "It's a chance, and I'm gonna take it."[60] Based on the film *Alice Doesn't Live Here Anymore* (for which Ellen Burstyn won an Academy Award in 1974), the series has a theme song, "There's a New Girl in Town," with a familiar ring to it. Mary Richards had been a new girl in town only a few years earlier. Throughout the nine-year run of the series, Alice struggles to avoid getting sidetracked, while waiting tables at Mel's Diner. In the series finale, she fully commits to her dream (now that she no longer has a teenage son to support) by moving to Nashville to be the lead singer in a band. She proves that it's never too late to go after something you want.

One of television's best examples of successful working women involves a group of Southern women who run their own interior design firm. The show, of course, is *Designing Women.* While Murphy Brown succeeds by butting heads with her male bosses, on this show, the women *are* the bosses. They aren't the only ones. In the spring of 1987, Kate and Allie started their own catering business. At last, women-owned businesses were no longer rare on television, paralleling the lives of actual women. (Today, women are the fastest-growing group of small business owners.)

Designing Women revels in depicting a successful women-owned business. Unlike most television shows in the '80s, it was overtly feminist, tackling real-life struggles, including the Clarence Thomas and Anita Hill hearings, sexual harassment, and job discrimination. Critics described it as a blend of social commentary and feminist humor, and they loved it. So did audiences, who went to bat for the show when CBS threatened to cancel it in the spring of 1987. The network was bombarded with letters and phone calls from women demanding they keep it on the air, proof of the power female viewers wielded in influencing television content. The show went on to run for seven seasons.

The *Designing Women* characters are uniquely individual, if somewhat stereotypical: the brain, the beauty queen, the mom, and the innocent. They are, each in her own way, explicit about the challenges women face in a world run predominantly by men. Their connection to each other is cemented by these shared complexities of women's lives. Julia Sugarbaker, the matriarch of Sugarbaker & Associates, is the most sharp-tongued character on the show. Appropriately, her strongest words are reserved for defending their women-run business. In an episode in which a photographer wants to photograph the women in centerfold-like poses for a feature on "The Women of Atlanta," Julia Sugarbaker lets loose the cannons:

> **JULIA:** If you are looking for a woman to suck
> pearls, then I suggest finding yourself an oyster.

Because I am not a woman who does that. As a matter of fact, I don't know any woman who does that, because it's stupid. And it doesn't have any more to do with decorating than having cleavage and looking sexy has to do with working in a bank. When you start snapping photos of serious, successful businessmen like Donald Trump and Lee Iacocca in unzipped jumpsuits, with wet lips, straddling chairs, then we'll talk.[61]

Julia Sugarbaker, an intelligent and eloquent speaker, also exudes the real credibility of owning her own successful business. She and her cohorts were an important addition to the arsenal of strong women I was modeling myself after. I wanted the optimistic independence of Mary Richards, the unwavering determination of Murphy Brown, and the verbal mastery of Julia Sugarbaker. *Designing Women* further expanded TV's possibilities for women, increasing the range of opportunities opening to a generation of girls, myself included. *Designing Women* was a part of a culture in which women could indeed be business owners.

Mary and Beyond . . .

My mother and grandmother, like their mothers before them, were wives and mothers first and foremost. I saw Mary Richards and other small-screen heroines choose a different path, and it helped me do the same. It may sound ridiculous to admit to making life decisions based on a TV characters, but it seemed less arbitrary than basing those choices on the experience of one set of parents, one set of friends, or that of living in one town. Mary Richards's life was larger than that, and I wanted mine to be as well.

By the time the 1990s rolled around, it was a given that television moms could also work. In the pilot episode of *Home Improvement* (a bastion of the male-centered sitcom), Jill Taylor has a discussion with her husband about her desire to work.

> **TIM:** What I mean is, you don't have to work.
>
> **JILL:** You don't really want me to work, do you?
>
> **TIM:** No, no, no, no. I make enough money for both of us—
>
> **JILL:** No, this is not about money. This is . . . this is about me having a life outside this house. My . . . my autonomy.
>
> **TIM:** Your autonomy?
>
> **JILL:** Yeah.
>
> **TIM:** How d'you spell that?[62]

In her book *Inventing Herself,* Elaine Showalter writes, "After the first London production of Ibsen's *Doll's House* in 1889, women lingered 'breathless with excitement . . . this was either the end of the world or the beginning of a new world for women.'[63] Where are our Saint Theresas and Noras of the 2000s, the women who leave us breathless with excitement?

Where are the women who embody womanhood's radiant, sovereign self?"[64] On television, of course. Whether married or single, with children or without, women on television want their autonomy. And *they* know how to spell it.

The prime-time sitcoms of the 1970s, 1980s, and 1990s showcased the lives of working women, from housekeepers to business owners, from waitresses to executives. These representations inspired generations of women, who increasingly found the working world more receptive to them than to women of previous generations. The sitcoms' relevance isn't simply that the women of prime time prove you can be a journalist, or an interior designer, or make your way in "the big city." They exist as substantive evidence that being a working woman is no longer an anomaly. Currently, women's participation in the labor force is almost indistinguishable from that of men. Even in top positions, women have made enormous gains; 46 percent of managerial jobs are now held by women.[65] I would like to think our working heroines on TV have had at least a little something to do with that. Women have moved closer than they've ever been to equality in a working world that Mary Richards helped open.

Chapter 7

Saying the Word
Pregnancy in Public

At one time, women on television weren't referred to as "pregnant" but as "expecting." In January 1953, Lucy Ricardo gave birth to a son on *I Love Lucy*, although how she got pregnant when she and Ricky slept in twin beds still eludes me. Little Ricky's birth was a cultural phenomenon (more than forty-four million people watched the show, which at that time represented 72 percent of the American audience). It was a phenomenon, though, that had no name.[1]

Television viewers were certainly excited about the birth of little Ricky, but if you were looking for insights into pregnancy and birth, you could forget it. Pregnancy was, and continues to be, a difficult issue for television to explore; on the one hand, it is a highly personal matter, and on the other, it is laden with traditional ideas about women's roles and priorities. In the fifties, those ideas meant ignoring the whole topic.

In the 1970s, women in the real world were delaying pregnancy to focus on their careers or education. (In the early part of that decade, women composed 46 percent of four-year college students; by 1980, they outnumbered male students.) As they had with other trends, family sitcoms slowly started to represent pregnancy as an option, chosen by women, not prescribed for them. In the late '80s, Roseanne reflects on her decision to become a mother and admits to being saddened by the fact that motherhood was the only thing that had been expected of her.[2]

Over time, television has dealt more openly with pregnancy and birth. No longer does a happy TV couple miraculously show up at home with a swaddled baby in hand. Today, TV portrays the difficulties of pregnancy with more honesty. Pregnancy and motherhood don't come easy to Jamie Buchman or Rachel Green. Women like Roz on *Frasier*, Maryann on *Cybill,* Lisa on *NewsRadio,* Elaine on *Seinfeld,* and Grace on *Will & Grace* are honest about their aversions to pregnancy and motherhood. By addressing the confusion and fear of pregnancy, TV has moved beyond omission into the murky questions that surround motherhood, questions that many women face.

Labor Pains

The new openness about pregnancy on TV has helped prepare me for an event I may one day go through. Watching women like Roseanne, Jamie Buchman, Murphy Brown, and others go through labor on television helped to demystify the process; the audience got to watch a vulnerable, angry, painful, meaningful, and often funny moment in a woman's life. I have seen so many sitcom episodes in which women go into labor and give birth that I now know that during this painful, emotional experience, it is acceptable, even encouraged, to scream, cry, curse, get angry and irrational, and, at moments, even give up. I know that television is a poor substitute for reality, but I also know that it has allowed me to glimpse everything from the excitement and love to the pain and fear of the childbearing experience.

We have all seen sitcom scenes in which a pregnant character goes into labor, screaming, cursing, admonishing the man who "did this to me," rudely yelling at nurses, doctors, and hospital staff, and generally acting any way she pleases because, let's face it, squeezing out an offspring has to be unbelievably painful.

On sitcoms such as *Roseanne, Friends, The Nanny, Mad About You,* and *Sex and the City,* I have heard a variety of opinions about pregnancy and seen a variety of childbirth scenes. Probably the most famous of these is the birth scene on *Murphy Brown.* Though Murphy's pregnancy was a controversial development in the series (see chapter 6), the birth episode was ultimately decidedly apolitical. As Murphy goes through the usual pains and anger alongside her work "family," we see a typical sitcom birth. After she has the baby, though, we see an entirely new side to Ms. Brown. After the tiny baby boy is brought into her room, she sits alone with him and begins to tear up. She introduces herself to her new son by quietly singing Aretha Franklin's "(You Make Me Feel Like) A Natural Woman" to him.

It is a moment that could melt even the hardest of hearts. It isn't simply that a woman like Murphy Brown, who certainly didn't seem like mother material, would decide to have a baby. It is the way in which the birth forces her to really let go and feel the intense emotion that accompanies giving birth. Seeing Murphy Brown vulnerable and emotional says a lot about the universality of women's experience and the utter humanity of even the most obstinate women. Her instant connection with her son, despite her ignorance regarding the needs of an infant, made me, a woman who is unsure about whether I want children, see that all types of women can be mothers, even those who have no idea what they are doing.

Candice Bergen admitted that she could barely hold in her real tears during this episode, because it was to be the last for Diane English, creator of the show. The actress described the overwhelming emotion felt on the set—partly because of the poignancy of the episode, and partly because of English's departure. Her tears seem real, as they probably were, and an appropriate response to an episode intended to be tender and emotional.

Mad About You also features an inspiring birth episode, when Jamie gives birth to a daughter. In the episode, Jamie's husband, Paul, goes through a series of antics to reach his about-to-give-birth wife. The most notable of these involves him being led by a slightly injured Bruce Willis (playing himself) through a secret maze in the hospital. Since the Buchmans are still undecided about the baby's name, Paul thinks Bruce Willis may be able to help. Not surprisingly, the names of the Willis children—Rumer, Scout, and Tallulah—do not impress Paul. Sans a baby name, Paul finally reaches Jamie's bedside, just when she needs him most.

Sitcom episodes in which a new life is brought into the world are always full of humor, but they also give writers and actors the chance to blend real feeling with the required jokes. When Jamie Buchman has been in labor for several hours and becomes increasingly tired and unmotivated, it is Paul who gives her the strength to go on. It is a rare television moment when both the man and the woman are truly "in it" together.

> **JAMIE:** I love you. *(Paul attempts to mime a response.)* What are you doing? What's the matter with you? Why aren't you saying anything?
>
> **PAUL:** Now? Now it's okay to talk?
>
> **JAMIE:** Yes! Oh, no, it's just during the contraction that I can't stand the sound of your voice.[3]

Paul will clearly do anything Jamie needs, even providing complete silence or allowing her to break his hand with her pain.

> **DOCTOR:** Okay, Jamie, now one more push. Ready?
>
> **JAMIE:** I can't. No, I really can't. I just can't.

PAUL: Yeah, you can, sweetie, yeah you can. You can do anything.

JAMIE: I can?

PAUL: Yes.

Although their words are few, the actors state them so forcefully that you can see how a real partnership between a husband and wife—a pretty equal one as far as sitcoms go—can help save a situation in which many women feel alone.

Debra Barone of *Everybody Loves Raymond* makes constant fun of the fact that her husband was too busy to support her during the birth of her twins. He was too busy buying a hoagie as he passed the time before the birth. Sitcom story lines abound about how pregnancy and childbirth are a woman's realm, while the men are clueless, anxious, sometimes useless accompaniments to the birthing process. Though men's absence from or uselessness in the birthing room is a common joke, when TV women give birth, I have always found the support from their lovers, husbands, friends, and family both inspiring and comforting.

In some shows, a woman's best friend or sister offers comfort and support during the pain and the pushing. Roseanne stays in the delivery room as her sister Jackie gives birth, just as Ross from *Friends* is present for the birth of both his children.

When Rachel Green gives birth to her baby during the second-to-last season of *Friends*, all her friends are there to support her; but as her labor progresses at a snail's pace, she is quite unhappy.

> **RACHEL:** Dr. Long, I've been at this for seventeen hours! Three women have come and gone with their babies; you gotta give me some good news! How many centimeters am I dilated? Eight? Nine?
>
> **DR. LONG:** Three.
>
> **ROSS:** Just three?! Dilated three!
>
> **DR. LONG:** We are moving along, just slowly. *(Rachel lies back on the bed, sighing.)* Don't worry, you're doing great. I'll be back soon. *(Dr. Long exits.)*
>
> **RACHEL:** Hey, y'know what? I'm not waiting! I'm gonna push this baby out! I'm doing it! I mean, it's what? Three centimeters? That's gotta be like this! *(She holds her hands a couple of inches apart.)*
>
> **ROSS:** Actually it's more like this *(pushing her hands to less than an inch apart)*.
>
> **RACHEL:** Oh, stupid metric system!

As four women in labor come in and out of Rachel's semi-private hospital room, she gets increasingly angry and yells at a nurse.

> **RACHEL:** Okay! Okay, wait! You listen to me! You listen to me! Since I have been waiting, four women, that's four, one higher than the number of centimeters that I am dilated, have come and gone with their babies! I'm next! It's my turn! It's only

fair! And if you bring in one more woman and she has her baby before me I'm going to sue *you!* Not this hospital, I'm going to sue you! And my husband . . . *(pointing at Ross)* he's a lawyer!

MONICA: I can't believe this is taking so long. How are you doing?

RACHEL: Oh, not bad. Do you know that feeling when you're trying to blow a Saint Bernard out your ass? *(A woman and her child are wheeled past.)* Oh, that's five, Ross. Five women have had five babies! And I have had no babies! Why doesn't she want to come out?

ROSS: Y'know what I think it is? I think you've made such a nice home for her over the last nine months that she just doesn't want to leave.

RACHEL: Oh. Look at you, making up crap for me. Oh, God! *(Another contraction starts as Dr. Long enters.)*

DR. LONG: Twenty-one hours. You're a hero.

RACHEL: Doctor, you gotta do something! I think you gotta give me drugs or you gotta light a fire up in there and just smoke it out.

DR. LONG: Actually, I think you're ready to go to the delivery room.

RACHEL: What?

DR. LONG: Ten centimeters—you're about to become a mom.

RACHEL: My God. Okay. *(Another woman enters.)* Ha, ha, ha! Beat ya, sucker![4]

It isn't just during the actual childbirth that women need support. In *Mad About You,* there is a short time during her pregnancy when Jamie's gynecologist puts her on bed rest and orders Paul to serve Jamie's every need because she cannot leave her bed. He runs around trying to make her comfortable in every way—cooking potato pancakes, keeping her away from stress, and making sure she knows that he is there solely to serve her.

TV births have shown viewers that pregnancy and childbirth is a great time to ask for and utilize the help of friends and family, whether from a husband or any other loved one: as Lamaze coaches, as birthing partners, and for all the other support a woman needs.

On *Friends,* Rachel, who at first decided to be a single mother and do it all on her own, realizes she needs some help. During her first sonogram, she becomes upset because she is unable to see her fetus on the monitor. It is Ross, her ex and the father of the baby, who helps her locate the black-and-white blob on the screen which represents their growing fetus. Simply being unable to "read" a grainy sonogram makes Rachel feel as though she is already an unfit mother. "I can't even see my own child," she cries.[5] In the end, the help of her friends, and Ross in particular, gets her through the most frightening and uncomfortable experience of her life. Women can become mothers on their own; but as with so many major life changes, TV has shown us that relying on friends and family can make everything just a little easier.

Home from the Hospital. Now What?

Television shows have depicted new mothers experiencing a wonderful mix of fear, excitement, and complete fumbling idiocy. Every tentative step we see shows us the universal trials and joys of being the parent of a newborn. When Murphy Brown brings her son home from the hospital, she is amazed at the changes in her body: "My body is making milk! This is like discovering one day that you can get bacon out of your elbow."[6] Roseanne points out to her daughter that pregnancy and birth give your body a host of unwanted physical ailments, like hemorrhoids, mood swings, and the inability to hold your bladder while coughing or laughing. (Who knew that pregnancy occasionally entailed incontinence? My mom conveniently left that out.)

When Paul and Jamie bring their daughter, Mabel, home from the hospital, they cannot get her to stop crying. They've heard about the trick of soothing a crying baby by keeping it in motion for at least ten minutes. So, they run around New York looking for ways to keep the baby moving. A taxi doesn't work because they end up in a high-speed police chase. The streets of New York don't allow for an easy walk with the stroller. The elevator in their building stops too frequently. The Buchmans finally end up at their gym at three o'clock in the morning with their baby in her stroller on a speeding treadmill. Hey, whatever works! Because every baby is different, new parents have to do whatever they can to keep their baby happy and themselves sane.

After Rachel from *Friends* brings home her baby, Emma, she too has no idea how to stop her from crying. Eventually, Rachel finds that singing the rap song "Baby Got Back" is the only thing that quiets her. Embarrassed to admit to Ross that this is the only song that works, she explains, "What can I do? She loves the ass."[7] Rachel's inability to deal with "baby stuff" is comforting for those of us who aren't sure whether we were born with that "mommy" gene. Watching TV women struggle with their newborns reminds us that bringing home a baby from the hospital is exciting, but also scary and unpredictable. Though rapping to a newborn may not work for everybody, it serves to remind us that there is no one way to be a mother—no matter what June Cleaver did. Our funny sitcom moms prove that no mother is perfect, on TV or in real life.

The "Scourge" of Single Motherhood

Single motherhood has been a television staple since *Julia* (starring Diahann Carroll). After her husband is killed in the Vietnam War, Julia works as a nurse while raising her son, Corey. The majority of single mothers on television (Ann Romano, Alice, Kate, Allie, Florida Evans) do not choose to be single mothers, but have to raise their children alone because of death or divorce. The obstacles of raising children outside a marriage never prevent them from trying to be the best single mothers they can be.

While divorce or death created sitcoms' single mothers

in the '70s, single mothers since the '80s have increasingly chosen their path. They've reflected the changing landscape of the American home, one where marital status doesn't necessarily dictate childbearing and child rearing. As women have gained financial independence, they no longer need the support of a man or husband. In a world where a woman can do just about anything a man can do, why can't she be the head of her own household and the sole parent to her children?

Whether by accident, through family planning, or via artificial insemination, sitcom women are creating families on their own. Well, they aren't always on their own; many single TV women have their "makeshift" families composed of friends, coworkers, and extended family. Not all TV women who contemplate single motherhood go through with it, but the questions and issues that arise surrounding the responsibilities and difficulties of being a single mom are ones that real women deal with.

When Murphy Brown discovers she's pregnant, she decides that she has reached a point in her life when being a mother is a viable option. She is financially successful and reasonably settled; fate has given her an option she may not have chosen, but one she decides to be happy about. Watching Murphy decide to be a single mother was somewhat shocking to me because it seemed so out of character for the selfish, stubborn journalist. No matter how unmaternal she seems, Murphy is the kind of woman who commits unflinchingly to something she wants, and if a baby is what she wants, she will use all that ambitious energy to be the best mother she can be. But that was not to be the end of the issue.

When Dan Quayle attacked sitcom character Murphy Brown for her role in destroying the nuclear family, a common theme in Republican rhetoric, he made the mistake of criticizing a TV icon revered by millions of women. The irony is that Mr. Quayle only made reference to Murphy Brown in one sentence, but it created a media firestorm. His speech, broadcast on more than two hundred radio stations, discussed the lack of "values" in America, using a TV character as an illustration of the decline in American morals.

Few, including Quayle and the Bush camp, were prepared for what followed. The reaction was immediate.

> *Quayle's aides spent much of the next day trying to convince the White House that the speech was not a serious blunder. Bush initially refused to take questions on the matter. White House press secretary Marlin Fitzwater laughed it off by offering to marry Murphy Brown, until reminded that she was just a TV character and that Candice Bergen was already married.*[8]

As Susan Douglas and Meredith Michaels explain in their book, *The Mommy Myth: The Idealization of Motherhood and How It Has Undermined All Women,* "Few events in the early 1990s captured the importance and stupidity of the debates revolving around working mothers, and the rise of single mothers, than Dan Quayle's instantly infamous attack on the TV sitcom character played by Candace [sic] Bergen, Murphy

Brown."[7] Douglas and Michaels point out that many Americans already considered Quayle "dumber than a gerbil," but in the wake of discussions of welfare reform, the speech was actually "an attack on poor, inner-city (read *black*), unmarried mothers who were responsible for the 'lawless anarchy' and 'lack of structure in our inner cities.'"[10] Of course, the Republican answer to this "scourge" was marriage, as opposed to, say, subsidized abortion for women who could not afford it.

In response to the speech, *Murphy Brown* creator Diane English chose to focus her attention on that point: "If the vice president thinks it's disgraceful for an unmarried woman to bear a child without a father, then he'd better make sure abortion remains safe and legal."[11]

The response to his attack on Murphy Brown only served to embarrass the vice president even more than he already had been. He also was forced to eat crow when, as a public relations stunt, he watched the 1992 season premiere of *Murphy Brown* with a group of single mothers.[12] The show addressed the issue head-on, as though Murphy were a real person as opposed to a TV character. She chided the vice president for his comments and expressed pride in her decision to become a single mother.

As Diane English and Douglas and Michaels point out, the whole "brouhaha" over the issue missed the point: The crux of the issue was about government and social services abandoning women, particularly poor women, who faced single motherhood. As a viewer, I saw another issue that was being obscured. Why did Murphy Brown need to have a baby at all? Many feminists were surprised at Murphy's decision to become a mother, the implication being that a successful woman wasn't truly fulfilled unless she was a mother. Of course, we are dealing with the world of television, and to keep audiences interested season after season, writers occasionally make decisions that seem to go against the ethos of the show. As much as Murphy Brown served as an emblem of feminism, she was also a TV character, controlled, in the end, by the forces of CBS and advertising dollars. I cut the character and the show some slack because even our feminist icons aren't perfect and, in the end, Murphy's pregnancy brought to light the important issue of single motherhood in America. Murphy redeemed herself by doing what she always did—making sure she had the last word. The same year Dan Quayle criticized Murphy Brown, Candice Bergen won the Emmy for her portrayal of the character. In her acceptance speech, Ms. Bergen kindly thanked the vice president for helping her win it.

The Birth of Insemination

Choosing to become a mother without a man is a recent phenomenon, but surprisingly one that television has addressed more than once. Television has given us a variety of single mothers, who more often than not did not choose the situation but learned to thrive within it. With the recent advent of "sperm banks," women—straight, gay, old, and young—have even more ability to control almost every aspect of the process of becoming a mother. Control may be one of the most attractive factors of the artificial insemination route: Women get to decide what kind of man, or sperm, they want, usually after examining a series of men's confidential profiles.

In a particularly funny episode of *Friends,* titled "The One with the Jam," out-of-work chef Monica Geller has just broken up with a man twice her age. The man, Richard (played by the dapper Tom Selleck), did not want to have any more children, and Monica refused to envision her future without them. After her breakup and losing her job, she realizes she needs something to focus on while she is unemployed. At first, she decides to start a business selling homemade jam, then realizes she can't make a profit with the amount of work the "jam plan" entails.

> **RACHEL:** Well, what happened to your jam plan?
>
> **MONICA:** I figured out I need to charge seventeen bucks a jar just to break even. So, I've got a new plan now. Babies.
>
> **CHANDLER:** Well, you're gonna need much bigger jars.
>
> **ROSS:** What are you talking about?
>
> **MONICA:** I'm talking about me having a baby.
>
> **ROSS:** What?
>
> **RACHEL:** Are you serious?

MONICA: Yeah. The great thing about the jam plan was I was taking control of my life. So I asked myself, What is the most important thing to me in the world? And that's when I came up with the baby plan.

ROSS: Well, aren't you forgetting something? What . . . what . . . what is that guy's name? Dad!

MONICA: It took me twenty-eight years to find one man that I wanted to spend my life with. If I have to wait another twenty-eight years, then I'll be fifty-six before I can have a baby, and that's just stupid.

CHANDLER: That. That's what's stupid?

MONICA: I don't need an actual man, just a couple of his best swimmers. And there are places you can go to get that stuff.[13]

Clearly, Monica's brother Ross is not happy about her "baby plan," as he threatens to tattle to their parents. Monica Geller is no Murphy Brown: She's unemployed, depressed, jealous of her brother's connection with his son, Ben, and indulging in just about any irrational plan in an attempt to stabilize her life. She goes straight from making jam to motherhood. Clearly, her excitement over picking a sperm donor overshadows some of the more permanent, life-changing, realities of single motherhood.

MONICA: Okay, sperm donor number 03815, come on down! Okay, he's six feet two, 170 pounds, and he describes himself as a male Geena Davis.

CHANDLER: You mean there's more than one of us?

ROSS: Look, you can't do this, Mon. All right—if you do this, I'm, I'm gonna, I'm, I'm gonna . . .

MONICA: You're gonna what?

ROSS: I'm gonna tell Mom.

RACHEL: Honey, I'm sorry, but he's right. I love you, but you're crazy.

ROSS: Crazy.

MONICA: What? Why? Why is this crazy? So, this isn't the ideal way to something—

ROSS: *(Interrupting her)* Oh, it's not the ideal way—

MONICA: Lips moving, still talking! I mean, it may not be ideal, but I'm so ready. No, I, I, I see the way Ben looks at you. It makes me ache, you know?[14]

I'm sure many women relate to the desire to be a mother and have a child. As educated, mature individuals, we also need to research, investigate, and examine all the positives and negatives the decision entails. The decision to have a baby is very emotional and personal, and it is laden with everything from our primal urges to our desire to love. Thus, when you can plan a pregnancy, rationality would tell you that it is imperative to weigh all the options and think deeply about every aspect of bringing a new life into the world. This would seem to be the upside of insemination: There are no real surprises and a woman can plan her conception and pregnancy for her specific needs. The downside, however, is that a woman goes it alone. It is not a path most women take. There are women, like Monica, who use insemination as a substitute for the kind of family they really want, but don't think they will have. Having a baby as a substitute for anything is probably not the best decision, and, by the end of the episode, Monica realizes she does indeed want something different. As she discusses the issue with her friend Joey, Monica sees there are other alternatives, and she needn't be in a hurry to be a mother.

JOEY: Where you going?

MONICA: To the bank.

JOEY: Sperm or regular?

MONICA: Sperm.

JOEY: So you're really doing this, huh?

MONICA: Oh yeah—picked a guy, 37135.

JOEY: Sounds nice.

MONICA: 'Fraid so. Brown hair, green eyes . . .

JOEY: No kiddin'. Hmm.

MONICA: What?

JOEY: No, I . . . I figured you would've picked a blond guy.

MONICA: Really? Why?

JOEY: I don't know, I just always pictured you ending up with one of those tall, smart, blond guys, name like . . . Hoyt.

MONICA: Hoyt?

JOEY: It's a name, yeah. I saw you, you know, in this great house with a big pool.

MONICA: Really. Is he a swimmer?

JOEY: He's got the body for it.

MONICA: I like that. *(Joey starts laughing.)* What?

JOEY: You guys have one of those signs that says: "We don't swim in your toilet, so don't pee in our pool," you know.

MONICA: We do not have one of those signs.

JOEY: Sure you do—it was a gift from me. Oh! And you have these three great kids.

MONICA: Two girls and a boy?

JOEY: Yeah!

MONICA: And, and, and they wear those little water wings, you know. And they're, they're running around on the deck. Then Hoyt wraps this big towel around all three of them.

JOEY: Sure! *(Monica gets visibly depressed.)* But hey, you know, this way sounds good too.

MONICA: Yeah.

As Monica imagines the life she really wants, she realizes that insemination probably wouldn't fulfill her in the same way her imaginary husband, Hoyt, and their three children would.

Deciding to be a single mother, whether pregnant by choice or not, is no simple task. Murphy Brown thinks long and hard about what to do. She has never harbored happy married suburban fantasies. Monica, who does harbor them, fears she's running out of time. In the end, Monica's baby plan goes the way of the jam plan, and we have to wait to see if Monica will ever get what she wants.

Infertility: The New Anxiety

A diagnosis of infertility can be devastating to both men and women. According the Centers for Disease Control, there are two million infertile couples in America, yet more than nine million women have used fertility services at one point or another. It seems that the new American panic is not about what to do with all the babies who are already born—childcare, welfare, pre- and postnatal services—but about how to have more babies.

Infertility garners enormous media attention. However, the issue has had less exposure on sitcoms. Charlotte's trials with infertility on the sixth season of *Sex and the City* were a notable exception. The most conservative and traditional of our four fair women, Charlotte is married to her second husband and they are having trouble conceiving a child. The prospect of not being able to have a child is devastating for her; she has always wanted a baby.

In the episode titled "The Domino Effect," Charlotte decides to go to a fertility clinic. As she is sitting in the waiting room, she listens to a group of women talking about what they've "heard" works for infertility, from Chinese herbs to acupuncture to special teas. The camera focuses on Charlotte's face, and you see her increasing anxiety and confusion over a situation that feels utterly out of control. The truth, though, is no matter how many herbs or teas women invest in, there are a variety of options for women and couples who struggle to have children. Eventually, Charlotte and her husband are happy to have King Charles spaniel puppies. Who knows what will happen to Charlotte and her husband in the future.

In another beloved sitcom, *Friends* the ninth season brings married couple Chandler and Monica, some devastating news. After they are both tested to determine why they have been having trouble conceiving, the doctor calls with the results.

> **CHANDLER:** Hello? Oh, hi, Doctor Connelly. *(Pause)* No, she's not here, but, you know, I can tell her. Should I be sitting down for this? *(His smile fades as he listens.)* Oh. *(Pause)* Well, so what does that mean? *(Pause)* Okay. Okay, thank you. Thanks. *(He hangs up the phone.)*
>
> *(Monica enters the apartment.)*
>
> **MONICA:** Hey, sweetie.
>
> **CHANDLER:** Doctor Connelly just called.

MONICA: *(Speaking very quickly and wringing her hands)* With good news? Of course it's not good news, you just said *(speaking in a deadpan voice)*, "Doctor Connelly just called." If it was good news you would have said *(speaking excitedly)*, "Doctor Connelly just called!" But so what is it? Is there a problem? Is there a problem with me or with you?

CHANDLER: Actually it's both of us.

MONICA: What?

CHANDLER: Apparently my sperm have low motility and you have an inhospitable environment.

MONICA: Oh . . . what does that mean?

CHANDLER: It means that my guys won't get off their Barcaloungers and you have a uterus that is prepared to kill the ones that do. It means—

MONICA: Chandler?

CHANDLER: It means that we can keep trying, but there's a good chance this may never happen for us.

MONICA: *(Weeping)* Oh, my God!

CHANDLER: I'm sorry.

MONICA: I'm sorry too.

CHANDLER: *(Hugging Monica)* Well, we're gonna . . . we're gonna figure this out.

MONICA: I know.[15]

In the final season of *Friends*, Monica and Chandler adopt twins from a young woman who chooses to give her babies up for adoption. The series concludes with all of the *Friends* characters getting what they want, even though it was not how they originally planned it. Rachel never thought she would get pregnant, and has a baby; Monica, who wanted a baby her whole life never expecting she would have trouble getting pregnant, adopts. The beauty of television is that it wraps up all our "friends'" stories into neat, happy endings. Although real life may not always follow this twenty-two-minute formula, our sitcom families show us that, when it comes to having a baby, things don't always work out the way we think they will. Life is about adjustment, and we can all learn to be happy with our blessings, whatever they are.

Chapter 8

Women Over Fifty or Overweight Need Not Apply

Body Image and Aging on Television

> **DOROTHY:** Oh c'mon, Blanche, age is just a state of mind.
> **BLANCHE:** Tell that to my thighs.
> **—*The Golden Girls***

No subject can get women's blood boiling more than the representation—or lack thereof—of women on TV who are older than teenagers and heavier than supermodels. I grew up surrounded by women who wanted to *look* like Mary Richards, Murphy Brown, or the trendy *Friends* women (or the ultimate style symbols of *Sex and the City*) more than they wanted to *be* like these characters. That is why I rejoice in representations of women like those on *The Golden Girls* (all well over fifty), Maude (over fifty and not a classic beauty), Roseanne (feisty and overweight), Khadijah (played by Queen Latifah) on *Living*

Single, Carol Burnett, Esther Rolle on *Good Times,* Thea, Margaret Cho on *All-American Girl* (Asian and famously deemed "too fat" by network executives), Kathy Najimy on *Veronica's Closet,* Kirstie Alley in HBO's *Fat Actress,* and Ellen (a woman few would describe as exceptionally "feminine"). Seeing these (too few) women on TV may make us feel better about the fact that we don't wear a size 2 or stay twenty-five years old forever.

When *Sex and the City* appeared on the pop culture radar screen, the four women protagonists were all New York City glamour and gloss—but their addiction to fashion trends and high-end shoes was specific to them. When I watched the show, I longed for more varied representations of women TV characters. Why couldn't Charlotte or Samantha be black or Hispanic or weigh 150 pounds? Who were these white, skinny women who wore five-hundred-dollar Jimmy Choos? I understand that television—and film, for that matter—is a visual medium, and we like to look at pretty people, especially pretty women. I always do my best, however, to try to find one or two women on TV who look "normal," like our real moms, friends, and neighbors, assuming we don't live in a town full of supermodels (which is clearly where the women of *Desperate Housewives* live). Some women on TV *are* there because they are more funny than they are pretty (Bea Arthur, Roseanne, Ellen Degeneres) or more funny than they are thin (Queen Latifah, Kirstie Alley)—and for these few representations, I guess I can live with *Sex and the City's* well-coiffed fashionistas, as long as we all keep the pressure to look like them in check. We should always remind ourselves that every women we see on TV—and in magazines, music videos, and just about everywhere else in the entertainment world—has been made up, coiffed, and dressed by a team of professionals. With that much attention to our appearance, maybe we would all look like the women on *Desperate Housewives*.

The Power of Youth

In her 1991 bestseller, *The Beauty Myth: How Images of Beauty Are Used Against Women*, Naomi Wolf opens her examination of how images of beauty "strictly, heavily, and cruelly" weigh upon American women with a quote from Virginia Woolf: "It is far more difficult to murder a phantom than a reality."[1] Although I garner inspiration, strength, and laughter from the women on TV, I know they are creations. I know they are governed by a business—television in particular and visual entertainment in general—obsessed with youth, beauty, and getting large audiences. I also know that some absolutely amazing women have broken through the barrier and thrived alongside their gorgeous TV counterparts.

Being a feminist in our society isn't easy, and, unless we enjoy being depressed all the time, we have to search out representations on TV and elsewhere that make us feel normal and not like Cousin Itt. I don't think we should ever stop fighting how TV oppresses us with visions of youth and beauty, and we should also celebrate the woman who succeeds onscreen regardless of her dress size or sexual attractiveness to men.

Television has a long history of representing women as beautiful, pristine objects of youth and sexual desire. This is particularly true for TV wives and mothers. Before Mary Tyler Moore played working girl Mary Richards, she was the lovely Laura Petrie on *The Dick Van Dyke Show*. She was incredibly young and beautiful, and was often remembered for her spectacular legs—partly because she *(gasp)* wore pants in 1961 and partly because she began her career as a dancer and had the figure to prove it. This was typical for early television. Characters who were sidekicks and neighbors were allowed to look like "real" people, but leading women had to be gorgeous. Even Lily Munster was a babe. *I Dream of Jeannie, Bewitched, Gidget,* and *That Girl* all featured women who were young and extremely attractive. It wasn't until Edith Bunker on *All in the Family* in 1971 that we saw what a real working-class wife and mother looked like. Creator Norman Lear didn't stop there. Bea Arthur's character Maude was also introduced to America on the irreverent hit show, as was Louise Jefferson. These actresses and comediennes were cast because they were funny, versatile, and talented. Jean Stapleton's portrayal of Edith Bunker, America's favorite "dingbat," won her three Emmys and eight nominations. Not bad for the first character to go through menopause on prime-time television. Far from a feminist representation of the '70s woman, Edith was a character to whom older women going through "the change" could relate, especially when faced with a husband who had no understanding of the issue.

ARCHIE: If you're gonna have your change of life, have it right now! You have exactly thirty seconds.[2]

Edith Bunker wasn't exactly a role model for the wives and mothers of America, but at least she looked more like our real mothers than did Laura Petrie or America's favorite witch/wife/mom, Samantha Stephens (Elizabeth Montgomery) on *Bewitched*. By the time *Roseanne* aired, menopause and growing older were simply acknowledged parts of life. In fact, when her daughter Darlene misbehaves, Roseanne yells, "You're grounded until menopause!" Smart-mouth Darlene responds, "Yours or mine?" and Roseanne ends the joke by answering, "Your father's."[3]

As I got older, I realized that most of the women I'd seen on television my entire life were rarely over thirty and almost never over fifty. Part of the believability of *The Mary Tyler Moore Show* was that Mary Richards was in her thirties, as were the other women on the show. Had Mary been a perky twenty-one-year-old fresh out of college, would her rejection of marriage and entrance into the working world seem as revolutionary? Probably not; we would simply assume that after her twenties, America's "working girl" would give up her press pass for marriage vows and diaper pails. It was the fact that Mary was "getting older" that made her experiences all the more realistic to the people who watched her. And watch her they did: The show drew a weekly audience of forty-three million, a full fifth of the American population.[4]

These days, it hardly seems revolutionary for a woman of thirty to have her own sitcom; but in 1970, it created a buzz. One of the issues that had to be addressed was how to best present a woman of Mary's age. To launch a series featuring a woman "in her thirties" was a big deal. The producers wanted the character to "have a past."[5] Women in their twenties haven't had time to have much of a past. The "past" that writers had in mind also involved a much-debated issue. Originally, the character was supposed to be a divorcée, but CBS claimed that Americans didn't like divorced people (or New Yorkers or Jews, for that matter). They also didn't want to make Mary a widow like Julia.[6] The network prevailed, and Mary Richards was born, single and in her thirties. As sitcom historian Rick Mitz describes her, "She wasn't even young!" Bonnie Dow also points out that Mary was "not a 'girl' biding her time until marriage" like *That Girl*'s lead, Ann Marie.[7] Thank God for they took the bold step of featuring a woman in her thirties, countering the media's obsession with youth that continues to this today.

In a very funny episode of *The Golden Girls,* the ladies are invited to participate in a bachelorette auction. On the show, when Rose is offered breakfast, she says, "No thanks. I'm doing what we all should be doing, dieting for the bachelorette auction next Saturday." Bea Arthur's character, Dorothy, the most feminist of the group, counters, "Not all of us. I told you, Rose. Count me out. Even if it is for charity, I'm not gonna stand up there and allow myself to be sold to the highest bidder like some Holstein cow at a livestock auction. . . . I am not going. It is degrading."[8] Though Dorothy ends up participating, she makes clear her distaste for judging women based solely on their appearance, something TV shows rarely do.

In a media landscape that leans more to *Friends* girls than *The Golden Girls,* youth is sitcoms' prevailing paradigm. Every now and then, a good woman points out the superficiality and ridiculousness of this standard. Murphy Brown laments the attention always paid to Corky Sherwood's wardrobe and makeup instead of to Murphy's hard-hitting stories. On the show's pilot episode, Murphy lords her age over her new male boss, Miles Silverberg, a man who hasn't even reached thirty: "I can't help thinking that while I was getting maced at the Democratic convention in '68, you were wondering if you'd ever meet Adam West."[9] Murphy knows that her age gives her power and authority, even if many women who watch her show are more interested in Corky's newest look.

In *Where the Girls Are,* Susan Douglas describes how she and other baby boomer teen girls were "relentlessly" isolated as a "distinct market segment."[10] Young women became a critically important demographic, demonstrated by shows that appealed to young girls, like *Gidget,* and the Beatlemania that had taken over young women's lives. This also proved that young girls and women were increasingly desirable to advertisers. Today, appealing to the youth market is so vital that enormous effort and money are spent making products seem "hip" and "cool." The youth market remains a main advertising and marketing industry. Our culture prays at the altar of youth and beauty, and shows no indications of changing. Naomi Wolf's *Beauty Myth* was published in 1991; yet today's statistics about the amount women spend buying into the myth of permanent youth are even more striking than they were in the early '90s. Over nine million Americans—most of them women—underwent plastic surgery procedures in 2004, a trend that is expected to grow with the ongoing "scientific breakthroughs" in preventing and "treating" wrinkles.[11] We live in a country not simply obsessed with youth, but one that worships it.

In one episode of *Designing Women,* the women go on vacation with their husbands and boyfriends and children, and make the mistake of hiring a big-boobed, bikini-model-looking Norwegian to care for the children. The women feel threatened by "the former Miss Denmark" (as they dub her). Mary Jo complains, "I don't think we can compete with her."[12] In some ways, she is right: Young, beautiful women will always be attractive to men. But, as she does in most episodes, Mary Jo states that she is "a mature woman with a grown son" and she will not "participate in these pubescent teenage situations," watching the men in her life "drool in their socks over some Scandinavian import." The men eventually admit that their insecurity over their own "lost youth" has made them act the fools. They also tell their wives and girlfriends, "There are no women in the world like you three." The men involved with the *Designing Women* characters recognize that regardless of youth, beauty, or breast size, they love these women because of *who* they are, not how they look. Women like Julia Sugarbaker—witty, strong, successful, and over forty—are the ones to be reckoned with, women who are old enough to know that their worth is not measured in external beauty, but internal integrity. It's a lesson for us all. (That and doing our best to avoid watching TV ads, especially ones for wrinkle cream that feature eighteen-year-olds frolicking in their undies and splashing water on their lineless faces.) I like to think that women such as Maude, Roseanne, and the Golden Girls help sell feminism and accep-tance of aging more than advertising helps sell jars of beauty cream and tubes of concealer.

Fatties, Dogs, and Crones

Many sitcom women have succeeded more because of their talent than their appearance. This is not to say that television should abandon the American ideals of thinness, beauty, and youth; the media remains an area where feminism still has a lot of work to do. As Naomi Wolf defends herself and her book as not being "anti-beauty," I also believe it is our choice as women to look however we want, take pleasure in makeup, or work out to feel better about our bodies. But I echo Wolf's belief that "we deserve the choice to do whatever we want with our faces and bodies without being punished by an ideology that is using atti-tudes and economic pressure . . . regarding women's appear-ance to undermine us psychologically and politically."[13]

I hear unrelenting complaints from women about their bodies: wrinkles, thighs, breast size, sagging skin, thinning hair, skin tone, and countless other imperfections that we have been "trained" to look for—often in a ten-times magnifying mirror while locked in the bathroom. Few of us can fully escape the internal and external pressure to look perfect. We know that ideals of beauty and body image change depending on the time, culture, country, economy, and a variety of other factors. That doesn't seem to stop us from agonizing over imperfections and using them to demean ourselves as a whole. The responsibility for this lies with us as individuals and with a culture that values beauty over brains and thinness over thoughtfulness—if it didn't, none of us would have heard of Paris Hilton and her brilliantly creative catchphrase, "That's hot."

Some women have spent so much time thinking about what is wrong with their bodies, they lose sight of things that matter—like what kind of person they are and what gives them a sense of fulfillment. As one of the most economically successful and culturally influential mediums, television has not helped matters. As I see it, TV's beauty cult pales in comparison to that of women's magazines, movies, and advertising. I do my best to avoid these cultural demons and to find inspiration in women's deeds. I find physically imperfect but inspiring women on sitcoms and TV shows more than in any other media.

Consider Bea Arthur's *Maude*. Bea Arthur, who has an incredible ability to laugh at herself, has taken so many hits by comedians and writers about her appearance that these jokes are now considered "hack" or unoriginal. When *Maude* premiered in 1972, the lead character was created to be the female Archie Bunker—on the other side of the political spectrum. The show was meant to address politics as well as feminism and the experiences of middle-aged women. Even today, this remains an unpopular idea for a TV series. Imagine today, in the age of *Sex and the City*, writers pitching a show about a grandmother over fifty who goes through menopause on national television.

Women are allowed to be sexually active, aggressive, and noncommittal as long as they are gorgeous and young (or, at least, young looking). Older women on television are most often sideline characters who are the mothers of leading twenty-year-olds, in the same way that fat women can play best friends, but not leading women. That is why when women like Bea Arthur and Roseanne Barr are featured in their *own* sitcoms, I revel in their representations of women who may not be real, but definitely *look* real. Sitcom historian Rick Mitz describes *Maude* this way:

> Maude *was most significant in its exploration of the problems of upper-middle age. Maude had wrinkles. Most sitcom families were young and perky (Donna Reed never aged from week to week, season to season), and sitcom singles were usually forever young (*That Girl *never evolved into *That Woman, *and even Mary Richards canceled herself when she was nary thirty-seven). Maude Findlay was in her late forties, and every year she got older (and bolder).*

She was a grandmother. She went through menopause. She worried about aging. She had a facelift. She still looked her age.[14]

In fact, Maude does something we rarely see on TV—she turns fifty. Sure, she's aware of the importance of youth and beauty, but she also lives in the same world that we do. In fact, her fiftieth birthday is marked by a trip to a shrink where she laments, "I'm fifty and nobody loves me. . . . Oh God, if I could only repeal the law of gravity."[15] But *Maude* fights the images that imprison women in a jail of self-loathing and self-criticism. Personally, I think she does a good job and feel lucky I was able to watch reruns of the show as I was growing up. Even as a child, I wanted to be like Maude regardless of what she looked like. I cannot say the same for the women of *Friends* or *Sex and the City*.

Appearance is paramount when casting television shows, which makes me applaud the success of shows like *Maude, Roseanne, Grace Under Fire, Ellen,* and *The Golden Girls.* They eschew looks in exchange for likability they value substance over style.

While critics chided *The Golden Girls* as crones and ridiculed Roseanne for being fat, millions of women watched and continue to watch their shows. Even better, women created these shows. Susan Harris, who created *The Golden Girls*, says, "There's this myth that I would like to dispel: that when you grow older, you are no longer vital, attractive, sexy, and smart. There is life after forty."[16] Dorothy, Rose, Blanche, and Sophia are vital women who show the American audience how the lives of women senior citizens can be filled with laughter, fun, work, friendship, dating, and sex. This was news to many of us who'd never seen anything like it on TV before. As I imagine getting older myself, I would not balk at having the lives of these women. They have fuller lives than many young women I see on TV, especially the young wives and mothers from '50s and '60s sitcoms. Initially, Susan Harris was told repeatedly that a show about "old ladies" would never make it. In the end, *The Golden Girls* was an instant hit and stayed on the air for seven years. During its run, the show garnered ten Emmys, two for Best Comedy and one for each of the leading women—a rare accomplishment for ensemble sitcoms. Susan Harris's inspiration for the show was drawn from her own grandmother, who at eighty years old called her granddaughter to tell her about her new job. As Harris notes, "She obviously didn't think of herself as elderly, and I thought that was just wonderful."[17]

I Am Thin, Hear Me Roar . . .

Two images come to mind when I think of how television has dealt with the overwhelmingly common battle women face against their weight: Roseanne and Ally McBeal. These are the sitcom world's two extremes. In real life, most of us fall somewhere in the middle (generally closer to Roseanne than Ally).

Other than supporting actors playing housekeepers or grandmas, overweight women rarely appear on television.

Enter Roseanne Barr, one of television's first heroines to accept her fat. Audiences, for the most part, accepted her too. In a culture that spends thirty-three billion dollars a year on the dieting industry, Roseanne never apologizes for who she is, regardless of media attacks. During the show's run, women I knew loved Roseanne—I can't say the same for the men—for her strength, humor, power, and unique ability to bring feminism to the forefront with quick jabs and witty quips. Throughout the series, we rarely saw the character's insecurity and vulnerability, except when it came to her weight. Roseanne's character didn't ignore her "weight problem," she just had more important things to worry about—like raising three children, making financial ends meet, and keeping her marriage on track.

It wasn't that Roseanne accepted her body unconditionally, it was that she struggled with her weight the same way millions of American women do. I can't imagine how comforting it must have been to be an overweight woman in America and turn on the TV and see *Roseanne* instead of *Charlie's Angels.*

As most American women wear dress sizes in the double-digits, Roseanne is more representative of our collective appearance than television's ubiquitous waifs. During the course of the series, Roseanne addressed the issue of her weight many times. In an episode entitled "I'm Hungry," Roseanne and her overweight husband, Dan, decide to go on a diet. The episode opens with Roseanne at her new hair salon job at listening to all the women discuss their eating habits. When a thin, pretty twentysomething says that her eating is "out of control" because she eats breakfast, lunch, and dinner, Roseanne responds with, "Well, you just described my morning." Her boss then tells her a horrible thing that I'm sure many overweight women have had to endure: "You have such a pretty face. It's a shame you keep it hidden by all that extra weight." Roseanne makes an expression that clearly shows she's heard that one before.

> **CRYSTAL:** Roseanne doesn't have to worry about keeping slim. Dan's crazy about her no matter how she looks.
>
> **ROSEANNE:** Thanks, Crystal.
>
> **CRYSTAL:** *(Stuttering)* Oh, I'm sorry, Roseanne, I didn't mean for it to sound like—oh, uh, well, she's just so happily married, and *(to Roseanne)* you're just not on the market anymore.
>
> **ROSEANNE:** No, Crystal, you're right. I do need to lose weight. And I'll tell you what I'm gonna do. I'll start now by picking a day next week to go on a diet.
>
> **CRYSTAL:** Alright.
>
> **ROSEANNE:** *(Looking at a calendar)* Next week's bad. March is out.

Later, at home, Roseanne struggles to get her pants on, and at first wants to believe they shrank in the dryer. But she admits to Dan that she "just grew." He, equally fat, hugs her and says, "I think we've grown together."

ROSEANNE: We've gotta go on a diet.

DAN: What's this "we" jazz? My pants fit fine.

ROSEANNE: Well, my pants don't fit me.

DAN: Well, your pants don't fit me either.

ROSEANNE: Ha, ha, Dan. Let's burn the weight off with humor. Look at yourself—you're too fat. You've gotta go on a diet.

DAN: You go on a diet. I'm going to dinner.

As the family sits down to dinner, Roseanne continues to pressure Dan to diet with her.

BECKY: You guys going on a diet again?

ROSEANNE: Yes.

DAN: No.

DARLENE: I guess this means we're gonna have roast chicken for three nights, then get back to reality.

ROSEANNE: I mean, we're gonna look better and we're gonna feel better.

DAN: We won't eat better.

ROSEANNE: You know how we hate being like this.

DAN: You know what, Roseanne? We don't go out a lot. We don't have a big house. Food is the one luxury we can afford.

ROSEANNE: Food ain't supposed to be a luxury, Dan. It is supposed to keep you alive. It ain't supposed to provide entertainment value.

DAN: *(To the kids)* What do you guys think? Does your mom need to lose weight?

D.J.: *(Hugging Roseanne)* No, I like you mushy.

Becky, the Conners' eldest daughter, chimes in with her ideas about women, men, and fat.

BECKY: Men are supposed to get heavy when they get older. They all do, but it doesn't look good on women.

ROSEANNE: That is about the dumbest thing you've ever said.

DARLENE: Face it. You're both tanks.

ROSEANNE: Hey, you stay out of this. It's your fault I got fat in the first place.

DARLENE: Oh right, like I invented double dutch chocolate.

ROSEANNE: No, but I gained twenty pounds with that pregnancy.

DAN: Me too.

DARLENE: Twenty pounds?

ROSEANNE: Okay, forty pounds . . . with each kid.

DAN: Me too.

ROSEANNE: Remember when I was thin and beautiful?

DAN: You're still beautiful. You've had three beautiful kids.

ROSEANNE: Well, I can't use that excuse forever.

DAN: Sure you can.

ROSEANNE: No, I can't use that forever. A couple more years max, but not forever.[18]

Roseanne decides to take "drastic measures" and attempts to clean out the junk food from the pantry—but for the most part, she just notices that they have Mallomars. Just like the rest of us, she struggles with food and trying to keep healthy in a house full of sugar-eating kids. It isn't easy, but she goes on a diet—alone because Dan doesn't stick to it—and you see the difficulty many of us face as we battle extra pounds. Roseanne has trouble sticking to her diet, and sneaks into her bathroom to secretly eat potato chips. When her coworkers tell her that if she exercised, she could eat whatever she wanted, Roseanne really gets motivated. Her eyes light up at the very thought that she can "eat whatever she wants," as do mine and those of almost every other woman I know. This plan, however, does not really work for Roseanne.

The episode spells out the problems of trying to diet and to fit exercise into a busy work/home/family schedule. In a telling scene, Roseanne's daughters confront their aunt Jackie because they want to know why Roseanne is fat and her sister, Jackie, is thin. At first, Jackie tells them weight can be determined by genetics. Then she suggests it depends on whether a person was overweight as a child. And finally, she explains that the real problem for Roseanne, and most everyone who struggles with weight issues, is food.

> **JACKIE:** There's the environment and being pregnant three times and having kids around who need to eat constantly at all hours of the day. And there's also extra tartar sauce on her fish sticks, and extra mayo on her roast beef, and extra roast beef on her kaiser roll.
>
> **DARLENE:** So, basically you're saying Mom just eats a lot.
>
> **JACKIE:** No, no. Well, yeah, yeah.

The episode continues with Roseanne constantly having to fight her cravings for food as her kids eat ice cream and the television advertises fast food and sweets nonstop. Dan tries to give her a pep talk, but her desire for cookies is overwhelming. She denies herself the junk and continues on her diet and exercise program. Finally, Roseanne fits into the pants she had struggled to get into before.

> **ROSEANNE:** You know, I am so happy. I mean, I did it. It's not that much or nothing. But I mean, it's just a small thing, but my pants fit and, you know, I mean I feel really good about it. But, you know,

if I can do this good, maybe I can do even better. I mean, maybe we really can exercise every day and maybe I really can lose more weight. I feel great!

DAN: That's great, babe.

ROSEANNE: You know, I have time. You know what I'm gonna do? I'm gonna walk to work.

DARLENE: You're kidding.

ROSEANNE: No, I'm serious. I think it's about two and a half miles, and we probably walked farther than that this morning.

DAN: Easy.

ROSEANNE: Yeah, and then maybe I can walk home from work, too, and do that every day and that would be like an extra five miles a day.

DAN: Go for it.

ROSEANNE: I'm gonna do it. See you guys later.

KIDS: Bye, Mom. *(Roseanne leaves.)*

DAN: That's great. That is really great. I'm really proud of your mom.

ROSEANNE: *(Reenters the house)* Ooh, it's like thirteen degrees out there. I'm not walking to work.[19]

Designing Women also deals with the issue of weight. Toward the end of the series, Delta Burke's much-publicized weight problem became more apparent on television. The tabloids were barking about the actress's size and the network was pressuring her to return to the beauty queen physique she had when the show began. As with many sitcoms, the writers didn't ignore the issue, but instead decided to address it head-on. In an episode aptly titled, "They Shoot Fat Women, Don't They?" former beauty queen Suzanne Sugarbaker is preparing to attend a reunion where she knows people will notice and talk about how much weight she's gained since her pageant days. The episode is poignant, sad, and truthful in the way it addresses the problem.

> **JULIA:** Suzanne, it's just human nature. People love to see beautiful women get old or fat.

> **SUZANNE:** All my life I've had to fight my weight, and I admit, food has been my security blanket. But also, I just gain weight more easily than some people. Like you . . . you've always had that tiny waist and those skinny little legs. But I can't be that, and people have always tried to make me be that.

> **JULIA:** Suzanne, you're not alone. I'd be willing to bet most of the people in this country are overweight.

> **SUZANNE:** The point is it's different for women, especially beautiful women. Just look at Elizabeth Taylor. I bet I've seen *National Velvet* maybe twenty times, and if she never did anything else in her life, what a contribution *that* was. But all of a sudden, because she got fat, it was like she no longer had the right to live in this country. That's how I feel right now. Drugs, alcohol, cancer . . . whatever your problems, people are sympathetic

. . . unless you're fat, and then you're supposed
to be ashamed. I mean, everything is set up to tell
you that—magazine covers, clothes. "If you're not
thin, you're not neat, and that's it." And if looks
are all you've ever had . . . [20]

Suzanne has always defined herself by her beauty. She must face—as all women must—the fact that she is going to get old and wrinkled, and maybe even fat. So it's important to have something to be proud of other than appearance. Besides, physical changes don't alter who we are or what type of person we can still strive to be.

JULIA: What do you mean, "If looks are all you ever had"? Suzanne, first of all, don't be a dummy. Your looks will never be in the past tense. That face speaks for itself, and it's here to stay. And secondly, even if that weren't so—who cares?

SUZANNE: What do you mean?

JULIA: I mean, you and I are getting pretty far along in life, and I have been able to figure out a couple of things.

SUZANNE: Are you gonna give me the key?

JULIA: Yes, as a matter of fact I am. In the end it doesn't matter what anyone else thinks about you. You have to be exactly who and what you want to be. Most everyone is floating along on phony public relations: people who say being beautiful, or rich, or thin makes them happy, people who are trying to make their marriages and their children seem

better than they actually are . . . and for what?!
Appearances. Appearances don't count for diddly!
In the end, all that really matters is what was true,
and truly said, and how we treated one another.
And that's it.[21]

By the end of the episode, we know that Suzanne will go on struggling with her weight, yo-yo dieting, and stints at exercising. Watching her struggle reminds us that this character is based on real life, where food, weight, and exercise (or lack thereof) are problems for millions of women. Though many episodes of *Designing Women* didn't deal with Suzanne's weight problem, she, like Dan and Roseanne, is an icon for a TV reflecting the real world, where nobody's perfect.

Learning to Love Your Thighs

Since Mary Richards entered the working world, we have seen multitudes of strong, successful, ambitious women. We have to remember that it will always be a fight to feature women with both experience and wrinkles. Women who have experience, maturity, history, and life lessons to teach probably have breasts that don't stand at attention and skin with creases and lines from years of laughing, smiling, crying, having children, mediating crises, and living life. I think laugh lines and crow's-feet are beautiful. I would rather have a face that says "I have really lived" than a face filled with synthetic wrinkle-fillers.

In the end, though, the best part of feminism—every woman being able to choose her own path—applies to accepting the aging process as well. Whether we decide to have face-lifts or liposuction or deal naturally with the ravages of gravity, we all must face aging in our own way. As much as I would love to see women of all ages and sizes accept their bodies, I also understand the inclination to have a nip or a tuck here and there. One of our cultural icons (as well as plastic surgery icons), Cher, was interviewed about her predilection toward plastic surgery. When asked if she would have additional procedures, she said, "If I want to put my tits on my back, it's my business." Her answer sums up the idea that when it comes to aging and body image—to each her own.

I doubt the media or television will ever worship age the way they worship youth. As women, the best we can do is remember that media images—no matter how strong the intent to make characters seem "real"—are phantoms that can haunt us, but only if we let them. Susan Douglas explains that "some images and messages are harder to resist than others, like the one that insists that a forty-year-old woman should have thighs like a twelve-year-old boy's, and that no self-respecting woman should ever have wrinkles."[22]

Few of us can forget the episode of *Sex and the City* when Samantha decides to get a chemical peel before Carrie's book party. When she shows up looking like a seriously scarred burn victim, Carrie is shocked at her appearance, and tells her it would be perfectly acceptable to "go home."

Not even beautiful TV characters are immune to the cult of youth and beauty.

When I think about what Murphy Brown would do in response to growing older, I believe she would accept aging as a part of life, the way all women must. I think she would grow old with grace and dignity. There is little grace in filling your face with "ass fat" or paralyzing it with Botox. I would like to think my idol would agree, but who knows. We have to live with our bodies every day. Even if we decide to enhance or alter them, at the very least, we can learn from *Roseanne, The Golden Girls,* and other shows to try to accept our bodies as best we can.

Chapter 9

The Wonder of Womanhood

TV Friendship

> **FRAN:** We're talking about mean, vicious, backstabbing women!
> **MR. SHEFFIELD:** Then why are you going?
> **FRAN:** Because they're my friends!
>
> **—*The Nanny***

One of the most enduring staples of the woman-centered sitcom is the relationship between women—often strained, commonly problematic, and exceptionally vital. At various times in my own life, my friends and I have compared ourselves to Mary or Rhoda, or the women on *Friends* or *Sex and the City*. Whole sitcoms are based on the "situation" of women's friendships—*The Golden Girls, Sex and the City, Cybill, Kate & Allie, Designing Women, Living Single, Girlfriends* (often referred to as the African American *Sex and the City*), and *Friends*, to name a few. Watching women who help, support, strengthen, and give to each other makes us thankful for the women in our own lives. For the most part, television has been willing to deal with the imperfections, idiosyncrasies, and, ultimately, realities of women's relationships with each other.

I Got My Girls

In featuring women's relationships, television takes its cue from the ultimate career woman show, *The Mary Tyler Moore Show,* which featured a strong relationship between Mary and her neighbor Rhoda. The friendship was so integral to the show that in the 1990s, when Mary Tyler Moore and Valerie Harper filmed a TV movie reunion based on their characters, it was titled *Mary and Rhoda.* It is difficult to think about Mary without thinking of Rhoda as well. They are the perfect example of female TV friendship. Throughout the run of *The Mary Tyler Moore Show,* their relationship grows increasingly intimate and important. As different as the two characters are, they go through many of the same experiences at the same time. They are both "new women" working and dating and figuring out "how to make it" in a big city, which, without friends, can be lonely. At first, it isn't clear they'll become best friends. As Phyllis shows Mary an available apartment, they open the curtains, and there is Rhoda Morgenstern, described by Phyllis as "that dumb awful girl who lives upstairs." The first words Rhoda utters to her future friend are, "This is my apartment. Get out!" Mary decides to fight her for the apartment—not an ideal way to begin a friendship. After sizing Mary up, Rhoda tries to exert the power of her personality to convince Mary to let her have the apartment. Mary does her best to stand up to Rhoda. They eventually realize that they have more in common than their interest in the same apartment.

> **MARY:** You think I'm some kind of pushover, don't you?
>
> **RHODA:** Right.
>
> **MARY:** Well, if you push, I might just have to push back—hard.
>
> **RHODA:** Come on. You can't carry that off.
>
> **MARY:** I know.[1]

Rhoda calls Mary's bluff at her attempt at fearlessness, and Mary seems to appreciate that Rhoda already sees her for who she is and accepts her for it. During the course of the series, the two friends complement each other in a variety of ways. Rhoda usually helps Mary stand up for herself, and Mary helps Rhoda counter her inferiority complexes—about her weight, her mother, her lack of a husband. The morning after Mary moves into the apartment, Rhoda knocks on the door.

> **RHODA:** How do you come off looking that good in the morning? Who'd you get that nightie from? Tricia Nixon?[2]

Rhoda consistently serves as a sort of real-life counter to Mary's naive and idealistic nature. She is also able to make fun of Mary, and we all know that, deep down, these women truly love each other. When Valerie Harper left for her own show in 1973, many viewers were sad to see this great friendship break up. Although we knew Mary and Rhoda would stay friends, it was not the same as the two of them living in the same building. Every time I've had a friend living in the same building, I've always thought of us as Mary and Rhoda, two friends similar in age and experience, going through the same trials and tribulations, and finding in each other someone to lean on.

The relationship between Mary and Rhoda set a precedent for future sitcoms. Most woman-centered shows since then have included a best friend or, even better, a few best friends. Occasionally, the entire premise of a series is based on women's friendships. On *Laverne & Shirley* the two lead characters live together, work together, date together, get in trouble together. They are a team, often a ridiculous one, but no matter what happens with the men in their lives, they still have each other. Friends since high school, the two are inseparable. Shirley wrote a poem in Laverne's high school yearbook that sums up both their friendship and their silliness.

> *If in heaven, we don't meet,*
> *Hand in hand, we'll bear the heat,*
> *And if it ever gets too hot,*
> *Pepsi-Cola hits the spot.*[3]

It seems these two will be sharing a can of soda for all of eternity.

Women on TV indulge in their friendships, and during those common, schmaltzy emotional moments, TV women are able to tell each other how much their friendships mean and how important their mutual support has been. We've seen it over and over, and I hate to admit it, but I well up when I see two friends express their affection for each other. I've always related to the need for other women in my life, women who don't just happen to be there when you need them, but *choose* to be.

Sometimes sitcom friendships are cemented through working together, like the waitresses on *Alice,* or studying together, like the students on *The Facts of Life.* Sometimes the relationship that serves as the "best friend element" is between sisters, as on *Designing Women* (the Sugarbakers) and *Roseanne* (whose protagonist always takes care of her little sister and best friend, Jackie).

The show *Friends* premiered in 1994 and aired for a decade as the six leading twentysomethings created an unforgettable ensemble comedy. The show's title and its theme song, "I'll Be There for You," refer to three men and three women who are young New Yorkers beginning their adult lives and finding their identities. They support each other, make fun of each other and themselves, and genuinely care for each other. Over the years, they grow and mature, their lives change, they find different interests—but they still face the future together. Although their romances always get the most press and attention—the never-ending Ross and Rachel relationship played out over years—I always feel most connected to the show when the three female leads are together. Monica and Rachel were in high school together and were best friends who had lost touch. In the pilot episode, they're reunited and become roommates. Their apartment is usually where all the action happens (although "action" generally means a lot of pithy conversation).

For many people, the show is funny and entertaining, at times even poignant, but, for me, the bond between Phoebe, Rachel, and Monica has more heart than other aspects of the show. I love the episodes where the three women get in trouble together, help each other, and discuss issues they can't talk about when the guys are around. One Valentine's Day, they all lack dates or boyfriends; so together they burn old photos and letters from the men who've disappointed them in the past. One season, Monica and Phoebe start a catering business together.

Their friendship isn't perfect, and much of the show's comedy results from the fights among the three women. This rings true for any woman who has ever had a best friend (or two). There is one particular sentence from the show that truly exemplifies their friendship—fights and all. In the episode, Rachel has been dumped by her new boyfriend, and Ross, her ex who also happens to be engaged (something that is deeply disturbing to Rachel), is trying to comfort her. When Ross asks Rachel if she'll be all right, she turns to Phoebe and Monica, who are always there when she needs them, and simply says, "Yeah. I got my girls."[4]

I can't imagine my life without my makeshift family of friends, just as Monica, Phoebe, and Rachel couldn't. The camaraderie of womanhood allows us to share even the most personal aspects of our lives. Few women haven't felt the pain of menstrual cramps, the embarrassment of getting naked in front of someone for the first time, or the realization that the lipstick looked much better in the store than on our face. And it is the same for many sitcom friendships; from the roommates in *The Golden Girls* to the women of *Sex and the City*, female friendships often take precedence on television, and those connections are both affirming and inspirational. When I am having a hard time dealing with life, I know (like Rachel) that "I got my girls" and am eternally grateful for it.

Boston Marriages

As women have always known, we all need a little help from our friends to get through life, and as such some shows are based solely on the relationship between two women. *Kate & Allie* premiered in 1983 and explored the lives of two New York City divorced mothers who lived together and raised their children, almost in the same way a married couple would. Like women of nineteenth-century Boston who often lived together to pool resources, these two women did the same in the 1980s. According to sitcom historian Rick Mitz, there are some female stereotypes represented in sitcoms that often ring true: "Although sitcoms are most often written and directed by men, they are very often about women."[1] In the tradition of Mary and Rhoda and Laverne and Shirley, Kate and Allie are two very different women who come together to help one another get through the ups and downs of divorce, motherhood, work, and dating. In the '60s, Kate was a hippie, while Allie wore traditional pearls and sweater sets. They both married, had children (Kate had one daughter; Allie, a son and a daughter), and got divorced. Moving in together in New York City sets the stage for a friendship that will weather the same kind of storms traditional TV marriages face. At first, Allie plays the dutiful "wife" to the career-driven Kate, but eventually she decides to work outside the home as well. They help each other face the pain of divorce and the difficulties of being single mothers in New York City.

Some have said that the show was the first sitcom ever *about* women's friendship, the crux of the comedy based on the sometimes-rocky, long-lasting, meaningful relationship between these two women. In a twist that I enjoy, the women's two daughters also become best friends, although they essentially live as sisters with their two mothers serving as parents. Originally, both the lead actresses, Susan Saint James and Jane Curtin, were averse to doing the show: Curtin remarked that all the shows she loved took place outside the home, and Saint James wasn't keen on working on a show with children. But the show, created by Sherry Coben, appealed to many women who saw Kate and Allie as their own friends as well. Susan Saint James feels the show was a success "because people can identify with us, it reflects real life."[6] I think many of us identify with Kate and Allie because we can see our own friendships in their relationship, or, if we are not lucky enough to have that kind of friend, we look to these two as an example of the connection that can exist between friends. Unlike many other sitcoms, the show never has extreme plot twists—no new babies, husbands (Allie does marry toward the very end of the series, but her husband works in another city, essentially leaving the premise unchanged), or neighbors, themes usually explored on sitcoms when they have been on the air for a long time and ratings begin to fall. The key strength of the show, which was an instant hit, is that the friendship was enough to keep it going strong for five seasons.

"Frenemies": Friends We Love and Hate

No matter how close two women are—on TV or in real life—there are bound to be those "friends" we feel stuck with, friends we both love and hate at the same time. That is clearly the situation with Maude and her moronic friend, Vivian (played by Rue McClanahan, who would later star opposite Bea Arthur again in *The Golden Girls*), who seems to annoy Maude more than help her. Some friendships between women and relationships between sisters are fraught with resentment, jealousies, competition, and frustrations. Even women who love each other as much as Roseanne and her sister, Jackie; Kate and Allie; or Carrie, Miranda, Samantha, and Charlotte have their share of problems. This is, of course, the nature of dealing with other humans on an intimate level. What I love so much about the TV women I have grown up with is that they have endured the difficulties of female friendships as much as they have reaped the benefits. Comedy is most often gleaned from conflict, and relationships between women aren't safe from these trials and tribulations.

Much of the comedy on *The Golden Girls* stems from differences between the four women: Dorothy is the feminist voice of reason; her mother, Sophia, always makes verbal jabs at Blanche, the sexpot; and Rose is the idiotic country bumpkin.

> **BLANCHE:** My life is an open book.
>
> **SOPHIA:** Your life is an open blouse.[7]

Even the relationship between Dorothy and Sophia, mother and daughter, is full of verbal sparring and insults. In one episode, Dorothy and Sophia are forced to share the same bed. Sophia's response to the situation is not kind.

> **SOPHIA:** That's it. I'm outta here. . . . Your feet—it's like having two size-nine Fudgesicles pressed up against my butt.[8]

Sometimes our friends are there to give us a little jab in the side, to help us recognize when we are acting crazy, selfishly, or irrationally. The same kind of verbal sparring that occurs on *Designing Women,* although usually the beauty queen, Suzanne, takes the brunt of the abuse. Even the women of *Sex and the City* call one another out on Samantha's sluttishness, or Charlotte's naïveté, or Carrie's insanity. Beneath the insults and jokes, most of the TV women love and count on one another no matter how much they fight or disagree. Even mother and daughter can learn to be friends, as Dorothy and Sophia do on *The Golden Girls*.

DOROTHY: You're a good mother.

SOPHIA: You're a crazy lady—I love you.[9]

No matter how crazy friends can make us, we're lucky to have them around, even if it is simply to put us in check once in a while.

As with all female friendships—and friendships in general— things don't always go smoothly. Thus, *Sex and the City*'s Carrie Bradshaw created the term "frenemies" to describe those relationships frought with both love and tension, sympathy and envy. In the episode "Frenemies," we see just how friends can be both supportive and critical. As the four ladies have their usual lunch, Samantha characteristically discusses sex. But Charlotte has had enough.

CHARLOTTE: *(to Samantha)* How can you not know anything about him? You slept with him.

SAMANTHA: I fucked him. He made me come six
   times. That's good enough for me.

CHARLOTTE: Stop it! Why do you always have to talk
   about sex like that?

SAMANTHA: Because I can.

CHARLOTTE: I can't take this anymore. Sex is
   something special that is supposed to happen
   between two people who love each other.

SAMANTHA: Or two people who love sex.

CHARLOTTE: God, you're such a . . .

SAMANTHA: A what? What am I, Charlotte?

CHARLOTTE: When are you gonna learn that you
   can't just sleep with everything that comes along?

SAMANTHA: Hey, Mrs. Softy, at least I'm getting laid.

Carrie attempts to discuss the situation, but Charlotte
explains that she simply needs a break from Samantha. No matter how close friends can be, sometimes conflicting personal
issues (like the fact that Charlotte's seemingly perfect husband
is impotent) can color even the most solid friendships.

In the hopes of feeling more connected to women whom
she believes are just like her, Charlotte reunites for lunch with
her conservative, sweater-set-and-pearl-earring college sorority sisters.

CARRIE, VOICEOVER: Uptown, Charlotte decided this
   would be a good time to spend with her real old

friends—the sisters of Kappa Kappa Gamma. She knew they would understand her. After all, they were all married too.

SYDNEY: I remember being a newlywed. We hardly ever got out of bed.

WOMAN #2: *(Shocked)* Sydney!

SYDNEY: What? It's just us girls.

CHARLOTTE: My husband can't get it up. I'm so frustrated. I mean, don't you ever just want to be really pounded hard? You know? Like when the bed is moving all around and it's all sweaty and your head is knocking up against the headboard and you feel like it just might blow off? Damn it! I just really want to be fucked, just really fucked!

WOMAN: You know, Charlotte, this is really inappropriate.

SYDNEY: What's wrong with you, Charlotte? You're such a . . .

CHARLOTTE: What? What am I, Sydney?

CARRIE, VOICEOVER: Charlotte realized how much they'd all changed since college. *(Charlotte gets up and leaves.)* Her friends had become frenemies, and she had become Samantha.[10]

Sometimes it takes a conflict or two to help you realize who your real friends are.

Clearly, not all interactions between friends go smoothly. In one of America's favorite sitcoms, *Friends,* humor is garnered from the fights that occur between the women characters. One of the most memorable fights occurs when Rachel injures her foot and realizes she has no health insurance. Monica allows Rachel to pretend she is Monica so that she can use her insurance. Unfortunately, they meet two cute doctors and have to keep up their switched-identity charade on their double date with the physicians.

DR. ROSEN: So, Monica, how's the ankle?

MONICA: It's, uh . . .

(Rachel coughs discreetly in warning.)

MONICA: *(As Rachel)* . . . Well, why don't you tell them? After all, it *is* your ankle.

RACHEL: *(As Monica)* You know what, it's feeling a lot better, thank you. Um, well, listen, why don't you two sit down and, and we'll get you some glasses. Okay? *(The doctors don't know what to do with their coats, and Monica points to the living room.)*

(Rachel joins Monica in the kitchen area as she opens a bottle of wine. Rachel checks that the doctors aren't listening, then lowers her voice anyway.)

RACHEL: Okay, listen. I'm thinking, why don't we just tell them who we really are? I mean, it'll be fine. I really think it'll be fine.

MONICA: It will *not* be fine. We'll get in trouble.

RACHEL: Oh, Monica! Would you *stop* being such a wuss?

MONICA: A wuss? Excuse me for living in the real world, okay?

(On the couch, Dr. Mitchell and Dr. Rosen seem to be concerned about the women's conversation.)

DR. MITCHELL: So?

DR. ROSEN: So . . . they sss . . . still seem normal.

DR. MITCHELL: That's because they are.

DR. ROSEN: *(Nervously)* Okay, but you have to admit that every time we go out with women we meet at the hospital—it turns into . . .

DR. MITCHELL: Will ya relax? Look around. No pagan altars, no piles of bones in the corners. They're fine. *(Baring his teeth to clean them with his finger)* Go like this. *(Dr. Rosen obeys.)*

MONICA: *(To Rachel, who is at the sink)* I said we are not going to do it, okay? Sometimes you can be such a, a big baby.

RACHEL: *(Resentfully)* I am not a baby! You know what? I swear to God, just because you get so uptight every time we—

MONICA: Sure—every time, you're such a princess . . .

RACHEL: You know what?

MONICA: What?

RACHEL: You know what?

MONICA: What?!

RACHEL: You know what?

MONICA: *(Getting angry)* What?!

RACHEL: Every day, you are becoming more and more like your mother.

(Smiling, Rachel limps across the apartment with glasses of wine for the doctors, leaving an open-mouthed Monica in her wake.)

RACHEL: Hello! Here we go!

DR. ROSEN: This is a great place. How long have you lived here?

RACHEL: *(As Monica)* Thanks! I've been here about six years, and Rachel moved in a few months ago.

MONICA: *(As Rachel)* Yeah . . . *(Joining the others)* See, I was supposed to get married, but, um, I left the guy at the altar.

(Rachel tries to hide her alarm, but she squirms in her chair.)

DR. MITCHELL: Really?

MONICA: *(As Rachel)* Yeah. Yeah, I know it's pretty selfish, but ha ha. Hey, that's me. *(Pointing to a dish on the table)* Why don't you try the hummus?

DR. ROSEN: So, Monica, what do you do?

RACHEL: *(As Monica)* Ah. I'm a . . . chef at a restaurant uptown.

DR. ROSEN: Good for you.

RACHEL: *(As Monica)* Yeah, it is, mostly because I get to *boss* people around, which I just *love* to do.

DR. ROSEN: This hummus is great.

DR. MITCHELL: God bless the chickpea.

MONICA: *(As Rachel, laughing)* Oh God, I am so spoiled. . . . That's it!

(The doctors don't know what to make of all this.)

RACHEL: *(As Monica)* And by the way, have I mentioned that back in high school, I was a cow?

MONICA: *(As Rachel)* I used to wet my bed.

RACHEL: *(As Monica)* I use my breasts to get other people's attention.

MONICA: *(As Rachel, revealing her anger)* We both do that!

(The telephone rings. As the girls stare at each other, each silently daring the other to move first, the doctors both jump up to answer it. Dr. Mitchell gets to it first.)

DR. MITCHELL: *(Answering the phone)* Monica and Rachel's apartment. Er, yeah . . . ah, yeah, just one second. *(He hands the phone to Monica.)* Ah, Rachel, it's your dad.

MONICA: *(As Rachel)* Hi, Dad. No, no, it's me. *(She rises to move away from Rachel.)* Li . . . listen, Dad, I can't talk right now, um, but there's something, um . . . there's something that I've been meaning to tell you . . .

(Monica glares triumphantly across the room, scaring Rachel, who also stands up.)

RACHEL: *(As Monica)* Would you excuse me for a second?

MONICA: *(As Rachel)* Remember back in freshman year? *(Speaking quickly, before Rachel can reach her)* Well, Billy Dreskin and I had sex on your bed.

(Rachel almost loses her balance as she staggers
backward, eyes agog, gasping for breath.)[11]

The women may not always get along; they may tattle on each other or fight over a guy every now and then; but they always remain friends, living up to the series' title.

Our Real Other Halves

MR. SHEFFIELD: What do you and Val do together?

FRAN: We file our nails. We talk about our fantasies—when our parents are going to move to Florida, Häagen-Dazs, burning fat. You know, the usual.

—The Nanny

One common theme in television sitcom history is the carving out of makeshift families. Friends, relatives, coworkers, or a mixture of all three often compose a sitcom family, for better or worse. After Rachel on *Friends* gives birth to her daughter, she still hasn't settled on a name. She doesn't feel that her daughter is an "Isabella," the name she and Ross (the father of the baby) had originally decided on. Ross mentions that Monica has known the names of her future children since she was a child herself. When Rachel asks her what they are, Monica is hesitant to reveal her girl name for fear Rachel will use it. When Rachel promises that she won't, Monica discloses that she wants to name her daughter

Emma. As Rachel's eyes well up with tears, now clearly set on the name Monica had picked out, Monica tells Rachel to name the baby Emma, regardless of the fact that Monica had been holding on to the idea of naming her daughter Emma since she was a young girl. Some things mean more than childhood wishes.

> **RACHEL:** But you love that name.
>
> **MONICA:** Yeah, but I love you more.[12]

And there it is: The love between two friends transcends the dreams of a little girl for her future offspring.

I think *Will & Grace,* based on a fifteen-year friendship between a gay man and a woman, often exemplifies the ways in which friends need each other. On an episode titled "Coffee & Commitment," Will is annoyed with Grace's constant habit of taking her best friend for granted. At their friends' gay wedding, they realize how much their friendship means, no matter how often they fight, nitpick, ridicule, and tease each other. In the final scene, both Will and Grace read a poem for the wedding that they clearly see applies to their troubles with each other. As a friend, I take particular inspiration from the love Will and Grace feel for each other and express with such beauty and emotion.

> *When I'm feeling like there's no love coming to me,*
> *And I have no love to give.*

When I'm separated from the world,
And cut off from myself.
When I'm feeling annoyed by every little thing,
Because I'm not getting what I want.
I'll remember that there is an infinite amount of love
*   available to me,*
And I'll see it in you.
I'll remember that I am complete within myself,
So I'll never have to look to you to complete me.
And, most of all, I'll remember that everything I
*   really need I already have,*
And everything I don't have will come to me when I
*   am ready to receive it.*[13]

In an episode of *Murphy Brown* titled "The Morning Show," Murphy is cajoled into agreeing to host a morning show for one week, while the usual host is out. As she discusses the job with producer Miles, she remembers that morning shows rarely feature only one host.

> **MURPHY:** Hey, wait a minute. I'm not going to host the show alone. Who is my cohost going to be?
>
> **CORKY:** *(Entering excitedly)* Murphy, I just heard the news! We are going to have so much fun!

In a strange twist of fate, Corky excels as a morning show host, while Murphy's hard-nosed journalism—even when interviewing a children's author—evokes constant criticism of her performance. The majority of the staff encourages Murph to "lighten up."

MURPHY: C'mon, I'm not that bad, am I? Jim?

JIM: Frankly, Murphy, I've rarely seen anyone so ill-suited for a situation as you are for the morning show. You're acerbic, humorless, inflexible, and unprepared. In a nutshell, you make Sam Donaldson look like Pinky Lee.

MILES: Murphy, I feel terrible about this. It's all my fault. Who ever knew you could be so bad at anything?

MURPHY: I'm not bad, Miles, I'm just not good.

MILES: The morning show is harder than you thought, isn't it?

MURPHY: Yes; it takes a certain kind of person to ease people into their day. Corky knows how. I hate that.

MILES: Maybe there will be some things you just can't master.

Murphy decides she will put her mind to it and become a great morning host, but is thwarted when she is forced to attempt a cooking segment—a skill she lacks in spades. It is her friend, Corky who comes to her rescue.

CORKY: Murphy, it's all right. We'll get through this. Just tell yourself you can do this!

After the cooking segment ends in disaster due to Murphy's ineptitude, she realizes that she need Corky, as both a coworker and a friend.

MURPHY: I've been meaning to tell you something. You really surprised me this week. You were good.

CORKY: Oh, Murphy, thank you for saying that. It means a lot to me. I wish I could say the same about you.

MURPHY: It's okay. I've accepted my shortcomings . . . sort of.

CORKY: You know, this week you're probably feeling a lot like I do most of the time—somebody throws you into a situation you're not prepared for and you fall on your face a lot. But I believe a person can learn if they study hard and really apply themselves. At least, I hope they can. I really would love to be like you, Murphy.

MURPHY: Gee, guess that's about the nicest compliment anyone's ever given me.

CORKY: Come here, Murphy. *(They hug each other.)*[14]

We would all be incredibly lucky to have the kind of friendships experienced by many of our TV icons. Over the years, even professional rivals and complete opposites Corky Sherwood and Murphy Brown develop a friendship as Corky's marriage fails and Murphy becomes a mother, something Corky always wanted and was unable to achieve in her troubled marriage. Though Murphy whines and bellyaches when Corky tries to get close to her, by the show's finale, we know these women are not just coworkers and colleagues, but friends as well.

Chapter 10

Baby Steps

Sitcom Women Reclaim Some Power

> As we speed along this endless road to the destination called "who we hope to be," I can't help but whine, "Are we there yet?"
>
> **—Sex and the City**

When *Sex and the City* debuted in 1998, viewers reveled in the deliciously blunt representation of the four main characters. They openly discuss sex, chase men, and test society's boundaries of acceptable "ladylike" behavior. While my mother's generation grew up with role models like June Cleaver, we now have single mothers, career women, smart alecks, and ballbusters. Even young women have been included in our collective feminist history on television. Shows like *My So-Called Life*, *Blossom*, and *Gilmore Girls* give us a group of young women and teenage girls who, like their older TV counterparts, have a unique perspective and sense of themselves.

It is no longer a television novelty to see women cops and lawyers, women CEOs and soldiers. Work and motherhood are no longer mutually exclusive, even on more conservative programs. As far as we seem to have come, as with any examination of feminism, we must continually examine just how far we've come, onscreen and off, and how far we still have to go.

Examining real life can be more depressing than exploring our representation on television. Remember, women are nearly 52 percent of the population but only 8 percent of the United States Congress, paling in comparison to many other countries. Even the Muslim nation of Pakistan elected a woman prime minister, as have Canada and Great Britain. Most Scandinavian countries have an equal number of men and women in their parliaments. The good news, though, is that entertainment is inspired by and informs reality; in time, it helps us advance ideas about changing the inequalities still faced by not only women, but blacks and gays as well. Despite continued sexism and stereotyping, we can still revel in the gains we've made and ensure that this progress continues.

Today, feminism, in its many forms, is rarely mentioned explicitly on TV because many of its tenets have been accepted as norms. Most women, even those who refuse to call themselves feminists, believe in the most general doctrine of women's liberation: legal, political, and financial equality. This status quo makes it appear as though feminism has disappeared from TV altogether. When television executives pitch programs today, a series about a woman detective or politician is no longer met with the same sexist assumptions it would have been fifty years ago. Nevertheless, I am confident that, nine times out of ten, casting women for television shows is still nearly as offensive as casting cover models for *Maxim*. After all, TV executives had their hearts set on offering the part of Murphy Brown to bombshell Heather Locklear. Candice Bergen—a former model herself—had to fight for the part, and I can't say how happy I am that the executives eventually went with a woman with an average bra size. Regardless of the Barbie-doll cosmetically enhanced actresses cast for shows like *Buffy the Vampire Slayer* and *Alias,* at least we *have* shows in which women kick ass the way their male counterparts always have on television.

This is not to say that there is no more work to do; quite the contrary. Women's issues today differ from those we faced during the '60s and '70s, but the representations of women on television (and in other forms of mass media) will always require monitoring by those of us who believe women have more to offer the world than a pair of purchased breasts and the ability to shake our asses in front of a camera. Ratings may still be king, but more realistic female characters have claimed some rights to the throne and will most likely continue to do so. During the 2005 television season, ABC even gave us a woman president, incarnated by Geena Davis, in the drama *Commander In Chief.* In 2006, a show titled

Courting Alex premiered. In it, Jenna Elfman (formerly Dharma on *Dharma & Greg*) plays the successful head of a law firm. And *Seinfeld*'s Julia Louis-Dreyfus is trying her hand at sitcoms again (her first show after *Seinfeld* unfortunately failed) with the depiction of a modern, divorced working mother in *The New Adventures of Old Christine*. As with any new TV show, success isn't guaranteed, but with each new season, TV will continue to create women characters who are trying to live in the same postfeminist age as real women—juggling work, kids, and ex-husbands. Although many TV women (and real ones alike) take feminism as a given, it was Mary Richards who paved the road for us, throwing her hat in the air and, as cliché as it seems today, telling us that every woman can "make it after all."

How Far Have We Come?

MARY: I could've married him. Can you imagine what that life would've been like?

LOU: You feel good now?

MARY: No, I don't feel good. But I feel lucky.

—The Mary Tyler Moore Show

The television business is always introducing new series that essentially emulate the success of previous shows. When a network has a hit, it does everything to keep it running, keep viewers watching, keep bringing in more advertising dollars, and keep creating new shows based upon the same formula of that first hit—if it worked once, it may work again. In addition, the networks tend to compete with each other by trying to "copy" the successful series on other networks. The network with the success usually tries to create "spin-off" shows, featuring characters already familiar to the viewing public.

Some of the best shows on television have been created this way. For instance, *The Mary Tyler Moore Show,* a consistent example of intelligent programming that also garnered huge audiences, birthed two spin-offs: *Rhoda* in 1974 and *Phyllis* in 1975. *Maude* was a spin-off of *All in the Family,* and, in turn, created a spin-off of its own when the Findlays' housekeeper, Florida Evans, was given her own family sitcom, *Good Times.* Obviously, some of these shows have characters that are strong enough and likable enough to carry their own shows and move on to success; others do not. (*The Golden Girls* spin-off, *The Golden Palace,* did not fare well.) Like everything involved with television production and programming, creating TV shows is a crapshoot. Sometimes new shows are winners. More often than not, whether they are new shows or spin-offs, they are off the air before you can say "commercial break." In the endless cycle to fill prime-time airtime, more shows have come and gone than any of us can remember. That is why the ones that do make it and are met with either critical or commercial success (or both) are seen as the all-stars, and every network wants an all-star.

Since 1970, the first year that feminism openly showed its

face on television, we have seen great strides made for women on and off television. Mary Richards put a face, voice, and personality to the "career woman" of the seventies. The character is a compromise between traditional womanhood and feminism. Mary is a nurturer, generally soft-spoken, and takes on an almost maternal role at the television station where she works. As career women go, she is a great role model because she isn't a ballbuster or at all unlikable. This makes her both unthreatening to the men she works with as well as to the male audiences that watch her. At the time the show aired, Mary was also similar to many women in America. It would have been inconceivable for the first overtly feminist show to feature a woman like Maude, Roseanne, or Murphy Brown. Women's liberation had to be more generally accepted before television could trot out its most vehement feminists. As with any social change, it doesn't only occur slowly, but needs time to let audiences get used to the idea that a woman in her thirties would shun marriage for work and could create a fulfilling life on her own, without a man or husband.

The great thing about Mary was because she wasn't threatening, she was able to gain strength and confidence during the course of the series. In one episode, she even refers to herself as the "woman with the big mouth." She knows she must stand up for herself when she has to, just as she did in the interview scene with Mr. Grant in the pilot episode. But she also becomes the den mother for the makeshift family she creates at work. To me, this idea was revolutionary for 1970, although it wasn't until much later that I realized how important it was for Mary to be on her own, celebrating her independence, and to create a support group of friends who helped her as much as she helped them. When I became a "career girl" myself, living independently in New York City, I did much the same thing. My friends and I carved out our own versions of a family and support system in the wake of feminism, knowing that having husbands "take care" of us was not an option. Mary led the way for those of my generation to live out the dreams our mothers never could; she also blazed the feminist trail on television for a multitude of feminist TV icons that helped inspire viewers to push the limits of what women could do.

Murphy Brown was the woman Mary would have been had she grown up watching career women on television. The women I knew growing up were wives and mothers, excluding the occasional teacher or nurse. At that time a woman's job was to run her home, but not necessarily her life. Baby boomers lived for quite a long time with such traditional messages, and it took a special type of person to break out of the mother-wife suburban mold. In her book about the history of women intellectuals in our country, Elaine Showalter discusses her own experiences growing up before the effects of feminism:

> I have put some of my own history into this book, in places where it intersects with the history of feminism in our time. And as I've studied the lives of my heroines, of course I've also asked whether these patterns describe and help explain phases in my own life. I never met a feminist when

*I was growing up. I never met a "career girl," as she would
have been called in the forties and fifties. None of the
women in my huge extended family—aunts, cousins, cousins
once or twice removed—had a job outside her home.*[1]

I, too, have connected the experiences of the women I
saw on TV with the changes I saw growing up—when feminism was not just an idea, but a movement that was allowing
more and more women to explore areas traditionally reserved
for men. By the time *Murphy Brown* aired, its heroine *could*
be the ballbusting "Mike Wallace in a dress" who may have
made some sacrifices in her personal life, but took great pride
in her successful career.

Reclaiming the "F-Word"

Though America has been dramatically changed by feminism,
the word itself has been redefined in ways that obscure and
denigrate its true meaning. Many women today would be
loath to call themselves feminists, an unappealing term that
has in essence become the "f-word." I never balk at calling
myself a feminist. I feel that the word defines our desire to
have the same equality and opportunities as men. The term
also reminds us that options previously denied us are now
available. In a particularly poignant episode of *Friends*, Rachel
faces her mother's jealousy and unhappiness with Rachel's
own independence and freedom. The contrast between mother
and daughter is striking. Rachel decided not to marry a suc-

cessful doctor, wanting instead to live on her own, even though that means being a waitress and facing the challenges and frustrations any twentysomething feels when she leaves her parents' home for the "real world." Her mother, on the other hand, acquiesced to the mores of her generation. The episode captures the effects of feminism in our lives.

Rachel is nervous about her mother seeing the life she is living on her own, but receives a completely unexpected response from her.

> **JOEY:** I can't believe you're so uptight about your mom comin'.
>
> **RACHEL:** I know, but it's just . . . it's the first time, and I just don't want her to think that because I didn't marry Barry, that my life is total crap, you know?
>
> **MRS. GREEN:** *(Entering the coffee shop)* There she is.
>
> **RACHEL:** Mom!
>
> **MRS. GREEN:** Sweetie! So this is where you work? Oh, it's wonderful! Is it a living room? Is it a restaurant? Who can tell? But I guess that's the fun.
>
> **RACHEL:** Pretty much.
>
> **MRS. GREEN:** So, what do you think of my daughter in the apron with the big job?
>
> **RACHEL:** Oh, Mom!
>
> **MRS. GREEN:** If you didn't pour the coffee, no one would have anything to drink.

CHANDLER: Believe me, sometimes that happens.

MRS. GREEN: This is just so exciting. You know, I never worked. I went straight from my father's house to the sorority house to my husband's house. I am just so proud of you.

RACHEL: Really?

MRS. GREEN: Yes.

Later Mrs. Green is spending time with the girls at their apartment. She is not only happy for her daughter's independence, but seems to feel that the life Rachel is living is one that she herself is sad, to have had.

MRS. GREEN: *(Laughing)* You have *some* life here, sweetie.

RACHEL: I know. And Mom, I realize you and Daddy were upset when I didn't marry Barry and get the big house in the suburbs with all the security and everything, but this is just so much better for me, you know?

MRS. GREEN: I do. You didn't love Barry. And I've never seen you this happy. I look at you and I think, *Oh, this is what I want.*

RACHEL: For . . . me.

MRS. GREEN: Well, not just for you.

RACHEL: Well, what do you mean?

MRS. GREEN: I'm, uh, considering leaving your father.

Rachel discusses the issue with her friends and cannot believe that she was fearful that her mother would not approve of her life, when in fact she feels Rachel made the right choice.

ROSS: And you had no idea they weren't getting along?

RACHEL: None.

JOEY: They didn't fight a lot?

RACHEL: No! They didn't even talk to each other. God, how was I supposed to know they were having problems? I just can't believe this is happening. I mean, when I was little, everybody's parents were getting divorced. I just figured as a grownup I wouldn't have to worry about this.

MONICA: Is there any chance that you can look at this as flattering? I mean, she's doing it because she wants to be more like you.

RACHEL: Well, then, you know, couldn't she have just copied my haircut?

CHANDLER: You know, it's funny; when my parents got divorced, they sent me to this shrink, and she told me that all kids have a tendency to blame themselves. But in your case it's actually kinda true.

Rachel tries to process the fact that her parents' marriage may be over. She realizes how close she came to becoming the dissatisfied woman that her mother admits to being.

MRS. GREEN: This is so much fun, just the girls. You know what we should do? Does anybody have any marijuana?

RACHEL: God!

MONICA: All right, look, nobody's smoking pot around all this food.

MRS. GREEN: That's fine. I never did it. I just thought I might. So, what's new in sex?

RACHEL: Oh! What's new in sex?

MRS. GREEN: The only man I've ever been with is your father.

MONICA: *(Cutting vegetables in the kitchen area)* I'm dicing . . . I'm dicing . . . I don't hear anything.

MRS. GREEN: I mean, this is no offense to your dad, sweetie, but I was thinking there might be more.

RACHEL: Oh, I'm sorry. You know what? I cannot have this conversation with you. I mean, God, you just come in here, and drop this bomb on me, before you even tell Daddy. What? What do you want? Do you want my blessing?

MRS. GREEN: No.

RACHEL: You want me to talk you out of it?

MRS. GREEN: No.

RACHEL: Then what? What do you want?

MRS. GREEN: I guess I just figured of all people you would understand this.

RACHEL: Why on earth would I understand this?

MRS. GREEN: You didn't marry your Barry. I did.

RACHEL: Oh.[2]

The Future of Women on Prime Time

Many TV seasons have been heralded as "The Year of the Woman." Often, this title is laughable, as there are few new shows featuring women. In fact, in the '80s nearly four out of five characters on television were male. Miraculously, that didn't prevent us from getting some great women characters. That said, I would much rather have had Roseanne and Murphy Brown to inspire me than today's *Sex and the City* women. It is not that I don't like Carrie, Samantha, Miranda, and Charlotte. They just don't possess the same strength as Roseanne and Murphy. We live in a time when women are conflicted about everything from career choices to relationships to sexual freedom. We take for granted many rights and freedoms. TV's feminists, such as Maude, Roseanne, and Murphy Brown, have helped usher in an era in which women characters rarely need to explicitly acknowledge feminism. This historical force paves the way for women, like the friends on *Sex and the City,* to take their careers and independence for granted, and address the more personal issues women face.

To me, Roseanne, a feminist raising a son, represents the real experience of a woman who has to work and is uniquely verbal about the inequality between men and women—how much more work she has to do versus her husband.

> **ROSEANNE:** Me and your dad are exactly equal in this house. You know why? Because that's the way I want it![3]

In Roseanne's marriage and family, everyone has accepted the fact that Roseanne is in charge and that she should be. She was being the most capable wife and mother we had seen on TV for quite some time. As a working-class woman, Roseanne doesn't have the choices of, say, the women of *Sex and the City*. She is, however, more in charge of her relationships than those women seem to be. While it's hardly fair to compare TV women from different times and generations, Roseanne serves as a role model for women dealing with the real problems of financial struggle, finding time for your family and for yourself, and always having to compromise. It's a dose of realism that TV women in later years seem to sidestep.

I don't feel that all our TV women should be Roseanne or Murphy Brown, but I honor the history of our collective TV past and realize that there would not have been a woman president on television in 2005 without those trailblazers. If no one ever acknowledged the fallacy of the fifties' idealized nuclear family, the satire of *Desperate Housewives* would not be as funny and so easy for audiences to relate to. The greatest thing about that show is that it peers behind those perfect picket-fenced homes and exposes the unhappiness, deviance, and problems that were never acknowledged in early family series. When the show's narrator explains that she always worked to "polish her home to a gleaming shine"—before she commits suicide—it is women like Roseanne who help us understand the nature of the facade. *Roseanne* is so appealing precisely because it doesn't do what the women on Wisteria Lane do; it doesn't hide the imperfections in the Conner home, marriage, children, and lives.

We can hope for future prime-time sitcoms to present women we can be proud of and relate to. Sadly, those women seem to appear only once or twice a decade. The icons of history are few and far between in life and on television. Elaine Showalter points out that "as we come to the end of a century in which women have made enormous gains, we still lack a sense of the feminist past."[5]

I have done my best to honor the feminist past on television because TV, historically directed toward women audiences, is a part of our past, and generation after generation watches more and more television. The images we see, both good and bad, stay with us, and we have the choice to pick and choose what to be proud of from pop culture past. I am certainly proud of TV's feminists and know many other women who have been inspired by the girls and women they have invited into their homes through the television screen.

What Would Murphy Brown Do?

I think about what Murphy Brown would do in a variety of real-life situations, because I feel that too often, women get the short end of the stick, and I would like to help level the playing field between the sexes. That includes establishing equality in work, pay, law, and politics, as well as in our personal lives. Thirty-five years after the women's movement got off the ground, the personal is still political. Women still face discrimination, violence, and a host of difficulties that simply don't affect men in the same way.

Because she is my measure of strength, I ask myself what Murphy would do. Within our collective television past, each of us can find a character trait from which to draw inspiration—whether it's Roseanne's acerbic toughness or Rachel Green's haircut. We can look to our entertainment for clues about the direction in which our society is moving. We may not always be happy with TV's depiction of women, but we can all rest assured that the stereotypes of June Cleaver and *Charlie's Angels* are only one part of a much larger context. Women as accessories will continue to be featured on TV with every new television season, but we'll find our new icons too. When I think of future generations of girls and women, I think of Susan Douglas's hopes for her daughter and the popular culture she will see and take in throughout her lifetime:

> *I don't believe I can insulate my daughter from the mass media, nor do I want to. There are pleasures there for her, ones she already knows and ones she will learn. The*

sitcoms, records, magazines, and movies she grows up with will form, for better and for worse, the culture she will share with other people she barely knows. . . . I will try to teach her to be a resistant, back-talking, bullshit-detecting media consumer, and to treasure the strong, funny, subversive women she does get to see. . . . This, at least, is my hope. For she will see with her eyes and feel in her spirit that despite all this, women are not helpless victims, they are fighters. And she will want to be a fighter too.[6]

If one day I have a daughter of my own, I will also teach her to "read" the images she sees, the way my mother did for me. With her guidance, I learned to recognize programs and media that meant to scare women back into subservience, just as I learned to celebrate women like Murphy Brown, who was a great fighter and helped make me one as well.

Appendix

Women Behind the Scenes

At the same time that women in the '70s were blazing a trail on the TV screen, so were the women behind the scenes. While male writers generally outnumber women five to one in the film industry, the ratio is three to one in television. In addition, there is "only" a small wage gap (5 percent) between men and women TV writers.[1] The same cannot be said for the much larger wage gaps between men and women in other industries (sometimes 25 percent). Of course, we can legitimately argue that no wage gap is justified, and that there aren't enough women working in TV or film, but we have to take our gains where we can get them. In fact, there are a large number of successful women in television. Marcy Carsey, one of the most accomplished TV producers in history, along with her partner, Tom Werner, created television monoliths like *The Cosby Show* and *Roseanne* and produced countless others, including *3rd Rock from the Sun* and *That '70s Show*. The list of successful women in television also includes Marta Kaufman (cocreator of *Friends*), Diane English (creator of *Murphy Brown*), and Amy Sherman-Palladino (producer of *Gilmore Girls, Veronica's Closet,* and *Roseanne*). TV veteran Susan Harris began writing on *All in the Family* and went on to create the show *Soap*. She also wrote the infamous *Maude* abortion episode and won a 1987 Emmy for *The Golden Girls*. If that isn't enough, she is one of the founding partners of the highly successful Witt/Thomas/Harris Productions.

Many people believe that women are different from men and thus bring a different sensibility to the workplace. Harry Thomason describes his wife and creative partner, Linda Bloodworth-Thomason (the two are cocreators and executive producers of *Designing Women* and *Evening Shade*), as "much more interested in ideas; I'm more interested in details."[2] Sometimes, in their own unique way, women transform the workplace. Tom Werner explains what partner Marcy Carsey brings to the table: "I was at an extremely male-oriented network, and I think that most workplace relationships are more about competition and ego than about doing the job well. My relationship with Marcy has always been about doing good work, having fun, caring for each other, and positive reinforcement. At the network, it was more about 'You didn't do this' or

'We have to increase our sales this month by X percent,' which seemed more of a male idea."[3] Roseanne describes it this way: "Today you can't tell the difference between something produced by a woman and things produced by a man, and it disturbs me. When women's voices sound like men's, then women have effectively been censored."[4]

Women in television, as in any field, must pay their dues. CBS executive Sunta Izzicupo reveals that "women do not have for the most part meteoric rises. Women have to prove themselves to men. And the women I know have had to have every job along the way. You don't just show up as a vice president. Often the steps that men don't have to go through, we do twice. We skip nothing."[5] This is true for most career fields, as journalist and author Anna Quindlen notes: "The other day, a very wise friend of mine asked: 'Have you ever noticed that what passes as a terrific man would only be an adequate woman?' . . . She was absolutely right."[6]

The women who have thus far proven themselves in the television field are extremely impressive. Take, for instance, the first all-female front line in the control room. On the hit CBS show *The Nanny*, women held the positions of director, technical director, associate director, and script supervisor; more than half of the producers were women, including the star of the show, Fran Drescher.[7] Additionally, Linda Bloodworth-Thomason is the first American writer in television history, male or female, to write thirty-five consecutive episodes of a series. I call *that* impressive.

Appendix

Prime-Time Refresher[1]

Alice

First Airdate: August 31, 1976

Last Airdate: July 2, 1985

Network: CBS

Cast:

Linda Lavin as Alice Hyatt

Philip McKeon as Tommy Hyatt

Vic Tayback as Mel Sharples

Polly Holliday as Florence Jean "Flo" Castleberry

Beth Howland as Vera Louise Gorman

The sitcom *Alice* was based on the film *Alice Doesn't Live Here Anymore,* which told the story of a widowed single mother and aspiring singer who takes a job as a waitress at a diner. The TV show was one of the first sitcoms that addressed the trials and tribulations of a working mom with a teenage son. At Mel's Diner, Alice befriended her coworkers, Flo, a Southerner who spoke her mind with rare censorship ("Kiss my grits" was her trademark phrase), and shy, naive Vera. The diner was owned by gruff and narrow-minded Mel Sharples, who, deep down, loved the women who waited tables at his diner.

The character of Alice was strong, independent, and levelheaded, providing a great contrast to her coworkers. The show marked the progress women had made in the '70s by featuring a single, working-class mother who never gave up on her own dreams. In fact, the series finale found Alice leaving her Mel's Diner "family" to finally live out her dream as the lead singer of a band in Nashville.

All in the Family

First Airdate: January 12, 1971

Last Airdate: January 25, 1979

Network: CBS

Cast:

Carroll O'Conner as Archie Bunker

Jean Stapleton as Edith Bunker

Sally Struthers as Gloria Bunker Stivic

Rob Reiner as Mike "Meathead" Stivic

Though not a particularly feminist sitcom, *All in the Family* is emblematic of the changes occurring during the 1970s as the women's movement was taking place.

Whether you loved or hated Archie, who incessantly referred to his wife as "dingbat" and made racist comments about friends and neighbors, the show was groundbreaking in its ability to address very serious topics with humor and frankness. The show wasn't all Archie ranting against women, blacks, and immigrants, however. Over the course of the series, wife Edith went through menopause, a first for TV at that time, was nearly raped in one episode, and increasingly learned to stand up to her insensitive husband.

Norman Lear, the creator of the show, whom many believe changed the format of the sitcom forever, was no sexist himself. It was Lear who created one of the most feminist characters in TV history. Maude, played by Bea Arthur, first appeared on the small screen as Edith Bunker's cousin. In 1972, she would go on to have her own successful series.

Ally McBeal

First Airdate: September 8, 1997

Last Airdate: May 20, 2002

Network: Fox

Cast:

Calista Flockhart as Ally McBeal

Courtney Thorne-Smith as Georgia Thomas

Greg Germann as Richard Fish

Lisa Nicole Carson as Renee Raddick

Jane Krakowski as Elaine Vassal

Gil Bellows as Billy Thomas

Portia de Rossi as Nell Porter

Peter MacNicol as John Cage

Lucy Liu as Ling Woo

Ally McBeal, as a television series, became inextricably linked to two terms: *dramedy* and *postfeminism.* The hour-long show, about a neurotic Boston attorney, was part comedy, part drama. Ally struggled with her work life, her personal life, and her fantasy life, and the latter was often portrayed in the show through dream sequences and character voiceovers. Much of the drama and comedy on the show was garnered from Ally's ability to make remarkably poor decisions—as so many real women do—such as her decision, in the show's pilot, to take a job at a law firm where her childhood sweetheart also worked.

When they weren't addressing Calista Flockhart's weight (the actress was bone-thin), the media scrutinized the show, labeling Ally as a representative of a new kind of feminism—one in which women saw having a career as a given but struggled endlessly with the more private aspects of their lives: sex, love, insecurity, loneliness, and mother-hood. The series, whether women considered it feminist or not, undeniably addressed many of the struggles real working women faced—and did so using both humor and pathos.

Cagney & Lacey

First Airdate: March 25, 1982
Last Airdate: May 16, 1988
Network: CBS
Cast:
Tyne Daly as Mary Beth Lacey
Sharon Gless as Chris Cagney
Al Waxman as Bert Samuels
Carl Lumbly as Mark Petrie
Martin Kove as Victor Isbecki
Sidney Clute as Paul La Guardia

Cagney & Lacey was one of the first police shows featuring a law-enforcement partnership between two female detectives. The show was an overtly feminist creation—the two main characters consistently addressed the sexism of their coworkers, the uniqueness of being a female cop, and the intricacies of their personal lives: Lacey was married, and Cagney was single.

The series is most famous not for what viewers saw on the show but for their reaction to its cancellation. CBS dropped the series in 1983 and faced an onslaught of angry women viewers who championed the program. Amid protests and media attention as well as an Emmy win, CBS succumbed and brought the show back. Even today, it serves as a reminder that women viewers are indeed a powerful bunch.

Caroline in the City

First Airdate: September 21, 1995

Last Airdate: April 26, 1999

Network: NBC

Cast:

Lea Thompson as Caroline Duffy

Malcolm Gets as Richard Karinsky

Eric Lutes as Del Cassidy

Amy Pietz as Annie Spadaro

Andy Lauer as Charlie

Caroline in the City, a sitcom based on the creator of a female-centered comic strip called *Caroline in the City,* essentially followed the personal and love life of a young successful urban woman. It rarely dealt with her work and focused more commonly on her love life, but the show also explored her relationship with her best friend, Annie, her ex-boyfriend, Del, and the complicated, burgeoning romance between Caroline and her illustrator, Richard. Though the show was not overtly feminist, it still followed a successful, independent woman through the early years of her life.

The Cosby Show

First Airdate: September 20, 1984

Last Airdate: September 17, 1992

Network: NBC

Cast:

Bill Cosby as Dr. Heathcliff "Cliff" Huxtable

Phylicia Rashad as Clair Huxtable

Sabrina Le Beauf as Sondra Huxtable

Lisa Bonet as Denise Huxtable

Malcolm-Jamal Warner as Theodore Huxtable

Tempestt Bledsoe as Vanessa Huxtable

Keshia Knight Pulliam as Rudy Huxtable

Generally considered the most successful sitcom of the 1980s, *The Cosby Show* was a typical family sitcom with a few twists. Bill Cosby's character, Cliff, was an obstetrician, and wife Clair was a lawyer. Both were highly involved in their children's lives. Cliff and Clair were equals. In fact, it was Cliff who worked at home, establishing his office in the basement of the family's New York brownstone, and successful attorney Clair who left the home each day to head to her office.

Cybill

First Airdate: January 2, 1995

Last Airdate: July 13, 1998

Network: CBS

Cast:

Cybill Shepherd as Cybill Sheridan

Christine Baranski as Maryann Thorpe

Tom Wopat as Jeff Robbins

Dedee Pfeiffer as Rachel Blanders

Alicia Witt as Zoey Woodbine

Alan Rosenberg as Ira Woodbine

Cybill, a sitcom, followed the ups and downs of an over-forty actress who happened to have two daughters and two ex-husbands.

The show was unique in that Cybill was still friendly with her exes and struggled with aspects of aging, especially as an actress in Hollywood. The show addressed themes seen rarely on prime time. Over the course of the series, Cybill lost acting jobs to younger women, dated all kinds of men, and became a grandmother. As sitcoms go, the show included some very unique characters and was overtly feminist as Cybill continually fought the stereotypes so often heaped onto middle-aged women.

The Days and Nights of Molly Dodd

First Airdate: May 21, 1987

Last Airdate: April 13, 1991

Network: NBC (1987–1988)

Lifetime (1989–1991)

Cast:

Blair Brown as Molly Dodd

Allyn Ann McLerie as Florence Bickford

William Converse-Roberts as Fred Dodd

Sandy Faison as Mamie Grolnick

James Greene as Davey McQuinn

Victor Garber as Dennis Widmer

This drama was a big hit with female audiences; the show followed a pensive thirtysomething divorcee living in New York City. Molly was a precursor to Ally McBeal, but Molly wasn't nearly as successful in the workplace. She had a number of jobs over the course of the series, but she fretted equally over romance, success, and life in general. One of the biggest successes of the show was that after its cancellation from NBC, the women's network, Lifetime, picked up the show and even produced new episodes to please an audience of women who wanted to watch Molly's life each week.

Designing Women

First Airdate: September 29, 1986

Last Airdate: May 24, 1993

Network: CBS

Cast:

Dixie Carter as Julia Sugarbaker

Annie Potts as Mary Jo Shively

Delta Burke as Suzanne Sugarbaker

Jean Smart as Charlene Frazier Stillfield

Meshach Taylor as Anthony Bouvier

The sitcom *Designing Women* followed four women who ran an interior design firm in Atlanta. The show wasn't simply feminist; it made a feminist statement. These women were outspoken and owned and operated their own successful business. The four women themselves were quite different: Julia Sugarbaker, the head of the business and the best orator this side of the Mississippi, was always making a speech in defense of women, against sexism, or regarding current politics. Her sister, Suzanne, was a former beauty queen and unabashedly superficial. Mary Jo was a divorced single mother, and Charlene embodied the sweet, naive Southerner. The show addressed a range of issues of concern to women head-on—from the Anita Hill hearings to body image and PMS.

Dharma & Greg

First Airdate: September 24, 1997

Last Airdate: April 30, 2002

Network: ABC

Cast:

Jenna Elfman as Dharma Finkelstein

Thomas Gibson as Greg Montgomery

Mimi Kennedy as Abby O'Neil

Alan Rachins as Larry Finkelstein

Susan Sullivan as Kitty Montgomery

Mitchell Ryan as Edward Montgomery

Shae D'lyn as Jane Cavanaugh

Joel Murray as Pete Cavanaugh

Dharma & Greg was a sitcom that explored the question of what life would be like if a free-spirited hippie married a San Francisco blue-blood attorney. The show demonstrated that women and men could bridge their differences without either side losing power or integrity. It also illustrated many of the compromises married couples must face, whether from similar backgrounds or not.

Ellen

First Airdate: March 30, 1994

Last Airdate: July 29, 1998

Network: ABC

Cast:

Ellen DeGeneres as Ellen Morgan

Joely Fisher as Paige Clark

Arye Gross as Adam Green

Clea Lewis as Audrey Penney

Jeremy Piven as Spence Kovak

David Anthony Higgins as Joe Farrell

The beginning of this sitcom, created for standup comic Ellen

DeGeneres, was marked by some cast changes and even a name change. It was originally called *These Friends of Mine*. As that title suggests, the show revolved around a Los Angeles woman, Ellen Morgan, and her gang of friends: Paige, an adventurous movie executive; Adam, a dorky photographer; Audrey, an annoying hanger-on, and Spence, Ellen's neurotic cousin. Though the show's early days were a little unstable, it eventually came into its own as Ellen morphed into a business owner, buying her own bookstore and dealing with her friends' love lives.

Though Ellen dated men throughout the series (with little luck), a source of much humor was found in the character's coming out as a lesbian and her traditional parents' ensuing disappointment. This was groundbreaking: She had some lesbian relationships on the show, including one with celebrity Laura Dern, who appeared in a cameo as the object of Ellen's crush. At the same time, actress Ellen DeGeneres also came out, and the media went wild. The focus moved from the character Ellen to the actress Ellen, and that proved to be the undoing of the show. After four seasons, it was canceled. *Ellen* will always remain an important piece of television history. (Ellen DeGeneres went on to host her own successful talk show.)

Family Ties

First Airdate: September 22, 1982

Last Airdate: September 17, 1989

Network: NBC

Cast:

Meredith Baxter Birney as Elyse Keaton

Michael Gross as Steven Keaton

Michael J. Fox as Alex P. Keaton

Justine Bateman as Mallory Keaton

Tina Yothers as Jennifer Keaton

Marc Price as Erwin "Skippy" Handelman

This sitcom is still one of the most memorable family sitcoms of the 1980s. The Keaton parents were progressive—once hippies in the '60s, they now found themselves "grown up" with a family. Providing much fodder for humor, that family included an ultraconservative son in the form of Alex P. Keaton, a Reagan- and Nixon-loving Republican. Alex's politics were in sharp contrast to his parents, who were trying to hold on to their age-of-Aquarius ideals during the superficial '80s.

One unique aspect of the show was the relationship between parents Elyse and Steven. Elyse, an architect, was the main breadwinner, and Steven worked for public television. The show refuted the idea that men still financially dominated the dual-income couple. Filling out the cast were teenager and clotheshorse Mallory and wisecracking younger sister Jennifer. The show exemplified the difficulties of a decade in which women were trying to be "superwomen" both at home and at work.

Friends

First Airdate: September 22, 1994

Last Airdate: May 6, 2004

Network: NBC

Cast:

Jennifer Aniston as Rachel Green

Courteney Cox as Monica Geller

Lisa Kudrow as Phoebe Buffay

Matt LeBlanc as Joey Tribbiani

Matthew Perry as Chandler Bing

David Schwimmer as Ross Geller

One of the most successful sitcoms of the 1990s—and possibly ever—followed six twentysomethings in New York City as they sought to establish everything from their careers to their love lives and friendships. Each character had his or her own story when the show began: Ross was divorcing a pregnant lesbian, Rachel ran out on her own wedding, Monica was working toward becoming a chef, Chandler hated being a corporate drone, Phoebe expressed her hippie attitude and worked as a masseuse, and Joey was a dim but attractive wannabe actor.

Over the course of the series, the characters grew up. They got married, had children, found new careers, or achieved new heights in the ones they already had—leaning on each other for support and friendship throughout. The show's immense popularity created a genre of its own: the twentysomething urban angst sitcom.

Girlfriends

First Airdate: September 11, 2000

Network: UPN

Cast:

Tracee Ellis Ross as Joan Clayton

Golden Brooks as Maya Wilkes

Jill Marie Jones as Toni Childs-Garrett

Persia White as Lynn Searcy

Reggie Hayes as William Dent

This show follows the love lives of four black women and is often referred to as "the black *Sex and the City*." The women on the show are strong, independent, and successful, yet often at a loss about their romantic encounters. Thus, they do what all women do: They talk frankly to each other and dissect the actions of the men in their lives. Like so many sitcoms based on female friendship, the women stick together, support each other, and, like in so many sitcoms, use humor to address women's real fears, difficulties, and successes.

The Golden Girls

First Airdate: September 14, 1985

Last Airdate: September 14, 1992

Network: NBC

Cast:

Bea Arthur as Dorothy Zbornak

Betty White as Rose Nylund

Rue McClanahan as Blanche Devereaux

Estelle Getty as Sophia Petrillo

This successful sitcom took the typical women's friendship-based series and changed one main thing: The women roommates were all in their fifties and older. Dorothy, played by eminent comedian Bea Arthur, served as the mature, levelheaded character amid her wacky roomies. These roomies included Rose, the naive, small-town widow; Blanche, the man-hungry diva; and Dorothy's wisecracking mother, Sophia.

The show not only was successful but demonstrated that women who weren't in their twenties or a size 2 could still be vital, funny, sexy, and irreverent.

Good Times

First Airdate: February 1, 1974

Last Airdate: August 1, 1979

Network: CBS

Cast:

Esther Rolle as Florida Evans

John Amos as James Evans

Jimmie Walker as James "J.J." Evans Jr.

Ralph Carter as Michael Evans

BernNadette Stanis as Thelma Evans

Ja'net DuBois as Willona Woods

Good Times, a spin-off from the show *Maude*, followed a working-class black Chicago couple and their three children. Florida and James were the parents of two teenagers, wacky J.J. and self-involved Thelma. The show was rounded out by sweet son Michael and Florida's best friend and neighbor, Willona. The story line demonstrated the difficulties black families faced in the '70s as James moved from job to job and Florida worked hard both in and out of the home.

Grace Under Fire

First Airdate: September 29, 1993

Last Airdate: February 17, 1998

Network: ABC

Cast:

Brett Butler as Grace Kelly

Julie White as Nadine Swoboda

Casey Sander as Wade Swoboda

Dave Thomas as Russell Norton

Geoff Pierson as Jimmy Kelly

Grace Under Fire, a vehicle for comic Brett Butler, was a sit-com based on a very serious concept: a single mother who escaped an abusive husband. Butler's southern drawl and dry humor helped create a show that consciously addressed some of the very real problems women face, from single parenting and job discrimination to alcoholism. The character of Grace was strong, outspoken, and adept at just "being one of the guys." At the same time, she did all the things women "should not"—resisted authority, worked men's jobs, and raised children without the help of a man.

Grace had been through a lot in her life, including surviving an abusive husband, abandoning dreams of writing, giving up a child for adoption, and working to improve her life and the lives of her children. In this working-class comedy, Grace worked in an oil refinery, where she addressed real women's issues with Butler's dark humor and snappy one-liners. As TV women go, Grace was a memorable feminist, mother, and worker.

Kate & Allie

First Airdate: March 19, 1984

Last Airdate: September 11, 1989

Network: CBS

Cast:

Jane Curtin as Allie Lowell

Susan Saint James as Kate McArdle

Ari Meyers as Emma McArdle

Frederick Koehler as Chip Lowell

Allison Smith as Jennie Lowell

The sitcom *Kate & Allie* addressed a common theme in the 1980s: the life of the divorcée with children. This show, though, changed the formula of a divorced man and woman coming together (like in *The Brady Bunch*) by exploring what life would be like if two divorced women and their children all lived together in New York City. One of the few shows actually filmed in New York, the urban setting was background for a friendship so strong that it imitated a marriage.

Kate and Allie, best friends since high school and both divorced, were very different from each other, a source of both friction and comedy. Kate was strong, independent, and career-driven. She was easygoing in the raising of her only daughter, Emma, and contrasted sharply with Allie's traditional, uptight, sweater-set ways. Allie's daughter, Jennie, and son, Chip, offered up the typical sitcom-kid problems, but with varying responses from Kate and Allie. The idea that two very different women could make a life for themselves (when life didn't turn out the way they thought it would) was progressive and offered up hope, suggesting that divorce didn't have to ruin a woman's life but instead could be a catalyst in creating a whole new one.

Laverne & Shirley

First Airdate: January 27, 1976

Last Airdate: May 10, 1983

Network: ABC

Cast:

Penny Marshall as Laverne De Fazio

Cindy Williams as Shirley Feeney

Eddie Mekka as Carmine Ragusa

Phil Foster as Frank De Fazio

David L. Lander as Andrew "Squiggy" Squiggman

Michael McKean as Lenny Kosnowski

This sitcom was a spin-off of the popular show *Happy Days*, and it featured two best friends living together in the 1950s and '60s. Laverne and Shirley worked at a bottling factory, surrounded by predominantly male coworkers. They also lived together in a basement apartment, where they were often interrupted by their strange and annoying neighbors, Lenny and Squiggy.

Though the show rarely dealt with any serious issues— much of the comedy was slapstick—the friendship between Laverne and Shirley was something audiences could count on. Through their fights, dates, mistakes, and achievements, it was clear that these two women would be friends forever, making it through life with determination and the support of a friend.

Living Single

First Airdate: August 22, 1993

Last Airdate: January 1, 1998

Network: Fox

Cast:

Queen Latifah as Khadijah James

Kim Coles as Synclaire James

Kim Fields Freeman as Regine Hunter

Erika Alexander as Maxine Shaw

T. C. Carson as Kyle Barker

John Henton as Overton Jones

Occasionally referred to as the "black *Designing Women*," this sitcom followed the lives of four women who live together in Brooklyn. They were all successful working women; in particular, Khadijah was the editor of a magazine aimed at black women. Synclaire, her cousin, worked as her assistant. Rounding out the roommates was the man-obsessed Regine and the intellectual Max, who was also an attorney.

Just as so many shows have done for white women, *Living Single* explored the experiences, both personal and professional, of middle-class black women struggling to find success, love, and happiness.

Mad About You

First Airdate: September 23, 1992

Last Airdate: August 5, 1999

Network: NBC

Cast:

Paul Reiser as Paul Buchman

Helen Hunt as Jamie Buchman

Anne Ramsay as Lisa Stemple

John Pankow as Ira Buchman

Leila Kenzle as Fran Devanow

Richard Kind as Dr. Mark Devanow

During the 1990s, not all sitcoms were about divorce, women's friendship, or suburban parenting. *Mad About You* was a sweet comedy about a newly married New York couple, Paul and Jamie Buchman, who were simply living their lives and learning how to be married. Created by comic Paul Reiser, the show was an attempt to explore marriage from the inside, revealing a couple's banter about both the minutiae and the big stuff.

The couple's lives included Jamie's unhinged sister, Lisa, Paul's erratic cousin, Ira, their neurotic friends, Fran and Mark, and, on occasion, the in-laws. The essence of the show was that, regardless of their differences, Paul and Jamie were on equal footing in their marriage. They argued, compromised, and supported each other through a series that eventually saw them become parents in addition to spouses. Though their daughter came later in the series, it was clear that Paul was a new kind of TV husband, one willing to help with everything, including the housework and other duties previously portrayed as "woman's work" on television.

The Mary Tyler Moore Show

First Airdate: September 19, 1970

Last Airdate: September 3, 1977

Network: CBS

Cast:

Mary Tyler Moore as Mary Richards

Edward Asner as Lou Grant

Valerie Harper as Rhoda Morgenstern

Gavin MacLeod as Murray Slaughter

Ted Knight as Ted Baxter

Cloris Leachman as Phyllis Lindstrom

Georgia Engel as Georgette Baxter

Betty White as Sue Ann Nivens

Premiering in 1970, *The Mary Tyler Moore Show* created the independent, single, working woman sitcom genre. Mary Richards had left her fiancé and moved to Minneapolis to try to make it on her own. She found an apartment and landed a job as a TV news associate producer. At WJM, she worked with a group of eccentric characters, including her closest work friend, Murray; the egotistical and dumb anchor, Ted; flaky Phyllis; and her gruff but lovable boss, producer Lou Grant. Along with her new best friend and neighbor, Rhoda, Mary decided to live her life on her own terms.

Mary Richards, for so many television viewers, represented the new opportunities opening for women during the 1970s. No longer was life preplanned with marriage and motherhood. Mary Richards is an emblem of early feminism: While she was sometimes stereotypically female in that she had trouble speaking her mind, she also made decisions—both personally and professionally—that were strong and independent.

Maude

First Airdate: September 12, 1972
Last Airdate: April 29, 1978
Network: CBS
Cast:
Beatrice Arthur as Maude Findlay
Bill Macy as Walter Findlay
Adrienne Barbeau as Carol
Conrad Bain as Arthur Harmon
Rue McClanahan as Vivian Harmon

An icon of the political and social changes of the 1970s, Maude, to this day, is one of the most consciously feminist television sitcom characters in history. Played by actress Bea Arthur, Maude Findlay, a suburban housewife, was anything but stereotypical. She had been married four times, was a mother and grandmother, and, unlike countless TV women before her, was hard as nails.

The show was a spin-off of *All in the Family*, and the dominant, outspoken Maude served as an opposing counterpart to Archie Bunker. She was equally as strong as Archie, but she was a woman, and a liberal one at that. Maude was always in control. Married to the meek Walter, Maude never had trouble speaking her mind—to anyone.

For a sitcom in the 1970s, *Maude* was way ahead of its time. It is still amazing that audiences supported a show whose controversial lead character had an abortion and a face-lift, turned fifty, faced her husband's infidelity and alcoholism, became involved in politics, and went through menopause.

Murphy Brown

First Airdate: November 14, 1988
Last Airdate: August 10, 1998
Network: CBS
Cast:
Candice Bergen as Murphy Brown
Charles Kimbrough as Jim Dial

Joe Regalbuto as Frank Fontana

Faith Ford as Corky Sherwood

Grant Shaud as Miles Silverberg

Set at a fictional TV network newsmagazine, *Murphy Brown* was a whole new kind of workplace comedy. The lead character and most successful broadcast journalist of the bunch was not only a woman, but also a complicated, flawed, and exceptional one at that. The series begins right after hard-driven, unrelenting reporter Murphy Brown completes a stint in rehab for alcoholism. Audiences were suddenly introduced to a successful woman who struggled with her demons, like everyone else.

Murphy Brown could be manipulative, calculating, and insensitive, but she was also sympathetic and lovable. No matter how much she annoyed her coworkers, they loved and supported her through everything from being uninvited to the White House to becoming a single mother and getting breast cancer.

My So-Called Life

First Airdate: August 25, 1994

Last Airdate: January 26, 1995

Network: ABC

Cast:

Claire Danes as Angela Chase

Bess Armstrong as Patty Chase

Tom Irwin as Graham Chase

Lisa Wilhoit as Danielle Chase

A. J. Langer as Rayanne Graff

Wilson Cruz as Rickie Vasquez

Devon Gummersall as Brian Krakow

Jared Leto as Jordan Catalano

Devon Odessa as Sharon Cherski

As the quintessential teen angst drama, *My So-Called Life* explored the humiliation, insecurity, and absurdity of being a teenager. The twist was that the show was narrated by a teenage girl, Angela Chase, and the events of the series were often filtered through her eyes.

The show examined the life of a typical teenager in a suburban family who was always obsessing over either her crush, Jordan, or the antics of her new friend Rayanne. Angela was abandoning old friends and discovering new ones, while opening her eyes to what went on in the world outside her traditional middle-class home.

Angela, as tortured as she seemed, was also exceptionally smart, caring, responsible, and as uncomfortable with herself as real teenage girls were. Whether she was aspiring to be a writer or skipping class for the first time, audiences watched this young girl learn how to be a woman. The short-lived show is still considered one of the best teen dramas seen in prime time and has developed a cult following.

The Nanny

First Airdate: November 3, 1993

Last Airdate: June 23, 1999

Network: CBS

Cast:

Fran Drescher as Fran Fine

Charles Shaughnessy as Maxwell Sheffield

Lauren Lane as C. C. Babcock

Daniel Davis as Niles

Nicholle Tom as Maggie Sheffield

Benjamin Salisbury as Brighton Sheffield

Madeline Zima as Grace Sheffield

Renee Taylor as Sylvia Fine

Rachel Chagall as Val Toriello

This sitcom was based on the clash of cultures that occurs between a Jewish woman from Queens takes a position as a nanny for a wealthy British theater producer and his three children. Though this sitcom featured a brash, ballsy, sometimes childish woman running a wealthy man's household, the real focus on women occurred behind the scenes. More than half the staff members of the show were women, a great stride in the production of network sitcoms.

Once & Again

First Airdate: September 21, 1999

Last Airdate: April 15, 2002

Network: ABC

Cast:

Sela Ward as Lily Manning

Billy Campbell as Rick Sammler

Jeffrey Nordling as Jake Manning

Susanna Thompson as Karen Sammler

Shane West as Eli Sammler

Julia Whelan as Grace Manning

Evan Rachel Wood as Jessie Sammler

Meredith Deane as Zoe Manning

This midlife drama, created by the team behind *thirtysomething* and *My So-Called Life,* was an attempt to examine the lives of recently divorced parents. Lily Manning, a typical suburban mom with two daughters, and Rick Sammler, a divorced dad raising two teenagers, began to fall in love. The feelings and experiences were new to both divorcées, as were the inevitable problems dating caused when there were children involved.

The constant conflicts between parents and children as well as spouses and ex-spouses attempted to realistically address the problems faced by a whole new generation of forty- and fiftysomething women who were thrust back into the dating scene and suddenly had to face the difficulties of trying to juggle new romance *and* motherhood.

One Day at a Time

First Airdate: December 16, 1975

Last Airdate: September 2, 1984

Network: CBS

Cast:

Bonnie Franklin as Ann Romano Royer

Mackenzie Phillips as Julie Cooper Horvath

Valerie Bertinelli as Barbara Cooper Royer

Pat Harrington Jr. as Dwayne Schneider

Richard Masur as David Kane

Michael Lembeck as Max Horvath

After her divorce, Ann Romano found herself living in an apartment in Indianapolis with her two teenage daughters, Julie and Barbara. Ann had been married for nearly twenty years and now had to start her life over as a single mother and an advertising executive. The show garnered much of its comedy from the typical clashes between the teen-age girls and their mother, and common fights between the teens themselves.

Over the course of the show, Ann dated various men and occasionally found herself in a serious relationship. In addition, her oldest daughter, Julie, got married while still in college, and Julie and her new husband moved in with Ann for a short time. This show was almost totally woman-centered, though much comedy was sparked by the building's handy-man, Schneider, and his endearing relationship with Ann.

Throughout, the show explored the real issues that single mothers were facing in the '70s and '80s and addressed these topics with sensitivity and humor.

Roseanne

First Airdate: October 18, 1988
Last Airdate: August 26, 1997
Network: ABC
Cast:
Roseanne as Roseanne Conner
John Goodman as Dan Conner
Lecy Goranson and Sarah Chalke as Becky Conner
Sara Gilbert as Darlene Conner
Michael Fishman as D.J. Conner
Laurie Metcalf as Jackie Harris

In a decade marked by the excess of shows like *Dynasty*, ABC acquired this working-class comedy based on the stand-up routine of Roseanne Barr, who had made a name for herself skewering the lives of housewives and mothers, referring to them as "domestic goddesses." The show was an extension of Roseanne's real working-class life as a wife and mother.

Though there were multiple plot twists over the course of the series, the essential Conner family consisted of Roseanne—wife, mother, and domestic dictator—and her husband, Dan, a construction worker and mechanic; daughter

Becky, a blond overachiever; Darlene, a brooding pre-teen; and D.J., a strange but sweet young son.

Roseanne may have achieved the remarkable success it did because the show dealt with issues many real parents must face but rarely discuss. For example, it pushed the social-standard envelope when Roseanne's boss had the first prime-time gay wedding, when Roseanne got hit on (and kissed) by another woman, and when her mother admitted that she was both an alcoholic and a lesbian.

The show made huge strides in addressing the real problems working-class American families faced. Roseanne never backed down from her assertion that, for too long, women had been handed the short end of the stick.

Sex and the City

First Airdate: June 6, 1998
Last Airdate: February 22, 2004
Network: HBO
Cast:
Sarah Jessica Parker as Carrie Bradshaw
Kim Cattrall as Samantha Jones
Kristin Davis as Charlotte York
Cynthia Nixon as Miranda Hobbes

Premiering in 1998, this HBO show broke new barriers when it came to women's frank discussions of sex and love. Blunt conversations about blow jobs, one-night stands, and the intricacies of relationships defined this show and consistently brought female audiences back from week to week. The show, partly due to its airing on cable versus network television, made huge strides in making a woman's view of sex and relationships part of the popular culture.

thirtysomething

First Airdate: September 29, 1987

Last Airdate: September 3, 1991

Network: ABC

Cast:

Ken Olin as Michael Steadman

Mel Harris as Hope Steadman

Timothy Busfield as Elliot Weston

Patricia Wettig as Nancy Weston

Melanie Mayron as Melissa Steadman

Polly Draper as Ellyn Warren

Peter Horton as Gary Shepherd

This hourlong drama is often considered a hallmark of the backlash against women in the 1980s. Set in suburban Philadelphia, *thirtysomething* followed the lives of two couples, Michael and Hope Steadman and Elliot and Nancy Weston. The Steadmans were presented as the perfect, neotraditional couple; Hope's kindness and maternal demeanor made her seem happy to change diapers and appease her anxious husband. The Westons represented the problems so many couples and women faced: how to explain divorce to children, deal with infidelity, and start a new life after a marriage dissolves.

Though many feminists chided the show for being a throwback to 1950s-era gender stereotyping (e.g., all the nonmarried characters were neurotic and miserable), there were occasional elements of feminism, including both Hope and Nancy's dissatisfaction with the abandonment of their career goals. The show may have been representative of a neoconservative time, but the female characters still clearly were products of a new generation, one that may have forced them back into the home but could never keep them there permanently.

Will & Grace[2]

First Airdate: September 21, 1998

Last Airdate: May 18, 2006

Network: NBC

Cast:

Eric McCormack as Will Truman

Debra Messing as Grace Adler

Megan Mullally as Karen Walker

Sean Hayes as Jack McFarland

Shelley Morrison as Rosario McFarland

This groundbreaking sitcom created a new formula for the women-best-friend genre. Instead of women living together and supporting each other, as in *Kate & Allie* and *The Golden Girls, Will & Grace* made one of those friends a gay man.

Though Grace often exhibited some stereotypical female traits—she was desperate to get married, she was overly needy and dependent, and she loved to be taken care of—she was also the sole owner and founder of a successful business and, through the course of the series, learned to find strength in herself as a woman and, eventually, as a wife and mother.

The show is consistently credited with breaking down the stereotypes of gay men, but it also provided a realistic female character, Grace, who was as complex and flawed as so many of the women watching her.

Yes, Dear[3]

First Airdate: October 2, 2000
Network: CBS
Cast:
Anthony Clark as Greg Warner
Mike O'Malley as Jimmy Hughes
Liza Snyder as Christine Hughes
Jean Louisa Kelly as Kim Warner

This sitcom is a new version of *The Odd Couple*, but as opposed to garnering comedy from two very different individuals, the show does the same thing with two very different married couples. Greg, a movie studio accountant, and Kim, a stay-at-home mom, represent the traditional nuclear family. Self-righteous and responsible, they are forced to accept that friends and fellow parents Jimmy and Christine are different and will manage their family accordingly.

The show is a good example of the fact that all American parents raise their children and run their households in different ways. Through fun, fights, births, and deaths, the couples must learn to get along regardless of their differences and show America that there is certainly more than one way to be a family.

Acknowledgments

This book came about partly because of my obsessive television-watching, but also because of the exceptional scholarship of the women's historians who have found television and other forms of the mass media an important component of women's history: Susan Douglas, Bonnie Dow, Barbara Ehrenreich, Susan Faludi, Molly Haskell, Naomi Wolf, Elaine Showalter, and countless others whose scholarship made this book and the idea of examining the representation of women on TV possible.

In addition, the book would not have been possible without the exceptional editing power of Elizabeth Woodman and the support of my editor, Jill Rothenberg. I would not have been able to complete this project without the assistance, both personal and professional, of the amazing agent (and great guy) Dan Lazar.

I would also like to acknowledge the continued support of my friends, who have allowed me to patch together a family of people who inspire me every day, including: Julie, Rachel, Farah, Stephanie, Vanessa, Cherine, Jillian, Narges, and Josh. Finally, I would like to thank my family: the Kleins; my beautiful sister, Fara; my brother Andrew; and one of the best male feminists I've met (and one of my best friends), my brother Evan. The constant support of my stepdad, Stuart, will always mean the world to me.

Last but not least, I would like to thank all the women on TV and off who have inspired me, made me mad, made me want to be a feminist, made me want to be strong, and made me who I am. Of all these women, the one who deserves the most credit by far is my mother, Lynn, whose pride in me and support of my every endeavor have allowed me to live a life I never imagined. She will always be the first woman who inspired me to watch TV consciously and look for women to admire on the screen. Clearly, I have found so many TV women to look up to, but none more amazing and incomparable than my own mother. She will always be my first Murphy Brown.

Endnotes

Introduction

1. Jon Gertner, "Our Ratings, Ourselves," *The New York Times Magazine,* April 10, 2005.

2. Susan Douglas, *Where the Girls Are: Growing Up Female with the Mass Media* (New York: Random House, 1994): 3.

3. Ibid., 7.

4. Bonnie Dow, *Prime-Time Feminism: Television, Media Culture and the Women's Movement since 1970* (Philadelphia: University of Pennsylvania Press, 1996): 32.

5. Molly Haskell, *Holding My Own in No Man's Land* (New York: Oxford University Press, 1997): 197.

6. Douglas, *Where the Girls Are,* 9.

7. Ibid., 9.

Chapter 1

1. *Murphy Brown.* Pilot Episode: "Respect." Written by Diane English. Airdate: November 14, 1988.

2. Rick Mitz, *The Great TV Sitcom Book,* 159.

3. Susan Douglas, quoted in Sheila Rowbotham, *A Century of Women: The History of Women in Britain and the United States in the Twentieth Century* (New York: Penguin, 1997): 460.

4. Betsy Israel, *Bachelor Girl: The Secret History of Single Women in the Twentieth Century* (New York: HarperCollins, 2002): 209.

5. Ibid., 208-209.

6. Ibid., 208.

7. Ibid., 208.

8. Davis, quoted in Dow, *Prime-Time Feminism,* 27.

9. Mitz, *The Great TV Sitcom Book,* 213.

10. *The Mary Tyler Moore Show.* Pilot Episode: "Love Is All Around." Written by Allan Burns and James L. Brooks. Airdate: September 19, 1970.

11. Mitz, *The Great TV Sitcom Book,* 159.

12. Ibid., 159.

13. Davis, quoted in Dow, *Prime-Time Feminism,* 24.

14. Alley and Brown, Dow, *Prime-Time Feminism,* 25.

15. Dow, *Prime-Time Feminism,* 25.

16. Mitz, *The Great TV Sitcom Book,* 213.

17. Ibid., 213.

18. Israel, *Bachelor Girl,* 233.

19. Ibid., 234.

20. Ibid., 254.

21. Ibid., 232.

22. Douglas Bauer, ed., *Prime Times: Writers on Their Favorite*

TV Shows (New York: Crown, 2004): 133.

23. Mitz, *The Great Sitcom Book,* 213.

24. Ibid., 214.

25. *Ellen.* Episode: "The Promotion." Written by David Rosenthal. Airdate: April 20, 1994.

26. *The Nanny.* Episode: "The Fifth Wheel." Written by Jayne Hamil. Airdate: January 29, 1997.

27. Stephanie Coontz, *The Way We Never Were: American Families and the Nostalgia Trap* (New York: Basic Books, 1992): 182.

28. Ibid., 263.

29. *Murphy Brown.* Episode: "It's Just Like Riding a Bike." Written by DeAnn Heline and Eileen Heisler. Airdate: May 2, 1994.

30. *Friends.* Episode: "The One with the Thumb." Written by Jeffrey Astrof and Mike Sikowitz. Airdate: October 6, 1994.

31. *One Day at a Time* dialogue quoted in Mitz, *The Great TV Sitcom Book,* 301.

32. *Kate & Allie* dialogue quoted in Mitz, *The Great TV Sitcom Book,* 351.

33. *The Nanny.* Episode: "Rash to Judgment." Written by Ivan Menchell. Airdate: January 7, 1998.

34. *Sex and the City.* Pilot Episode: "Sex and the City." Written by Darren Star. Airdate: June 6, 1998.

35. Marcelle Clements, *The Improvised Woman: Single Women Reinventing Single Life* (New York: Norton, 1999): 69.

Chapter 2

1. *Everybody Loves Raymond.* Episode: "Win, Lose or Draw." Written by Kathy Ann Stumpe. Airdate: November 8, 1996.

2. Glenda Riley, quoted in Rowbotham, *A Century of Women*, 454.

3. Douglas, *Where the Girls Are*, 36.

4. Ibid., 4.

5. Mitz, *The Great TV Sitcom Book*, 251.

6. Ibid., 255.

7. Douglas, *Where the Girls Are*, 47.

8. Susan Faludi, *Backlash: The Undeclared War Against American Women* (New York: Anchor Books, 1991): 142.

9. Ibid., 142.

10. Ibid., 143.

11. Ibid., 143.

12. Douglas, *Where the Girls Are*, 273.

13. Faludi, *Backlash*, 160-161.

14. *Roseanne.* Pilot Episode: "Life and Stuff." Written by Matt Williams. Airdate: October 18, 1988.

15. Jon Caramanica, *The New York Times*, September 25, 2005.

16. *Roseanne.* Pilot Episode: "Life and Stuff."

17. Douglas, *Where the Girls Are*, 43.

18. Ibid., 16.

19. Todd Gitlin, *The Whole World Is Watching* (Berkeley: UC Press, 1980), quoted in Douglas, *Where the Girls Are*, 16.

20. *Roseanne.* Pilot Episode: "Life and Stuff."

21. Ibid.

22. Caramanica, *The New York Times*, September 25, 2005.

23. Coontz, *The Way We Never Were*, 14.

24. *Mad About You.* Episode: "Romantic Improvisations." Written by Danny Jacobson and Paul Reiser. Airdate: September 23, 1992.

25. Ibid.

26. *Dharma & Greg.* Episode: "Shower the People You Love with Love." Written by Bill Prady. Airdate: October 8, 1997.

27. Arlie Hochschild, *The Second Shift* (New York: Penguin, 1989): 11.

28. Ibid., 12.

29. Ibid., 13.

Chapter 3

1. Nina Liebman, "Comedy, Domestic Settings," Museum of TV Archives, 2004.

2. Rowbotham, *A Century of Women*, 320.

3. Douglas, *Where the Girls Are*, 44-45.

4. Ibid.

5. Reka Hoff, quoted in Toni Carabillo et al., *Feminist Chronicles: 1953-1993.* Quoted in Rowbotham, *A Century of Women*, 321.

6. Douglas, *Where the Girls Are*, 51.

7. *Roseanne.* Episode: "The Clip Show: All About Rosey (2)." Written by Perry Dance and Rob Ulin. Airdate: March 1, 1995.

8. *Roseanne.* Episode: "Husbands and Wives." Written by Kevin Abbott. Airdate: March 22, 1995.

9. Douglas, *Where the Girls Are*, 285.

10. *Roseanne.* Episode: "A Stash from the Past." Written by Kevin Abbott. Airdate: October 5, 1993.

11. *Roseanne.* Episode: "No Talking." Written by Norma Safford Vela. Airdate: December 12, 1989.

12. Ibid.

13. *Murphy Brown.* Episode: "It Came from College." Written by Anne Beatts. Airdate: November 4, 1991.

14. *Alice.* Episode: "Sex Education." Written by Donald Reiker and Patricia Jones. Airdate: November 6, 1976.

15. Mitz, *The Great TV Sitcom Book,* 301.

16. Ibid., 303.

17. *Roseanne.* "Troubles with Rubbles." Written by Joel Madison. Airdate: March 26, 1991.

18. *Yes, Dear.* Episode: "Baby Fight Club." Written by Patrick McCarthy and Eric Shapiro. Airdate: October 15, 2001.

19. *Roseanne.* Episode: "A Bitter Pill to Swallow." Written by Amy Sherman-Palladino and Jennifer Heath. Airdate: September 17, 1991.

20. *Yes, Dear.* Pilot Episode. Written by Gregory Thomas Garcia and Alan Kirschenbaum. Airdate: October 2, 2000.

21. *Roseanne.* Episode: "Direct to Video." Written by Michael B. Kaplan. Airdate: December 5, 1995.

Chapter 4

1. *Friends.* Episode: "The One Where Eddie Won't Go." Written by Michael Curtis and Greg Malins. Airdate: March 28, 1996.

2. Rowbotham, *A Century of Women,* 468.

3. *Maude.* Episode: "Walter's Problem (1)." Written by Bob Weiskopf and Bob Schiller. Airdate: September 11, 1973.

4. Deborah Felder, *A Century of Women: The Most Influential Events in Twentieth-Century Women's History* (Secaucus: Birch Lane Press, 1999): 231.

5. Ibid., 231.

6. Mitz, *The Great TV Sitcom Book,* 213.

7. Felder, *A Century of Women,* 231.

8. *Ladies' Home Journal*, quoted in Felder, *A Century of Women*, 231.

9. *Sex and the City*. Episode: "Secret Sex." Written by Darren Star. Airdate: July 12, 1998.

10. Douglas, *Where the Girls Are*, 61-62.

11. Ibid., 62-63.

12. *Murphy Brown*. Episode: "Angst for the Memories." Written by Rob Bragin. Airdate: September 27, 1993.

13. Ibid.

14. Cathi Hanauer, ed., *The Bitch in the House: 26 Women Tell the Truth About Sex, Solitude, Work, Motherhood, and Marriage* (New York: William Morrow, 2002): 123.

15. *Sex and the City*. Episode: "Secret Sex."

Chapter 5

1. Coontz, *The Way We Never Were*, 186.

2. Douglas, *Where the Girls Are*, 45.

3. John Fiske, quoted in Douglas, *Where the Girls Are*, 16.

4. Coontz, *The Way We Never Were*, 180.

5. Ibid., 36.

6. Ibid., 36.

7. Douglas, *Where the Girls Are*, 57.

8. Ibid., 57-58.

9. Dow, *Prime-Time Feminism*, 24.

10. Israel, *Bachelor Girl*, 234.

11. Ibid.

12. Ibid.

13. Dow, *Prime-Time Feminism*, 27.

14. Ella Taylor, *Prime-Time Families*, quoted in Dow, *Prime-Time Feminism*, 25.

15. Ibid., 25.

16. Andrea Press, quoted in Dow, *Prime-Time Feminism,* 26.

17. Mitz, *The Great TV Sitcom Book,* 253.

18. Mira Komarovsky, quoted in Douglas, *Where the Girls Are,* 17.

19. Douglas, *Where the Girls Are,* 17.

20. Faludi, *Backlash,* 143.

21. Douglas, *Where the Girls Are,* 57.

22. Hochschild, *The Second Shift,* xxiv.

Chapter 6

1. As quoted in Douglas, *Where the Girls Are,* 199, and Rowbotham, *A Century of Women,* 460.

2. Erica Jong as quoted in Barbara Ehrenreich, "The Women's Movements, Feminist and Antifeminist," *Radical America* 15, no. 1-2 (Spring 1981), 98; and Rowbotham, *A Century of Women,* 443.

3. Douglas, *Where the Girls Are,* 19.

4. Jennifer Baumgardner and Amy Richards, *Manifesta: Young Women, Feminism, and the Future* (New York: Farrar, Straus and Giroux, 2000): 151.

5. James L. Brooks and Allan Burns, *The Mary Tyler Moore Show Season 1* DVD Liner Notes, Twentieth Century Fox, 2002.

6. *The Mary Tyler Moore Show.* Pilot Episode: "Love Is All Around."

7. Rowbotham, *A Century of Women,* 252 and 258.

8. Ibid., 271 and 274.

9. Katha Pollitt, *Subject to Debate: Sense and Dissents on Women, Politics, and Culture* (New York: Random House, 2001): xxv.

10. Linda Seger, *When Women Call the Shots: The Developing Power and Influence of Women in Television and Film* (New York: Henry Holt, 1996): 158.

11. Herma Snider, "I Stopped Feeling Sorry for Myself," *Redbook* 115, no. 5 (December 1960). Reprinted in Gerda Lerner, *The Female Experience* (Oxford: Oxford University Press, 1997): 130-134.

12. Ibid.

13. Anna Quindlen, *Living Out Loud* (New York: Ballantine, 1988): 59.

14. Betty Friedan, *The Feminine Mystique* (New York: Norton, 1963): 15.

15. Marie Wilson, *Closing the Leadership Gap: Why Women Can and Must Help Run the World* (New York: Viking, 2004): xii.

16. Nancy Franklin, "Women Gone Wild," *The New Yorker,* January 17, 2005.

17. *Desperate Housewives.* Pilot Episode. Written by Marc Cherry. Airdate: October 3, 2004.

18. Rowbotham, *A Century of Women,* 320.

19. Lynn Spigel, *Private Screenings: Television and the Female Consumer* (Minneapolis: University of Minnesota Press, 1992): x.

20. *The Mary Tyler Moore Show.* Pilot Episode: "Love Is All Around."

21. *The Mary Tyler Moore Show.* Episode: "The Forty-Five-Year-Old Man." Written by George Kirgo. Airdate: March 6, 1971.

22. Faludi, *Backlash,* 156.

23. Horace Newcomb, ed., *Encyclopedia of Television* (online version), 2nd ed. (New York: Routledge, 2004).

24. Ibid.

25. Seger, *When Women Call the Shots*, 159 and 163.

26. *The Mary Tyler Moore Show.* Episode: "The Forty-Five-Year-Old Man."

27. Ibid.

28. Rowbotham, *A Century of Women*, 453-454.

29. Ibid., 320.

30. Ibid.

31. Dow, *Prime-Time Feminism*, xv.

32. Linda Seger, "How to Evaluate Media Images of Women," *Media & Values* 49 (Winter 1990).

33. *Friends.* Pilot Episode: "The One Where Monica Gets a Roommate." Written by Marta Kaufman and David Crane. Airdate: September 22, 1994.

34. Pollitt, *Subject to Debate*, xix.

35. Newcomb, *Encyclopedia of Television.*

36. Roseanne Barr, from the Turner Network documentary *Century of Women*, quoted in Seger, *When Women Call the Shots*, 161.

37. *Roseanne.* Episode: "The Blaming of the Shrew." Written by Laurence Brock. Airdate: May 3, 1995.

38. Ibid.

39. *Roseanne.* Episode: "Let's Call It Quits." Written by Grace McKeany. Airdate: May 2, 1989.

40. Ibid.

41. *Friends.* Pilot Episode: "The One Where Monica Gets a Roommate."

42. *Friends.* Episode: "The One with George Stephanopoulos." Written by Alexa Junge. Airdate: November 13, 1994.

43. Ibid.

44. Ibid.

45. Ibid.

46. *Roseanne*. Episode: "Guilt by Disassociation." Written by Tom Arnold. Airdate: September 26, 1989.

47. *Roseanne*. Episode: "Like, a New Job." Written by Jeff Abugov. Airdate: October 9, 1990.

48. Ibid.

49. *Caroline in the City*. Pilot Episode. Written by Fred Barron and Marco Pennette. Airdate: September 21, 1995.

50. *Mad About You*. Episode: "I'm Just So Happy for You." Written by Billy Grundfest. Airdate: October 28, 1992.

51. *Roseanne*. Episode: "Guilt by Disassociation."

52. *Roseanne*. Episode: "Confessions." Written by Brad Isaacs. Airdate: December 18, 1990.

53. Ibid.

54. Candice Bergen, interviewed on *60 Minutes,* CBS. Airdate: January 24, 2003.

55. *Murphy Brown*. Episode: "Devil with a Blue Dress On." Written by Korby Siamis. Airdate: November 21, 1988.

56. *Murphy Brown*. Pilot Episode: "Respect."

57. *Murphy Brown*. Episode: "Devil with a Blue Dress On."

58. B. Ricardo Brown, "Media Diversion(s): Dan Quayle, New Right Ideology and the Uses of Murphy Brown," paper presented at the annual meeting of the Eastern Sociological Society, March 1994.

59. *Murphy Brown*. Episode: "Devil with a Blue Dress On."

60. *Alice*. Pilot Episode. Written by Robert Getchell. Airdate: August 31, 1976.

61. *Designing Women*. Episode: "The Women of Atlanta." Written by Linda Bloodworth-Thomason. Airdate: May 1,

1989.

62. *Home Improvement.* Pilot Episode. Written by Carmen Finestra, David McFadzean, and Matt Williams. Airdate: September 17, 1991.

63. Edith Lees, "Olive Schreiner and Her Relation to the Woman Movement," *Book News Monthly,* February 1915.

64. Elaine Showalter, *Inventing Herself: Claiming a Feminist Intellectual Heritage* (New York: Scribner, 2001): 66.

65. "Women at Work," *Monthly Labor Review,* October 2003, 48. By 1985, 70 percent of all women worked outside the home, representing more than half of the total U.S. workforce.

Chapter 7

1. Anderson, Christopher. *I Love Lucy. Encyclopedia of Television.* Horace Newcomb, ed. 2004. The Museum of Broadcast Communications. Online at www.museum.tv.

2. Rowbotham, Sheila. *A Century of Women* (New York: Penguin, 1997): 443.

2. *Mad About You.* Episode: "The Birth Part 2." Written by Larry Charles. Airdate: May 20, 1997.

3. *Friends.* Episode: "The One Where Rachel Has the Baby (2)." Written by David Crane and Marta Kauffman. Airdate: May 16, 2002.

4. *Friends.* Episode: "The One Where Rachel Tells . . . " Written by Sherry Bilsing and Ellen Plummer. Airdate: October 11, 2001.

5. *Murphy Brown.* Episode: "Birth 101." Written by Korby Siamis and Diane English. Airdate: May 18, 1992.

6. *Friends.* Episode: "The One with Ross's Inappropriate Song." Written by Robert Carlock. Airdate: November 14, 2002.

7. Brown, "Media Diversion(s)."

8. Susan Douglas and Meredith Michaels, *The Mommy Myth: The Idealization of Motherhood and How It Has Undermined All Women* (New York: Free Press, 2004): 232.

9. Ibid., 232.

10. Ibid., 233. Dow, quoted from *Prime-Time Feminism*.

11. Ibid., 233.

12. *Friends.* Episode: "The One with the Jam." Written by Wil Calhoun. Airdate: October 3, 1996.

13. Ibid.

14. *Friends.* Episode: "The One with the Fertility Test." Written by Robert Carlock. Airdate: May 1, 2003

Chapter 8

1. Naomi Wolf, *The Beauty Myth: How Images of Beauty Are Used Against Women* (New York: Anchor Books, 1991): 10.

2. Mitz, *The Great TV Sitcom Book*, 208.

3. *Roseanne.* Episode: "Toto, We're Not in Kansas Anymore." Written by Grace McKeaney. Airdate: March 28, 1989.

4. Mitz, *The Great TV Sitcom Book*, 219.

5. Ibid., 213.

6. Ibid., 214.

7. Dow, *Prime-Time Feminism*, 30.

8. *The Golden Girls.* Episode: "Love for Sale." Written by Don Siegel and Jerry Perizigian. Airdate: April 6, 1991.

9. *Murphy Brown.* Pilot Episode: "Respect."

10. Landon Jones, quoted in Douglas, *Where the Girls Are*, 14.

11. American Society of Plastic Surgeons, statistics for 2005.

12. *Designing Women*. Episode: "Reservations for Twelve, Plus Ursula." Written by Linda Bloodworth-Thomason. Airdate: November 14, 1988.

13. Wolf, *The Beauty Myth*, 1.

14. Mitz, *The Great TV Sitcom Book*, 252.

15. *Maude*. Episode: "The Analyst (a.k.a Maude Bares Her Soul)." Written by Jay Folb. Airdate: November 10, 1975.

16. Mitz, *The Great TV Sitcom Book*, 362.

17. Ibid., 363.

18. *Roseanne*. Episode: "I'm Hungry." Written by Danny Jacobson and Norma Safford Vela. Airdate: February 13, 1990.

19. Ibid.

20. *Designing Women*. Episode: "They Shoot Fat Women, Don't They?" Written by Linda Bloodworth-Thomason. Airdate: December 11, 1989.

21. Ibid.

22. Douglas, *Where the Girls Are*, 16.

Chapter 9

1. *The Mary Tyler Moore Show*. Episode: "Love Is All Around."

2. Ibid.

3. Mitz, *The Great TV Sitcom Book*, 295.

4. *Friends*. Episode: "The One with the Wedding Dress." Written by Michael Curtis and Greg Malins. Airdate: April 16, 1998.

5. Mitz, *The Great TV Sitcom Book*, 351.

6. Ibid., 352.

7. Ibid., 362.

8. Ibid., 364.

9. Ibid.

10. *Sex and the City*. Episode: "Frenemies." Written by Jenny Bicks. Airdate: October 1, 2000.

11. *Friends*. Episode: "The One with Two Parts, Part 2." Written by Marta Kaufman and David Crane. Airdate: February 23, 1995.

12. *Friends*. Episode: "The One Where Rachel Has the Baby (2)."

13. *Will & Grace*. Episode: "Coffee & Commitment." Written by Adam Barr. Airdate: January 4, 2001.

14. *Murphy Brown*. Episode: "The Morning Show." Written by Kathryn Baker. Airdate: May 22, 1989.

Chapter 10

1. Showalter, *Inventing Herself*, 17.

2. *Friends*. Episode: "The One with the Lesbian Wedding." Written by Doty Abrams. Airdate: January 18, 1996.

3. *Roseanne*. Episode: "The Blaming of the Shrew."

4. *Desperate Housewives*. Pilot Episode.

5. Showalter, *Inventing Herself*, 19.

6. Douglas, *Where the Girls Are*, 306-307.

Women Behind the Scenes

1. Writers Guild Association, "Hollywood Writers Report," 1998.

2. *Hollywood Reporter*, Women in Entertainment Issue, December 12, 1995, quoted in Seger, *When Women Call the Shots*, 81.

3. Seger, *When Women Call the Shots*, 81-82.

4. *Hollywood Reporter*, Women in Entertainment Issue, quoted in Seger, *When Women Call the Shots*, 114.

5. Ibid., 263.

6. Quindlen, *Living Out Loud*, 32.

7. Seger, *When Women Call the Shots*, 262.

Prime-Time Refresher

1. Show airdates, networks, and cast lists compiled from Tim Brooks and Earle Marsh, *The Complete Directory to Prime Time Network and Cable TV Shows: 1946-Present,* 12th ed. (New York: Ballantine Books, 1999). All series descriptions are original.

2. Airdate and cast information for *Will & Grace* from NBC.

3. Airdate and cast information for *Yes, Dear* from CBS.

About the Author

Allison Klein is a former writer and associate producer for MTV News, where she produced the network's political news coverage, including *Choose or Lose,* a documentary about the issues facing young women in the 2000 presidential election. She also produced MTV's award-winning documentary series *True Life* and the behind-the-scenes series *Uncensored.* Most recently, she was a writer at the PR firm Ruder Finn, where she was a consultant on global women's issues, including the media representation of women, domestic violence, women's voting patterns, and women's activism. She received her bachelor's degree in journalism and women's studies from Northwestern University and her master's degree in American history from Brown University. She lives in the East Village in New York City.

Selected Titles from Seal Press

For more than thirty years, Seal Press has published ground-breaking books. By women. For women. Visit our website at www.sealpress.com.

Job Hopper: The Checkered Career of a Down-Market Dilettante by Ayun Halliday. $14.95, 1-58005-130-8. Halliday, quickly becoming one of America's funniest writers, chronicles her hilarious misadventures in the working world.

Dirty Sugar Cookies: Culinary Observations, Questionable Taste by Ayun Halliday. $14.95, 1-58005-150-2. Ayun Halliday is back with comical and unpredictable essays about her disastrous track record in the kitchen and her culinary observations—though she's clearly no expert.

The Big Rumpus: A Mother's Tale from the Trenches by Ayun Halliday. $15.95, 1-58005-071-9. Creator of the wildly popular zine *East Village Inky*, Halliday employs words and line drawings to describe the quirks and everyday travails of a young urban family, warts and all.

The Truth Behind the Mommy Wars: Who Decides What Makes a Good Mother? by Miriam Peskowitz. $15.95, 1-58005-129-4. A groundbreaking book that reveals the truth behind the "wars" between working mothers and stay-at-home moms.

Above Us Only Sky: A Woman Looks Back, Ahead, and into the Mirror by Marion Winik. $14.95, 1-58005-144-8. A witty and engaging book from NPR commentator Marion Winik about facing midlife without getting tangled up in the past or hung up on the future.

Indecent: How I Make It and Fake It as a Girl for Hire by Sarah Katherine Lewis, $14.95, 1-58005-169-3. An insider reveals the gritty reality behind the alluring facade of the sex industry.